Lecture Notes in Artificial Intellig

Subseries of Lecture Notes in Computer Science
Edited by J. G. Carbonell and J. Siekmann

Lecture Notes in Computer Science
Edited by G. Goos, J. Hartmanis, and J. van Leeuwen

Springer
Berlin
Heidelberg
New York
Barcelona
Hong Kong
London
Milan
Paris
Tokyo

Angélica de Antonio   Ruth Aylett
Daniel Ballin (Eds.)

Intelligent Virtual Agents

Third International Workshop, IVA 2001
Madrid, Spain, September 10-11, 2001
Proceedings

Springer

Series Editors

Jaime G. Carbonell, Carnegie Mellon University, Pittsburgh, PA, USA
Jörg Siekmann, University of Saarland, Saarbrücken, Germany

Volume Editors

Angélica de Antonio
Universidad Politécnica de Madrid, Facultad de Informática
Campus de Montegancedo, Boadilla del Monte, 28660 Madrid, Spain
E-mail: angelica@fi.upm.es

Ruth Aylett
University of Salford, Center for Virtual Environments, Business House
Salford, M5 4WT, UK
E-mail: r.s.aylett@salford.ac.uk

Daniel Ballin
BTexact Technologies, Radical Multimedia Lab
Ross PP1, Adastral Park, Martlesham, Ipswich, IP5 3RE, UK
E-mail: daniel.ballin@bt.com

Cataloging-in-Publication Data applied for

Die Deutsche Bibliothek - CIP-Einheitsaufnahme

Intelligent virtual agents : third international workshop ; proceedings /
IVA 2001, Madrid, Spain, September 10 - 11, 2001. Angélica de Antonio ...
(ed.). - Berlin ; Heidelberg ; New York ; Barcelona ; Hong Kong ; London ;
Milan ; Paris ; Tokyo : Springer, 2001
    (Lecture notes in computer science ; Vol. 2190 : Lecture notes in
    artificial intelligence)
    ISBN 3-540-42570-5

CR Subject Classification (1998): I.2.11, I.2, H.5, H.4, K.3

ISBN 3-540-42570-5 Springer-Verlag Berlin Heidelberg New York

Springer-Verlag Berlin Heidelberg New York
a member of BertelsmannSpringer Science+Business Media GmbH

http://www.springer.de

© Springer-Verlag Berlin Heidelberg 2001
Printed in Germany

Typesetting: Camera-ready by author, data conversion by PTP-Berlin, Stefan Sossna
Printed on acid-free paper   SPIN: 10840591   06/3142   5 4 3 2 1 0

Preface

Predicting the future is a risky game, and can often leave egg on one's face. However when the organizers of the Intelligent Virtual Environments workshop at the European Conference on AI predicted that the field of Intelligent Virtual Agents would grow and mature rapidly, they were not wrong. From this small workshop spawned the successful one on Intelligent Virtual Agents, held in Manchester in 1999.

This volume comprises the proceedings of the much larger third workshop held in Madrid, September 10-11, 2001, which successfully achieved the aim of taking a more international focus, bringing together researchers from all over the world. We received 35 submissions from 18 different countries in America, Asia, and Africa.

The 16 papers presented at the conference and published here show the high quality of the work that is currently being done in this field. In addition, five contributions were selected as short papers, which were presented as posters at the workshop.

This proceedings volume also includes the two prestigious papers presented at the workshop by our keynote speakers:

- Daniel Thalmann, Professor at the Swiss Federal Institute of Technology (EPFL) in Lausanne and Director of the Computer Graphics Lab., who talked about *The Foundations to Build a Virtual Human Society*.

- Jeff Rickel, Project Leader at the Information Sciences Institute and a Research Assistant Professor in the Department of Computer Science at the University of Southern California, who debated about *Intelligent Virtual Agents for Education and Training: Opportunities and Challenges*.

Many people and groups contributed to the success of this workshop. Our sincere thanks goes out to all of them. We would like to thank all the authors who contributed to this volume for their willingness to share their knowledge on this exciting new field. Significant thanks goes out to the local program committee in Madrid, for the efficient handling of all the tasks thrown at them:

Julia Clemente, *Universidad de Alcalá*
Pilar Herrero *Universidad Politécnica de Madrid*
Ricardo Imbert *Universidad Politécnica de Madrid*
Gonzalo Méndez *Universidad Politécnica de Madrid*
Jaime Ramírez *Universidad Politécnica de Madrid*
María Isabel Sánchez *Universidad Carlos III*

We would also like to acknowledge the hard work of the members of the Program Committee, who thoughtfully reviewed the submissions. The Program Committee consisted of the editors along with 22 distinguished researchers coming both from academia and business.

We invite readers to enjoy the papers in this book, and look forward to the next Intelligent Virtual Agents conference.

July 2001
Daniel Ballin
Ruth Aylett
Angélica de Antonio

Committee Listings

Conference Chair
Ruth Aylett - Centre for Virtual Environments, University of Salford
Daniel Ballin - Radical Multimedia Laboratory, BT exaCT

Local Conference Chair
Angélica de Antonio - Universidad Politécnica de Madrid

Local Organizing Committee
Julia Clemente - Universidad de Alcalá
Pilar Herrero - Universidad Politécnica de Madrid
Ricardo Imbert - Universidad Politécnica de Madrid
Gonzalo Méndez - Universidad Politécnica de Madrid
Jaime Ramírez - Universidad Politécnica de Madrid
María Isabel Sánchez - Universidad Carlos III

Panels Co-ordinator
Marc Cavazza - University of Teeside

Program Committee
Elisabeth André - DFKI - German Research Center for Artificial Intelligence
Riccardo Antonini - Consorzio Roma Ricerche
Angélica de Antonio - Universidad Politécnica de Madrid
Ruth Aylett - Centre for Virtual Environments, University of Salford
Norman I. Badler - University of Pennsylvania
Daniel Ballin - Radical Multimedia Laboratory, BT exaCT
Bruce Blumberg - MIT Media Lab
Joanna Bryson - MIT AI Lab
Justine Cassell - MIT Media Lab
Marc Cavazza - University of Teeside
Elisabeth Churchill - FX-PAL
Dave Cliff - Hewlett-Packard Labs Bristol
Kerstin Dautenhahn - University of Hertfordshire
Steve Grand - Cyberlife Research
Ricardo Imbert - Universidad Politécnica de Madrid
Brian Logan - University of Nottingham
Mike Luck - University of Southampton
Jan-Torsten Milde - University of Bielefeld
Ana Paiva - IST-Technical University of Lisbon
Todd Papaioannou - DALi Inc
Catherine Pelechaud - Università degli Studi di Roma "La Sapienza"
Paolo Petta - Austrian Research Institute for Artificial Intelligence
Dave Roberts - University of Reading
Ryohei Nakatsu - ATR Media Integration & Communications Research Laboratories
Phoebe Sengers - GMD - Institute for Media Communication
Demetri Terzopoulos - New York University

Table of Contents

Invited Speakers

Papers

Short Papers

The Foundations to Build a Virtual Human Society

Daniel Thalmann

Computer Graphics Lab
EPFL
CH 1015 Lausanne
Daniel.Thalmann@epfl.ch
http://ligwww.epfl.ch

Abstract. The simulation of the dynamics of human societies is not an easy task, and we propose a bottom-up approach, which consists in defining the human entity as a single, autonomous and independent entity (called Agent), and then immerse many of them in a common environment to let them interact and co-operate as the environment evolves. To achieve our goal and create Virtual Human societies, we try to extend the concepts we have developed for crowd simulations to encompass more autonomy at the level of individuals.

1. Introduction

The goal of our research effort is to develop a behavioral model for animation of believable virtual humans (actors) in virtual environments. In this context, believability means that the behavior of a synthetic actor has to be indistinguishable from that of a human. For instance, an actor inhabiting a typical virtual environment composed of objects and other actors, only concerned to perform a given task without reacting to objects or actors it encounters or to what these actors are doing would not look believable. The behavior of these actors would be more that of a robot than that of a human. To be believable, an actor has to be affected by what takes place around it and needs to engage in social behaviors with other actors. Therefore, the behavioral model of an actor needs to be versatile enough to allow a change of behavior, the emotional state of the actor must be reflected and must affect its behavior, the interpersonal relationships with the other actors must be taken into account and possibly bring the actor to engage in social interactions.

Our ultimate research objective is the simulation of Virtual Worlds inhabited by a Virtual Human Society (e.g. Fig.1), where agents will co-operate, negotiate, make friends, communicate, group and ungroup, depending on their likes, moods, emotions, goals, fears, etc. But such interaction and corresponding groups should not be programmed. Behaviour should emerge as a result of a multi-agent system sharing a common environment, in our case, sharing a virtual environment. For example in a panic situation we do not model the group behaviour, because each human reacts differently depending for example on its level of fear. If we model the individual entity, there will be groups of different behaviours (not programmed explicitly) as result of the interaction of common individual behaviours.

A. de Antonio, R. Aylett, and D. Ballin (Eds.): IVA 2001, LNAI 2190, pp. 1-14, 2001.

Fig. 1. A Virtual Human Society

The simulation of the dynamics of human societies is not an easy task, and we propose a bottom-up approach, which consists in defining the human entity as a single, autonomous and independent entity (called Agent), and then immerse many of them in a common environment to let them interact and co-operate as the environment evolves.

To achieve our goal and create Virtual Human societies, we try to extend the concepts we have developed for crowd simulations to encompass more autonomy at the level of individuals. For interactive training simulations such as modelling of crowd responding to emergency situations we extend our current crowd model with inclusion of multiple dynamic physical and emotional attributes for individuals in crowds. Such attributes are used to represent various states of agents such as levels of fear, aggressivity, tiredness or injuries on different body parts affecting both agents behaviours and rendering of agents appearances. Agents are able to access states of other agents and have possibly influence on it, e.g. for modelling of people calming down other people in panic decreasing thus their fear level.

We also extend and modify our generic behavioural control system to be usable in simulation of emergency situations, where combination of various levels of agents' state variables and perceived state of the environment produce both corresponding overt behaviours and change of internal states (e.g. when agents are inside toxic gas area their breathing capacity decreases of 10% each 10 seconds). For transitions between normal state background behaviours of crowd and behaviours corresponding to particular state of the emergency situation, system should also allow to specify different levels of priorities of behaviours. Real-time requirements of training simulations put constraints on complexity of individual behaviour, so the system using various levels of behaviour complexity can be useful for decreasing load of computational resources. For example rules for background behaviour associated with places in virtual urban environment common for all agents can be stored in informed environment database [1], then when an emergency situation occurs the state of agents change and priority system would accordingly switch to individual behavioural rules.

We also simulate the main steps of the groups' so-called "life-cycle": the initial formation, maintenance and closure stages. This includes the requirement of defining what are the necessary conditions for the transition from one stage to another, as well as a proper handling of members input and output through a mechanism of collective decision making. An interesting area for further research is modelling of the process of crowd formation. In previous works crowds have been always considered as already formed units with more or less uniform behavior placed in very particular environment corresponding only to narrow purpose of simulation e.g. pedestrian just fleeing from burning building or marching crowd during political demonstration. However in the real world there is no global controller of crowds assigning people to particular groups and determining their behaviors. Collective behavior emerges from interaction of individuals, crowds are dynamically assembled and disassembled and over time change their behavior. For such modelling notion of contagion from sociology can be useful. Contagion is process where crowd members become increasingly preoccupied with each other's behavior, and outlooks and events that would normally concern them become insignificant. Eventually each crowd member becomes so focused on other's activities that he or she loses self-consciousness, which usually is a "means of barricading oneself against influence of others".

Several group structures should emerge, each with a different configuration of the members' roles and status. Such issues as leadership, power distribution and roles conflict can be tackled. The internal evolution of the group, through dynamic members' roles distribution,

There are mainly three factors allowing to judge of such a Virtual Reality system: the autonomy, the interaction and the degree of presence. The autonomy expresses the ability of autonomous virtual humans to react to simulated stimuli. The interaction measures the number of adjustable parameters of the system and the presence measures the degree of immersion of the user in a virtual world and at which extent, he can interact with it using specialized devices.

2. Crowds

2.1 Characteristics of a Crowd

Crowds are ubiquitous feature of everyday life. People have long assembled collectively to observe, to celebrate, and to protest various happenings in their everyday lives. The collective assemblages or gatherings called crowds are ongoing features of the social word and, as a consequence, have long been the object of theorizing and inquiring, ranging from psychologistic renderings of LeBon [2] and Freud [3] to the more sociological accounts of Smelser [4] to the highly systematic and empirically grounded observations of McPhail [5].

With computers it become possible not only to observe human crowds in the real world, but also to simulate various phenomena from the domain of collective behavior in virtual environment. Collective behaviors have been studied and modeled in computers with very different purposes:

- To animate large number of characters for entertainment industry in movies and computer games [6].

- To populate simulated virtual worlds for training of military personnel [7] or policemen dealing with crowds [8].

- To model movement of a large number of people to support architectural design both for everyday use of a buildings and for emergency evacuation conditions [9][10].

- And finally, for applications concerning sociological and behavioral simulations [11].

There have been different approaches to modeling of the crowds, because of different purposes of the models required by various application domains. The modeling techniques range from those that do not distinguish individuals such as flow and network models, to those that represent each individual as being controlled by rules based on physical laws or behavioral models.

Advantage of macroscopic models is their low requirements on computational capacity making simulation of even very large crowds possible. However as noted by Sime [12], pedestrian movement models that represent people as "nonthinking objects" whose movement is modelled by analogy to laws of physical science neglect the psychological aspects that are important for effective modelling.

2.2 A Crowd Modelling

Animating crowds [13] is challenging both in character animation and a virtual city modeling. Though different textures and colors may be used, the similarity of the virtual people would be soon detected by even non-experts, say, "everybody walks the same in this virtual city!" . It is, hence, useful to have a fast and intuitive way of generating motions with different personalities depending on gender, age, emotions, etc., from an example motion, say, a genuine walking motion. The problem is basically to be able to generate variety among a finite set of motion requests and then to apply it to either an individual or a member of a crowd. It also needs very good tools to tune the motion [14].

The proposed solution addresses two main issues: i) crowd structure and ii) crowd behavior. Considering crowd structure, our approach deals with a hierarchy composed of crowd, groups and agents, where the groups are the most complex structure containing the information to be distributed among the individuals. Concerning *crowd behavior*, our virtual agents are endowed with different levels of autonomy. They can either act according to an innate and scripted crowd behavior *(programmed behavior)*, react as a function of triggered events *(reactive or autonomous behavior)* or be guided by an interactive process during simulation *(guided behavior)*. We introduced the term <guided crowds> to define the groups of virtual agents that can be externally controlled in real time [15]. Figure 2 shows a group guided by a leader.

Fig. 2. Group guided by a leader

In our case, the intelligence, memory, intention and perception are focalized in the group structure. Also, each group can obtain one leader. This leader can be chosen randomly by the crowd system, defined by the user or can emerge from the sociological rules. Concerning the crowd control features, The crowd aims at providing autonomous, guided and programmed crowds. Varying degrees of autonomy can be applied depending on the complexity of the problem. Externally controlled groups, *<guided groups>*, no longer obey their scripted behavior, but act according to the external specification. At a lower level, the individuals have a repertoire of basic behaviors that we call *innate behaviors*. An innate behavior is defined as an "inborn" way to behave. Examples of individual innate behaviors are goal seeking behavior, the ability to follow scripted or guided events/reactions, the way trajectories are processed and collision avoided. While the innate behaviors are included in the model, the specification of scripted behaviors is done by means of a script language. The groups of virtual agents whom we call *<programmed groups>* apply the scripted behaviors and do not need user intervention during simulation. Using the script language, the user can directly specify the crowd or group behaviors. In the first case, the system automatically distributes the crowd behaviors among the existing groups. Events and reactions have been used to represent behavioral rules. This reactive character of the simulation can be programmed in the script language (scripted control) or directly given by an external controller. We call the groups of virtual agents who apply the behavioral rules *<autonomous groups>*.

The train station simulation (Figure 3) includes many different actions and places, where several people are present and doing different things. Possible actions include "buying a ticket", "going to shop", "meeting someone", "waiting for someone", "making a telephone call", "checking the timetable", etc. This simulation uses external control (RBBS [16]) to guide some crowd behaviors in real time.

Fig. 3. Train station simulation.

3. Agents

3.1 Why Agents ?

The creation of groups of virtual humans capable of behaving and interacting realistically with each other in 3D environments requires the development of a specific agent architecture. Most current agent architectures are dedicated to the fulfilment of precise tasks/problem solving, e.g. Ingrand [17], or to the simulation of purely emotional behaviour, e.g. Botelho [18]. However, we think that pure goal oriented and emotional behaviour are not sufficient in order to fully model human interaction in groups.

In real life, we daily engage in many interactions and social activities with different people, adapting our behaviour to the situation, dealing with complex motivations and different cultures, and also simply following routines. Our social status, gender, age or cultural origin are, among others, very important criteria to explain why we enjoy interacting with some people and feel uneasy with others.

Sociologists have identified and described specific social mechanisms used by the individuals which are necessary to the creation and maintenance of groups, and have underlined the importance of the participants' social identity in the group's structure and behaviour, e.g. Forsyth [19].

These facts need to be taken into account in the development of an agent architecture allowing the simulation of group behaviour. The participating agents must be modeled at a higher level, adding social identities, social motivations and social reasoning to them, on top of their specific competency.

3.2 Behaviour and Mental States

One important point in the simulation is the believability of the individual virtual humans, they should behave as real humans, including capabilities such as: perception, language understanding and generation, emotions, goal-driven behaviour, reactivity to the environment, memory, inference, appearance of thought and personalities, interpersonal interactions, social skills and possibly others. A very important factor for the believability are emotions. Emotions must affect everything about the entity, the way it moves, the way it talks, the expression on its face (see Figure 4) , "The expression must be captured throughout the whole body as well as in the face" [20].

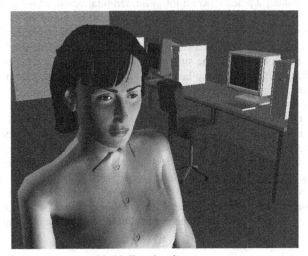

Fig. 4. Emotional state

3.3 Perception and Sensors

In order to implement perception, virtual humans should be equipped with synthetic or virtual sensors [21] like visual, tactile and auditory sensors. These sensors should be used as a basis for implementing everyday human behaviour such as visually directed locomotion, handling objects, and responding to sounds and utterances. The actor-environment interface, or the synthetic sensors, constitute an important part of a behavioral animation system. As sensorial information drastically influences behavior, the synthetic sensors should simulate the functionality of their organic counterparts. Due to real-time constraints, we did not think that it is necessary to model biological models of sensors. Therefore, synthetic vision [22] only makes efficient visibility tests using powerful graphics engine that produce a Z-buffered color image representing an agent's vision. A tactile point-like sensor may be represented by a simple function evaluating the global force field at its position. The synthetic "ear" of an agent will be represented by a function returning the on-going sound events. What is important for an actor's behavior is the functionality of a sensor and how it filters the information flow from the environment, and not the specific model of the sensor.

More precisely, each agent will be running an inference engine in a separated process, and this engine will be responsible of the high-level behaviours and decisions. That is, based on plans and input from the environment (visual perception, communications, etc.) or from internal states (tiredness, obligations...), the behavioural engine will select the proper actions to perform.

3.4 Emotional and Social Relationships

Let us now consider a place where a lot of human relationships take place like a work place office or factory for example. These relationships could be organized in two sets: social relations and hierarchical relations. While the hierchical relations change rarely, the social relationship, that is, all informal and inter-personal relations between the staff would evolve during the simulation. These relations are normally developed outside working hours, like coffe breaks or lunch time, and they are normally based on people likes, activities, fears etc.

In order to realistically simulate how humans interact in a specific social context, it is necessary to precisely model the type of relationship they have and specify how it affects their interpersonal behaviour. Sociologists have identified several dimensions that are important to provide for the simulation of any group behaviour: 1) power (dominance and submissiveness of the agents), 2) attraction (friendliness and unfriendliness), 3) instrumental control (hierarchical rank) and 4) emotional expressiveness. For the development of the agents' behaviour in an organizational context, taking into account the hierarchical relationship is of course crucial, but the importance of the more informal dimensions should not be underestimated.

3.5 Physical Parameters

Physical parameters such as hunger, tiredness, types and levels of injuries should have influence on both behaviours and visualisation of virtual humans. For example, according to their level of tiredness, people would be able to perform different types of activities and this would have different influence on person's fatigue; people burned by fire at various body parts would have their appearance changed appropriately; mobility of persons affected by toxic gas would decrease and eventually they could become unconscious.

These attributes should be perceivable and modifiable by other agents. For example in order to be able to simulate emergency situations in a factory where one worker is injured and other worker are helping him, agent should perceive other as injured, identify injured part of body so that it could apply appropriate first aid and also change its physical state to reflect effect of the aid (e.g. increasing mobility of the injured agent). Dynamic evolution of such attributes according to agent's interaction with environment and other agents should be possible to specify by a system of rules.

3.6 Social Parameters and Behavior

The agents' behaviour within a group is highly dependant on their location in the sociometric structures but also on their own social identity. This social characterization should be done using social-statistical variables, 1) culture, 2) gender and 3) age, and taking into account the agent's roles within the group. A distinction between 4) task roles (e.g. function), and 5) socioemotional roles (e.g. confident) is often used. An additional 6) status rating (prestige) can also be introduced.

A typical behavior of an actor for a party scenario may be the following. The actor arrives at the party and looks what happens around it. Some food and drinks may stand on a table. Probably, it will be surrounded by friends and unknown persons. The actor may decide to take a drink and some food or to have social interactions with other actors. These interactions may be friendly conversations or the courtship of another actor from the opposite gender. In a friendly conversation, two actors may also share a drink or an actor may be rejected by the other actor when their friendship is not reciprocal. Depending on the issue of a courtship, an actor may also leave the party with another one. The behavior for a supermarket scenario is mainly a sequence of tasks to achieve. The actor comes in the supermarket, takes all the needed articles and leaves the supermarket. Nevertheless, the actor may also be attracted by unforeseen articles or may interact with other actors. Both scenarios are the source of emotions. The objects like drink and food at the party or article in the supermarket are the source of liking and disliking emotions. Behaviors generated by these emotions may be to take a liked object or to ignore or avoid a disliked one. The actions of the actor itself or from other actors may generate pride and shame or admiration and reproach emotions. For instance, an actor knocking down an object will be ashamed and another actor will reproach it. An actor helping another actor to take an unreachable object will be pride and the other actor will admire it. Events like the ownership of an object or the acceptance of a communication by another actor may generate joy emotions or the lost of an object or the refusal of a communication may generate distress emotions. The emotions happy for, sorry for, resentment and gloating are generated when an actor sees another actor having joy or distress emotions. The emotions hope and fear, relief and disappointment, satisfaction and fears confirmed depends on prospective events like the possible ownership of an object or a special expectation from a communication.

3.7 Verbal and Non-verbal Communication

Social interactions requires to reproduce verbal communication. In such a graphical environment, inter-agents communication would be more than just an exchange of messages. We need to create models for sound propagation, which should be suitable for verbal communication. These models do not need to be as accurate as for accoustic simulations, but should carry enough information in order to avoid situations such as too people conversing while they are in two different rooms, for instance. We should also take into account some human interaction elements, such as, turn taking (ability to interrupt others while they are talking, or wait for pauses indicating that it the other agent is waiting for an answer), conversation tracking (that is, mainly the ability to suspend and continue a conversation, to handle multiple conversations and queries at the same time), interpretation and reactions to silences during the speech, gazing while conversing, etc.

Interesting implication of introducing communication abilities for agents could be in modelling of emergent collective behaviour. Emergent crowds can be formed based on transfer of both emotional states and behaviours for example by verbal and non-verbal communication between physically close agents. Such transfer can depend on personalities of involved agents, where charismatic persons will be more easily able to affect others, or where some agents with high level of dominance will be resisting to adopt crowd behaviour. Further possibility of such emotional and behavioural influences can be used to indirectly control the crowd, where one of the agents would be externally guided by real human user.

To increase the believability of behaviors resulting from emotions we included nonverbal communication elements. A nonverbal communication is concerned with postures and their indications on what people are feeling. Postures are the means to communicate and are defined by a specific position of the arms and legs and angles of the body. As stated in [23], 65 percent of the substance of a face to face communication is conveyed by nonverbal elements and many psychologists suggest that a posture is an important means of conveying interpersonal attitudes. The effects of nonverbal communication, though unconscious, are nevertheless important. Let us have an example: two persons communicating with each other and rejecting a third one. The first two persons are standing in an open triangle formation commonly used for friendly conversation. It leaves a potential opening for a third person to join them. Such a person attempts to join the group, but the first two respond by rejecting him out. One raises his left arm, forming a barrier. The other deliberately avoids making eye contact with the newcomer. They have formed a closed formation, suppressing any possibility for a new person to join them. The newcomer feels rejected and leaves unhappily. The interpersonal relationships between actors is represented by a structure that encodes the type of the relationship (friendly, hierarchical) and the level of that relationship (from 0 (not friend, subordinate) to 1 (very close friend, superior)). These values are used to evaluate the desire to communicate with another actor and are updated according to the issue of the communication.

The issue of a communication may be for example the transfer of an object from an actor to another one or the rejection of an actor by another one. Figure 5 shows an example.

Fig. 5. A non-verbal communication between two virtual humans

3.8 Our Agent-Based Architecture for Intelligent Actors

Automatically animating a virtual human is such a complex task, that one has to decompose it into simpler elements and distinguish between low and high-levels. Saying that a task belongs to low level does not means that it is something easier or faster to achieve! We will rather regroup in the low-level the physical elements (for the virtual human, this includes the body, and basic animations like locomotion or objects interaction), and the behaviour will be handled by the high-level, simulating the virtual human's brain process. As shown in Figure 6, our low-level component is called Agents' Common Environment (ACE) and the high-level decisions making (the IntelligentVirtual Agent or IVA).

To simulate the physical word, we have developed the ACE system [24] that understands a set of different commands to be able to control the simulations, like the creation and animation of 3D objects, virtual humans, and smart objects [25] . Virtual humans encapsulate various motion motors and may have facial expression. They are able to repeat a recorded animation (key-frames animation), can walk, or use Inverse Kinematics for better interactions with objects. Finally, they can visually perceive their environment. ACE is mainly coded in C++ to ensure high performances. For convenient user-interaction, it also provides a Python layer which interprets commands on the fly and animates the virtual humans.

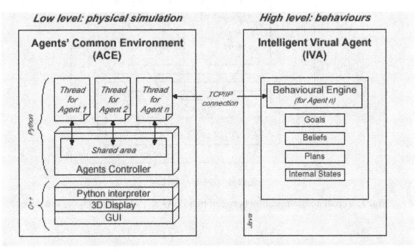

Fig. 6. Low and high level components in the system

IVA [26] relies on a Beliefs, Desires and Intentions architecture, as described by Rao and Georgeff [27], so that each agent manages its own beliefs and takes decisions by itself. While agents in the low-level have to share a common area and are handled by the Agents Controller, there is no such need for the IVA. Therefore, even if each IVA runs into a separated Java thread over the same application, there is no inter-threads communication.

This is demonstrated in Figure 7: when Agent 1 speaks to Agent 2, the message goes first to the low-level,then the thread for the first agent puts the message inthe shared area. Agent 2 is then able to retrieve the message and hear it.. This is in accordance with real human interaction: we do not have direct connections between our brains, but we need to use our body for communicating. The knowledge of the agent is decomposed into its beliefs and internal states (like the anxiety for instance), the goals to achieve and the plans, which are specifying a sequence of actions required to reach a specific goal. Based on these, the agent is then able to select the correct actions to perform in order to achieve its goals. Since beliefs and goals are subject to evolve over time, the agent is able to take into account new elements and dynamically react.

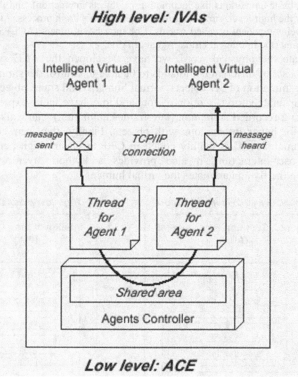

Fig. 7. Verbal communication between two IVAs has to go through the low-level

Conclusion

In this paper, we have shown that the simulation of the dynamics of human societies is a very complex task. We have proposed to use a agent architecture to build such a society. Our approach is bottom-up and consists in defining the human entity as a single, autonomous and independent entity (the Agent), and then immerse many of them in a common environment to let them interact and co-operate as the environment evolves. To achieve our goal and create these Virtual Human societies, we extend the concepts we have developed for crowd simulations to encompass more autonomy at the level of individuals.

Acknowledgment. The author is grateful to the people who contributed to this research, especially Marcelo Kallmann, Jean-Sebastien Monzani, Angela Caicedo, Anthony Guye-Vuillème, Branislav Ulicny, Soraia Musse, and Pascal Bécheiraz. The research was sponsored by the Swiss National Research Foundation.

References

1. Farenc, N., Boulic, R., Thalmann, D., "An Informed Environment Dedicated to the Simulation of Virtual Humans in Urban Context", Proc. Eurographics '99, Milano, Italy, pp.309-318, 1999.
2. LeBon, G., Psychologie des Foules, Paris:Alcan, 1895.
3. Freud, S., Group Psychology and Analysis of the Ego, London: International Psychoanalytical Press, 1921.
4. Smelser, N., Theory of collective behavior, Routledge & Keganpaul, London, 1962.
5. McPhail, C., The Myth of Maddening Crowd, NY:Aldine De Gruyter, 1991.
6. Character Studio 3, http://www2.discreet.com/docs/char_st_WHT.pdf
7. Varner, D., et al., "UMSC Small Unit Leader Non-Lethal Trainer", in Proc. ITEC'98, 1998
8. Williams, J.,R., A Simulation Environment to Support Training for Large Scale Command and Control Tasks, PhD thesis, University of Leeds, 1995.
9. Still, G., K., Crowd Dynamics, PhD thesis, Warwick University, 2000
10. Helbing, D., Molnar, P., "Self-Organization Phenomena in Pedestrian Crowds", Pages 569-577 in: F. Schweitzer (ed.) Self-Organization of Complex Structures. From Individual to Collective Dynamics, Gordon and Breach, London, 1997.
11. McPhail, C., Powers, W.,T., and Tucker, C.,W., "Simulating individual and collective actions in temporary gatherings", Social Science Computer Review, 10(1):1-28, Spring, 1992.
12. Sime, J., D., "Crowd psychology and engineering: Designing for people or ballbearings.", in R.A. Smith and J.F. Dickie, eds., Engineering for Crowd Safety, p. 119-130, Elsevier, 1993
13. Musse S.R., Thalmann D., A Behavioral Model for Real-Time Simulation of Virtual Human Crowds, IEEE Transactions on Visualization and Computer Graphics, Vol.7, No2, 2001, pp.152-164.
14. Emering L., Boulic R., Molet T., Thalmann D., Versatile Tuning ofHumanoid Agent Activity, Computer Graphics Forum
15. Musse, S.R., Babski, C., Capin, T. and Thalmann, D. Crowd, Modelling in Collaborative Virtual Environments. ACM VRST '98, Taiwan
16 Schweiss E., Musse S.R., Garat F.. Thalmann D., An Architecture to Guide Crowds Using a Rule-Based Behaviour System, Proc.Agents 99.
17. Ingrand, F.F., Georgeff, M.P., and Rao, A.S. (1992). An architecture for real-time reasoning and system control. IEEE Expert/Intelligent Systems, 7(6):34–44.
18. Botelho, L.M. and Coelho, H. (1998). Artificial autonomous agents with artificial emotions. In Proceedings of the Second International Conference on Autonomous Agents, pages 449–450, New York. ACM Press.
19. Forsyth, D. R. (1990). Group dynamics (2nd ed.). Pacific Grove, CA: Brooks/Cole.
20. Thomas F., Johnston O.. Disney Animation: The Illusion of Life. Abbeville Press, New York, 1981.
21. Thalmann D., A New Generation of Synthetic Actors: the Interactive Perceptive Actors, Proc. Pacific Graphics '96 Taipeh, Taiwan, 1996, pp.200-219.

22. Renault O., Magnenat-Thalmann N., Thalmann D., A Vision-based Approach to Behavioural Animation, Journal of Visualization and Computer Animation, Vol.1, No1, 1990, pp.18-21.
23. Argyle M., Bodily Communication, Methuen and Co Ltd. (1975)
24. Kallmann M, Monzani J.S., Caicedo A., Thalmann D., ACE: A Platfor for the Real time Simulation Of Virtual Human Agents in Real Time, Proc. Eurographics CAS 2000, pp.73-85.
25. Kallmann M., D. Thalmann D., A behavioral interface to simulate agent-object interactions in real-time. In IEEE Computer Society Press, editor, Proc. Computer Animation 99, pages 138–146, 1999.
26. Monzani J.S., Caicedo A., Thalmann D., Integrating Behavioural Animation Techniques, Proc. Eurographics 2001.
27. Rao A.S., Georgeff M.P., Modeling rational agents withing a bdi-architecture. In J. Allen, R. Fikes, and E. Sandewall, editors, Proceedings of the Third Inter-national Conference on Principles of Knowledge Representation and Reasoning. Morgan Kaufmann, 1991.

Intelligent Virtual Agents for Education and Training: Opportunities and Challenges

Jeff Rickel

USC Information Sciences Institute
4676 Admiralty Way, Suite 1001
Marina del Rey, CA, 90292
rickel@isi.edu
http://www.isi.edu/isd/rickel

Abstract. Interactive virtual worlds provide a powerful medium for experiential learning. Intelligent virtual agents can cohabit virtual worlds with people and facilitate such learning as guides, mentors, and teammates. This paper reviews the main pedagogical advantages of animated agents in virtual worlds, discusses two key research challenges, and outlines an ambitious new project addressing those challenges.

1 Introduction

Interactive virtual worlds provide a powerful medium for experiential learning. Navy personnel can become familiar with the layout and operation of a ship to which they will be assigned before they ever set foot on it. History students can learn about ancient Greece by walking its streets, visiting its buildings, and interacting with its people. Biology students can learn about anatomy and physiology through adventures inside the human body. The range of worlds that people can explore and experience is unlimited, ranging from factual to fantasy, set in the past, present, or future.

Our goal is to enrich such worlds with intelligent virtual agents – autonomous, animated agents that support face-to-face interaction with people in these environments in a variety of roles. Existing virtual worlds such as military simulations and computer games often incorporate virtual agents with varying degrees of intelligence. However, the ability of these characters to interact with human users is usually very limited; most typically, users can shoot at them and they can shoot back. Those characters that support more collegial interactions, such as in children's educational software, are typically very scripted, and offer human users no ability to carry on a dialogue. In contrast, we envision virtual agents that cohabit virtual worlds with people and support face-to-face dialogues situated in those worlds, serving as guides, mentors, and teammates. We call this new generation of computer characters *animated pedagogical agents* [1].

A. de Antonio, R. Aylett, and D. Ballin (Eds.): IVA 2001, LNAI 2190, pp. 15–22, 2001.
© Springer-Verlag Berlin Heidelberg 2001

2   Roles for Animated Pedagogical Agents

Research on animated pedagogical agents can draw on a long history of work in computer-aided learning, especially work on intelligent tutoring systems [2]. However, as discussed in detail by Johnson, Rickel, and Lester [1], animated pedagogical agents offer a variety of distinct new capabilities:

Interactive Demonstrations. A simulated mockup of a student's real work environment, coupled with an animated agent that inhabits the virtual world, provides new opportunities for teaching the student how to perform tasks in that environment. Perhaps the most compelling advantage is that the agent can demonstrate physical tasks, such as operation and repair of equipment. For example, Rickel and Johnson's Steve agent [3,4] cohabits a 3D mockup of a US Navy ship with students, and can demonstrate procedures while providing spoken commentary describing his objectives and actions. Steve can respond to interruptions from students and use planning to adapt the demonstration to the state of the virtual world, thereby providing more interactive demonstrations than alternatives such as video.

Navigational Guidance. When a student's work environment is large and complex, such as a ship, one of the primary advantages of a virtual mockup is to teach the student where things are and how to get around. In this context, animated agents are valuable as navigational guides, leading students around and preventing them from becoming lost. For example, as Steve demonstrates tasks, he uses a path planning algorithm to lead students around a complicated shipboard environment. Similarly, the WhizLow agent [5] uses path planning to guide students through the internals of a virtual computer.

Gaze and Gesture as Attentional Guides. To draw students' attention to a specific aspect of a chart, graphic or animation, tutoring systems make use of many devices, such as arrows and highlighting by color. An animated agent, however, can guide a student's attention with the most common and natural methods: gaze and deictic (e.g., pointing) gestures. For example, Steve uses gaze and pointing gestures to draw a student's attention to objects in the virtual world as well as to people and agents who are responsible for the next step in a task. Among other animated agents, Presenter Jack [6] is notable for its broad repertoire of deictic gestures, and Cosmo [7] is notable for its sophisticated criteria for choosing deictic gestures and accompanying referring expressions.

Nonverbal Feedback. One primary role of a tutor is to provide feedback on a student's actions. In addition to providing verbal feedback, an animated agent can also use nonverbal communication to influence the student, which allows more varied degrees of feedback than earlier tutoring systems. For example, the Adele agent [8,9] nods or smiles to indicate agreement with a student's actions, presents a look of puzzlement when the student makes an error, and shows pleasant surprise when the student finishes a task, while Herman the Bug [10] sometimes congratulates students by cartwheeling across the screen.

Conversational Signals. When people carry on face-to-face dialogues, they employ a wide variety of nonverbal signals to regulate the conversation and complement their verbal utterances. While tutorial dialogue in most previous tutoring systems resembles Internet chat or a phone conversation, animated pedagogical agents allow us to more closely model the face-to-face interactions to which people are most accustomed. For example, the agents of Cassell and her colleagues [11,12,13] use gaze and gestures to regulate turn taking, head nods to provide backchannel feedback, and gaze, eyebrow movements, head movements, and gestures to emphasize words.

Emotions and Personality. Motivation is a key ingredient in learning, and emotions play an important role in motivation. By modeling and expressing emotions, animated agents may improve student motivation by conveying enthusiasm for subject matter and appearing to care about the student's progress, and an animated agent with a rich and interesting personality may simply make learning more fun [14]. For example, Cosmo [15] employs a repertoire of emotive behaviors to advise, encourage, and (appear to) empathize with students.

Virtual Teammates. When students must learn to perform effectively in a team, they must master their individual role while also learning to coordinate their actions with their teammates. In such team training, animated agents can play two valuable roles: they can serve as instructors for individual students, and they can substitute for missing team members, allowing students to practice team tasks when some or all human instructors and teammates are unavailable. Steve supports such team training; a team can consist of any combination of Steve agents and human students, each assigned a particular role in the team [16]. Different Steve agents can be configured with different appearances and voices, and students can monitor the activities of their agent teammates as well as communicate with them through spoken dialogue. This capability for multiple animated agents to cohabit a virtual world with multiple people provides a rich environment for team training.

Story and Character. Engaging stories with interesting characters have a powerful ability to capture and hold our attention and leave a memorable impression. If such stories could be harnessed for education and training, and made interactive to allow active learning by students, the result could provide a potent tool for learning. For example, the Interactive Pedagogical Drama system [17] combines a rich story line and emotionally expressive animated agents to allow mothers of children with cancer to interactively control a character in a similar situation. Through a therapist character in the story, who reacts dynamically to the human mother's choices, the mother gains exposure to a problem-solving methodology developed by clinical psychologists to help such people cope with common problems.

3   Towards Broader Support for Experiential Learning

Despite exciting progress on animated pedagogical agents over the last five years, two main challenges remain. First, while such agents incorporate sophisticated capabilities from other areas of artificial intelligence, such as spoken dialogue and models of emotion, they do not represent the state of the art in those areas. More work is required to fully integrate the latest advances into animated agents. Second, each animated pedagogical agent developed to date incorporates only some of the capabilities described in the last section. We do not yet have a single agent architecture that integrates all of these capabilities, addressing all of their interdependencies.

We are currently addressing these two challenges in an ambitious new project [18,19]. In contrast to our prior work on Steve, which focused on teaching well-defined tasks, our new project focuses on leadership training and decision making in stressful situations. Figure 1 shows a screen shot from a prototype implementation of an example application, in which a young lieutenant (human user) is being trained for a peacekeeping mission. In the current implementation, there are three Steve agents that interact with the lieutenant: a medic (front right) that serves as his teammate, a Bosnian mother (front center) whose boy has been accidentally injured by one of the lieutenant's vehicles, and a sergeant (front left) who serves as both a teammate and mentor. All other characters (soldiers and an angry crowd of locals) are currently simple scripted agents. The bodies and animation algorithms for all the Steve agents and scripted characters were developed by Boston Dynamics Incorporated, and the expressive faces for the sergeant and medic were developed by Haptek Incorporated.

Fig. 1. An interactive peacekeeping scenario featuring (left to right) a sergeant, a mother, and a medic

This new type of training exploits all of Steve's prior capabilities, but it is pushing us in several new directions. First, we are addressing issues of story and character to make the learning experience more engaging and memorable. The basic story line was created by a Hollywood script writer, in consultation with Army training experts. As the simulation begins, a human user, playing the role of a U.S. Army lieutenant, finds himself in the passenger seat of a simulated vehicle speeding towards a Bosnian village to help a platoon in trouble. Suddenly, he rounds a corner to find that one of his platoon's vehicles has crashed into a civilian vehicle, injuring a local boy (Figure 1). The boy's mother and an Army medic are hunched over him, and a sergeant approaches the lieutenant to brief him on the situation. Urgent radio calls from the platoon downtown, as well as occasional explosions and weapons fire from that direction, suggest that the lieutenant send his troops to help them. Emotional pleas from the boy's mother, as well as a grim assessment by the medic that the boy needs a medevac immediately, suggest that the lieutenant instead use his troops to secure a landing zone for the medevac helicopter. The lieutenant carries on a dialogue with the sergeant and medic to assess the situation, issue orders (which are carried out by the sergeant through four squads of soldiers), and ask for suggestions. His decisions influence the way the situation unfolds, culminating in a glowing news story praising his actions or a scathing news story exposing the flaws in his decisions and describing their sad consequences.

Second, since the human user must collaborate with his agent teammates to formulate novel plans, rather than simply execute well-defined procedures, we are integrating state-of-the-art natural language understanding and generation algorithms into Steve, as well as extending those algorithms to handle multi-party conversations in immersive virtual worlds [20]. On one hand, virtual worlds are an ideal application for current spoken language technology: they provide a microworld where conversation can legitimately be restricted to the events and objects within its confines. On the other hand, they raise issues that have received relatively little attention in computational linguistics. First, face-to-face communication in virtual worlds requires attention to all the nonverbal signals (e.g., gaze, gestures, and facial displays) that accompany human speech. Second, conversations that are situated in a 3D world raise a host of issues, including the attentional focus of the conversants, whether and to what degree they can see and hear one another, and the relative locations of conversants and the objects they are discussing. Finally, since there will typically be multiple real and virtual people, virtual worlds require support for multi-party conversations, including the ability to reason about the active participants in a conversation as well as who else might be listening. While there has been some early work in the area of embodied conversational agents [21], and some of this work has addressed human-agent dialogues situated in 3D virtual worlds [3], there is currently no general model of such dialogues.

Third, to model the behavior of teammates in stressful situations, as well as create virtual humans that can induce stress in the human user by reacting emotionally, we have integrated a computational model of emotions into Steve [22]. For example, the mother in our peacekeeping scenario becomes increasingly angry at the lieutenant if his decisions thwart her goal of getting assistance for her boy. To handle the full range of emotions that arise in our scenario, we are incorporating a model of emotions arising from goals and plans [23] as well as a model of emotions arising from interpersonal relationships [17], and we are also working towards an outward expression of emotions that will be both believable and interpretable [24].

Our goal in this project is to create an architecture for animated pedagogical agents that integrates a broad range of capabilities. It is not sufficient to simply plug in a number of different modules representing the state of the art in spoken dialogue, affective reasoning, models of teamwork, motor control, etc. The state of the art in each area was developed independent of the others, so the fundamental research challenge is to understand the interdependencies among them. Our goal is an animated agent architecture that can be reused in a wide variety of applications and easily configured to model different styles and personalities.

4   Conclusion

Interactive virtual worlds combined with animated pedagogical agents offer an exciting new tool for education and training. While this tool builds on a long line of work in simulation-based learning and intelligent tutoring systems, animated pedagogical agents provide a variety of new capabilities. The last five years have seen exciting progress in this new technology, but most existing agents still have a limited range and depth of capabilities. To address this challenge, we are currently working on a single agent architecture that will incorporate a broader range of capabilities as well as integrating state-of-the-art modules for core capabilities such as spoken dialogue and affective reasoning. If successful, our work will lead to more sophisticated applications for animated pedagogical agents as well as a better understanding of the interdependencies among these different agent capabilities.

Acknowledgments. My research on animated pedagogical agents would not have been possible without the help of many talented people. Lewis Johnson collaborated with me on the original design of Steve's brain, and Marcus Thiebaux developed the models and animation algorithms for Steve's original body. Randy Stiles and his team at Lockheed Martin created the virtual world for Steve's shipboard training, and Allen Munro and his team at the USC Behavioral Technology Laboratories developed the simulation models for that virtual world. In our new project, Bill Swartout serves as the overall project director, Shri Narayanan is working on speech recognition, Randy Hill is working on perception, Ed Hovy is working on natural language understanding and generation, David Traum is working on dialogue management, Jon Gratch and Stacy Marsella are working on affective reasoning, Lewis Johnson and Richard Whitney are working on speech synthesis, Kate LaBore is developing the behaviors of the scripted characters, Larry Tuch wrote the story line with creative input from Richard Lindheim and technical input on Army procedures from Elke Hutto and General Pat O'Neal, Jay Douglas is working on interactive narrative issues, Ben Moore and Marcus Thiebaux created the simulation infrastructure, Chris Kyriakakis and Dave Miraglia are developing the immersive sound effects, and most of the graphics for the Bosnian town were created by Jacki Morie, Erika Sass, and Michael Murguia. The original research on Steve was funded by the Office of Naval Research under grant N00014-95-C-0179 and AASERT grant N00014-97-1-0598, and the new work is funded by the Army Research Office through the USC Institute for Creative Technologies under contract DAAD19-99-C-0046.

References

1. Johnson, W.L., Rickel, J.W., Lester, J.C.: Animated pedagogical agents: Face-to-face interaction in interactive learning environments. International Journal of Artificial Intelligence in Education **11** (2000) 47–78
2. Wenger, E.: Artificial Intelligence and Tutoring Systems. Morgan Kaufmann, Los Altos, CA (1987)
3. Rickel, J., Johnson, W.L.: Animated agents for procedural training in virtual reality: Perception, cognition, and motor control. Applied Artificial Intelligence **13** (1999) 343–382
4. Rickel, J., Johnson, W.L.: Task-oriented collaboration with embodied agents in virtual worlds. In Cassell, J., Sullivan, J., Prevost, S., Churchill, E., eds.: Embodied Conversational Agents. MIT Press, Cambridge, MA (2000)
5. Lester, J.C., Zettlemoyer, L.S., Gregoire, J., Bares, W.H.: Explanatory lifelike avatars: Performing user-designed tasks in 3d learning environments. In: Proceedings of the Third International Conference on Autonomous Agents, New York, ACM Press (1999)
6. Noma, T., Zhao, L., Badler, N.I.: Design of a virtual human presenter. IEEE Computer Graphics and Applications **20** (2000) 79–85
7. Lester, J.C., Voerman, J.L., Towns, S.G., Callaway, C.B.: Deictic believability: Coordinating gesture, locomotion, and speech in lifelike pedagogical agents. Applied Artificial Intelligence **13** (1999) 383–414
8. Shaw, E., Johnson, W.L., Ganeshan, R.: Pedagogical agents on the web. In: Proceedings of the Third International Conference on Autonomous Agents, New York, ACM Press (1999) 283–290
9. Shaw, E., Ganeshan, R., Johnson, W.L., Millar, D.: Building a case for agent-assisted learning as a catalyst for curriculum reform in medical education. In: Proceedings of the Ninth International Conference on Artificial Intelligence in Education, IOS Press (1999)
10. Lester, J.C., Stone, B.A., Stelling, G.D.: Lifelike pedagogical agents for mixed-initiative problem solving in constructivist learning environments. User Modeling and User-Adapted Interaction **9** (1999) 1–44
11. Cassell, J., Pelachaud, C., Badler, N., Steedman, M., Achorn, B., Becket, T., Douville, B., Prevost, S., Stone, M.: Animated conversation: Rule-based generation of facial expression, gesture and spoken intonation for multiple conversational agents. In: Proceedings of ACM SIGGRAPH '94, Reading, MA, Addison-Wesley (1994) 413–420
12. Cassell, J., Thórisson, K.R.: The power of a nod and a glance: Envelope vs. emotional feedback in animated conversational agents. Applied Artificial Intelligence **13** (1999) 519–538
13. Cassell, J., Bickmore, T., Campbell, L., Vilhjálmsson, H., Yan, H.: Conversation as a system framework: Designing embodied conversational agents. In Cassell, J., Sullivan, J., Prevost, S., Churchill, E., eds.: Embodied Conversational Agents. MIT Press, Cambridge, MA (2000)
14. Elliott, C., Rickel, J., Lester, J.: Lifelike pedagogical agents and affective computing: An exploratory synthesis. In Wooldridge, M., Veloso, M., eds.: Artificial Intelligence Today. Volume 1600 of Lecture Notes in Computer Science. Springer-Verlag, Berlin (1999) 195–212

15. Lester, J.C., Towns, S.G., Callaway, C.B., Voerman, J.L., FitzGerald, P.J.: Deictic and emotive communication in animation pedagogical agents. In Cassell, J., Sullivan, J., Prevost, S., Churchill, E., eds.: Embodied Conversational Agents. MIT Press, Cambridge, MA (2000)

16. Rickel, J., Johnson, W.L.: Virtual humans for team training in virtual reality. In: Proceedings of the Ninth International Conference on Artificial Intelligence in Education, IOS Press (1999) 578–585

17. Marsella, S.C., Johnson, W.L., LaBore, C.: Interactive pedagogical drama. In: Proceedings of the Fourth International Conference on Autonomous Agents, New York, ACM Press (2000) 301–308

18. Rickel, J., Gratch, J., Hill, R., Marsella, S., Swartout, W.: Steve goes to Bosnia: Towards a new generation of virtual humans for interactive experiences. In: AAAI Spring Symposium on Artificial Intelligence and Interactive Entertainment. (2001)

19. Swartout, W., Hill, R., Gratch, J., Johnson, W., Kyriakakis, C., LaBore, C., Lindheim, R., Marsella, S., Miraglia, D., Moore, B., Morie, J., Rickel, J., Thiébaux, M., Tuch, L., Whitney, R., Douglas, J.: Toward the holodeck: Integrating graphics, sound, character and story. In: Proceedings of the Fifth International Conference on Autonomous Agents, New York, ACM Press (2001) 409–416

20. Traum, D., Rickel, J.: Embodied agents for multi-party dialogue in immersive virtual worlds. In: Agents 2001 Workshop on Representing, Annotating, and Evaluating Non-Verbal and Verbal Communicative Acts to Achieve Contextual Embodied Agents, Montreal, Canada (2001) 27–34

21. Cassell, J., Sullivan, J., Prevost, S., Churchill, E., eds.: Embodied Conversational Agents. MIT Press, Cambridge, MA (2000)

22. Gratch, J., Marsella, S.: Tears and fears: Modeling emotions and emotional behaviors in synthetic agents. In: Proceedings of the Fifth International Conference on Autonomous Agents, New York, ACM Press (2001) 278–285

23. Gratch, J.: Émile: Marshalling passions in training and education. In: Proceedings of the Fourth International Conference on Autonomous Agents, New York, ACM Press (2000) 325–332

24. Marsella, S., Gratch, J., Rickel, J.: The effect of affect: Modeling the impact of emotional state on the behavior of interactive virtual humans. In: Agents 2001 Workshop on Representing, Annotating, and Evaluating Non-Verbal and Verbal Communicative Acts to Achieve Contextual Embodied Agents, Montreal, Canada (2001) 47–52

Eye Pattern Analysis in Intelligent Virtual Agents

Michael Li[1] and Ted Selker[2]

[1]MIT Media Lab, 20 Ames Street,
Cambridge, MA 02139, USA
mli@alum.mit.edu
[2]MIT Media Lab, 20 Ames Street,
Cambridge, MA 02139, USA
selker@media.mit.edu

Abstract. This research discusses a new approach that uses patterns of a person's eye motion to improve human computer interaction between intelligent virtual agents (IVA) and the people who interact with them. This approach adds new capability to current eye tracking interfaces that focus on eye fixations instead of patterns of motion. The analysis of eye motion on the pattern level can deliver three values to an eye tracking interface: speed, interaction reliability, and a more complete understanding of user attention. This research builds a system, called InVision, to demonstrate how the analysis of eye fixation at the pattern level can improve eye tracking interfaces for human computer interaction. An IVA is built using this eye pattern analysis technique.

1 Introduction

The analysis on the pattern level of a person's eye motion can allow intelligent virtual agents (IVA) a better way to understand the person they are interacting with. People say they want to meet to look into another person's eyes. What do they see? Eye tracking provides a channel through which IVA's can intelligently observe a human. The pattern-centric eye tracking approach discussed in this paper, can improve human computer interaction. The analysis of eye motion patterns can offer traditional eye tracking interfaces a quicker, more reliable mode of interaction where appropriate. Beyond the general improvement to eye tracking interfaces, this technique also has specific importance to the field of virtual agents and human computer interaction. Analyzing eye motion as a collection of patterns allows a system to think of broader meaning in eye motion, meaning that is associated with such things as context, social interaction and task. This type of eye tracking interface can give an IVA the ability to be aware of things such as context, social interaction, and task that can be determined to some extent from eye movement.

Analyzing patterns of eye motion can deliver three improvements to eye tracking interfaces: increased interaction speed, reliability, and a more complete understanding of user attention. Currently, eye fixation is the primary means of identifying user attention as well as selection for control purposes in present day eye tracking. Several problems plague interfaces that use traditional eye fixation techniques including slowness and unreliability. This work proposes the use of eye fixation patterns as solutions to these problems. Interaction speed is increased through the use of pattern

A. de Antonio, R. Aylett, and D. Ballin (Eds.): IVA 2001, LNAI 2190, pp. 23-35, 2001.

identification as a means of selection. Pattern correlation can help improve the reliability of an eye tracking interface. This approach also gives interfaces the capability to understand the context of a user's eye motion through pattern interpretation.

For the purposes of this research, an eye tracking interface tool called InVision is built that uses an eye pattern analysis approach. Specifically, this interface uses patterns of eye fixations to analyze and interpret eye motion data. Such an analysis moves beyond simple eye fixation identification and examines how the eye has moved around an image within the context of that image. Using the InVision interface tool, the three values proposed by this work that are offered by this pattern-based technique to the field of virtual agents are investigated and evaluated.

First, the performance of an eye pattern analysis approach in attentive selection is quantitatively evaluated. An experiment, the Eye Selection Test, is run for this purpose using the InVision system. The performance of the pattern approach is experimentally compared to that of an approach using simple fixation for selection. Two variables are measured: selection accuracy and selection time, reflecting system reliability and system speed respectively.

The second part of the work qualitatively studies how a virtual agent can use this proposed technique of examining a user's eye fixation patterns to reveal a more complete understanding of user attention. The Kitchen InVision project is a virtual agent that studies patterns of fixations for the purposes of identifying, interpreting and responding to user cognitive state. By understanding user attention on a more complete and contextual level through eye-motion pattern analysis, intelligent agents will be capable of better predicting and accommodating a user's interests, tasks and questions.

2 Background

Eye tracking can provide a channel through which IVA's can observe a human user on a contextual, emotional, and social level. The speed of interaction with an eye tracking interface can be incredibly fast. Ware and Mikaelian (1987) show that simple target selection and cursor positioning operations can be performed twice as fast using an eye tracking interface than using a mouse.

Fixation is an important phenomenon that is commonly used by eye tracking systems to provide an indication of local user attention. Most eye tracking interfaces use fixation as the basis for *target acquisition* which is the task of identifying a particular object. Target acquisition is generally an aspect of selection for eye tracking interfaces as well. Some eye tracking interfaces use eye fixation for both target acquisition as well as *selection*, such as IBM's Suitor project (Blue eyes: Suitor). The Suitor project, also known as Interest Tracker, distinguishes between a "glance" and a "gaze" by the amount of time a user has fixated on a particular area and uses a gaze as a means of selection. Techniques using fixation duration, or *dwell-time*, as a means of selection generally use a threshold value between 250-1000ms (Edwards, 1998). If a fixation lasts longer than the chosen threshold value, a selection is initiated. Interfaces using fixations for either for target acquisition or selection are referred to in this paper as *fixation-based* interfaces.

Fixation detection is an entire sub-field of eye tracking work While the physiological concept of a fixation is understood, many different algorithms for fixation detection (S. Zhai, personal communication, February 1, 2001) have been developed. A technique for fixation detection is used in this work that is similar to the fixation recognition approach described by Jacob (1995). It is believed that the specific choice of the fixation algorithm will not affect the results and conclusions of the work presented.

More recently, work has been performed regarding the use of eye motion patterns to understand user cognitive state. One of the earliest uses of eye motion pattern to understand user attention is in a system created by Starker and Bolt (1990) that displays a planet from "The Little Prince," a book by Antoine de Saint Exupery. It uses patterns of natural eye movement and fixation to make inferences about the scope of a user's attention. Edwards (1998) uses eye movement pattern identification in the Eye Interpretation Engine, a tool that can recognize types of eye movement behavior associated with a user's task. Perhaps one of the works that is most relevant to this work is done by Salvucci (1999) who describes a technique called fixation tracing, a process that infers user intent by mapping observed actions to the sequential predictions of a process model. This technique translates patterns of eye movement to the most likely sequence of intended fixations. Several pilot interfaces were implemented in developing this work. These interfaces studied grouping, patterns of association and identification in search. The use of eye motion patterns is still a relatively new research area that will become more prevalent as eye tracking technology improves.

3 Approach

Eye motion patterns are at the center of this work. Patterns of eye movement are comprised of a sequence of points representing the locations of the eye fixation points[i] over time. While research has been performed on patterns of object selection to infer user intention and state, this work explores a new direction: the use of *patterns of eye fixations*. Several advantages can be gained from analyzing patterns of eye motion in eye tracking interfaces. The technique of analyzing eye movement on the pattern level can have three significant effects on current eye tracking systems that this section will propose and discuss. Such a technique can offer speed, reliability and a better understanding of user attention and each of these three effects are individually discussed below.

3.1 Speed through Pattern Identification

Pattern identification in eye motion data can increase selection speed. Identifying a pattern of eye motion can be much quicker than detecting a sequence of object selections. The task of using eye fixations as a means of selection can take an unpredictably long period of time depending on how good the system accuracy and system calibration is. This can greatly delay a system's response time.

Eye-gaze tends to be both inaccurate and imprecise. A user's eye fixations, as recorded by an eye tracker, are often not centered over visual targets. Two things cause this inaccuracy: users can fixate anywhere within a one-degree area of the target and still perceive the object with the fovea (Jacobs 1995), and eye-trackers typically have an accuracy of approximately one-degree (Salvucci, 1999). Imprecision is introduced into eye-gaze data through the involuntary jittery motions produced by the eye. When the eyes appear to be looking at a single point, they are actually making a series of abrupt jumps. Research has demonstrated that impulses along the optic nerve occur only at the moment when the image changes on the retina (Babsky, Khodorov, Kositsky, & Zubkov, 1975). During constant application of light on visual receptors, impulses quickly cease along the corresponding optic nerve fibers and vision effectively disappears. For this reason, eye motion contains incessant imperceptible jumps that constantly displace the retinal image. This series of jumps stimulate new visual receptors and produce new impulses on the optic nerve, ultimately enabling the process of vision. Eye control is neither accurate nor precise enough for the level of control required to operate today's UI widgets such as scrollbars, buttons, hyperlinks and icons. Zhai, Morimoto, and Ihde (1999) show that the area represented by a user's fixation is approximately twice the size of a typical scrollbar, and much greater than the size of a character.

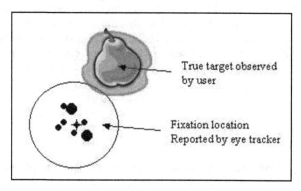

Fig. 1. A sample of eye movement that shows the inaccuracy and imprecision related to eyegaze.

Fixation-based interfaces are limited in their ability to handle and interpret eye tracking data because of this noise. By watching only for fixations, these interfaces adopt an easy technique for noise filtering, but at the same time end up ignoring important data as well. Consider the following problem: a user's eye gaze remains fixed on a point on the screen, but the eye tracking calibration is slightly off, resulting in a off-center fixation somewhere other than the location intended (see Figure 1). A fixation-based interface cannot effectively accommodate such noise.

Off-center fixations can undermine eye control reliability as well. An off-center fixation could fall on an object other than the one intended, producing an incorrect system response. Algorithms and techniques exist that attempt to map off-center fixations to intended targets. Similarly, cluster analysis methods can help determine likely target areas of attention (Goldberg & Schryver, 1995). These techniques do not always produce correct results however, especially as the number of target objects increase and the size of the target objects decrease.

The use of a pattern of fixations as a means of selection bypasses the need to select individual objects with fixations and thus can dramatically speed up selection time. Figure 2.a. displays a fixation path using a normal fixation-based method that requires a fixation to land on a target for a specified period of time. Figure 2.a. shows the need for several fixations per object selection when using fixation for selection. Figure 2.b. shows the use of eye fixation pattern for selection, which requires fewer fixation points to identify a selection. Because selection through pattern does not require many fixation points, selection speed for such a task is dramatically improved with little if no cost to accuracy. The InVision system records where a person's eyes look and filters this set of points for pre-defined patterns between one or more objects in the image. A selection pattern is identified by the system in Figure 2.b. based on the attention given to the 3 blue circles.

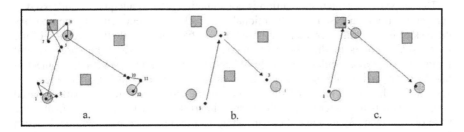

Fig. 2. Three different eye fixation paths are shown for the same task of selecting blue circles in the image. *a.* selection of three objects by fixation *b.* selection of three objects by pattern of fixation *c.* selection reliability through pattern correlation

3.2 Reliability through Pattern Correlation

This work demostrates that the technique of analyzing eye movement on the pattern level can improve reliability in eye tracking interfaces by increasing accuracy in target acquisition. In order for a pattern to be recognized, a very characteristic path must be taken by the user's eyes. Such a requirement can lead to a specificity that is hard to produce by either accident or luck. A system that is designed to listen for eye patterns waits for the user's eyes to move in a certain pattern before an event or action is initiated. This offers a much more reliable response than a system that looks only at the location of the user's gaze to initiate action.

Several features of an eye movement sequence can make pattern identification more reliable than fixation identification. The distance and vector angle between two points in an eye movement sequence are both attributes that can be used to help validate a pattern. Even the information concerning the location of where the eyes start and end can be used to help confirm a pattern. Identifying these features can provide data redundancy and correlation in noisy data from eye tracking systems. Figure 2.c. shows how pattern correlation can improve the reliability of a selection. This figure shows how the task of selecting blue circles can be distinguished from the task of selecting red squares based on the pattern of the eye fixation path. Using a pattern-based approach, a system can examine several validating factors to establish consistency in interpreting a user's intent, which ultimately improves the reliability of the interface.

3.3 Understanding User Attention through Pattern Interpretation

A system using an eye pattern based approach can better understand the concept of user attention. Several problems can be identified with the way fixation-based eye tracking systems determine user attention. Without looking at sequences of eye motion, it is difficult to appreciate attention on a complete level. Through examination of eye motion at the pattern level, the scope of a user's interest/attention can be better determined and identified.

The scope of user interest/attention is not something that is adequately addressed in current eye tracking systems. A traditional eye tracking system generally approaches the task of identifying user attention based on eye fixations. While the direction of the gaze usually points to the object of interest, this is not always the case. Several fixations within a particular area might indicate the user's interest in a single object in that location, or it could also be indicative of interest in a couple smaller objects. A system that has knowledge of the objects in the image and uses a pattern-based approach can better determine if the user is interested in a face, or specifically the nose on that face. By looking at eye tracking data in aggregate patterns, the data can be processed at a higher semantic level. The points of eye positions while giving little meaning themselves, can be grouped into patterns that have relevance to what the user is really looking at and what the user is concerned with.

Eye patterns can also give a better indication that a user has in fact given attention to a particular object. A system that can combine the history of a user's gaze with information about the objects in an image can build a better model of attention. The current location of a user's eye-gaze alone has proven insufficient for determining attention but the analysis of how the user's eyes moved in a given time period gives a much more complete picture. With this technique, the problem of distinguishing meaningful attentive vision from idle looking will be easier to approach.

Patterns of eye fixation can directly reflect user task. This represents a new area not emphasized by current eye tracking work which has primarily focused on patterns of object selections. Salvucci (1999) proposes similar work using fixation tracing to facilitate eye movement analysis to infer user intent at the fixation level. This work helps to better infer intended fixation location from recorded eye movement. Work performed by Edwards (1998) distinguishes eye movement into three mutually exclusive categories of behavior: searching, knowledge movement, and prolonged searching. From these characteristic patterns of eye movement, inferences can be made about user intent. This work investigates how aggregations of eye motion patterns can correlated to contextual user attention, such as user task. A computer user's eyes move in a specific way across the screen that is characteristic in part of the type of task, whether writing a paper, browsing the web, searching for a file, checking email or launching an application. Patterns promise the potential of helping eye tracking systems begin to understand the user on a much higher-level.

3.4 InVision Pattern-Based Approach

A description of the pattern-based approach used by the InVision system is provided. It is referred to as an *approach* rather than an algorithm since it describes a general method for defining a pattern of eye fixation within a set of eye-gaze data. This section describes how the InVision system examines eye tracking data for simple patterns between pre-defined objects in an image. More advanced pattern-analysis algorithms can be employed, but it is the intent of this research to demonstrate a general concept as opposed to a specific algorithm or the implementation of a specific system.

The pattern-based approach uses a measure of both angle of approach and distance traversed between two consecutive fixations in order determine the probability that two fixations belong to a pattern. Over a sequence of several fixations, the probability of a pattern being incorrectly determined is low since several points provide collective reinforcement. The angle of approach between two fixations is measured and compared with each angle in the set of angles between object pairs in the interface. If the value of the angle of approach is close (within a specified range) to the angle between one of the object pairs, the distance between the two consecutive fixations is measured and compared to the distance between that particular object pair candidate. If this distance falls within a designated range, then the next connecting angle of approach is measured. The process repeats until either a pattern is recognized or the system determines that no pattern in the interface exists that fits the angle and distance characteristics for that particular set of fixations.

4 Results

The quantitative results of the InVision research are presented and discussed in the following sections.

4.1 The Eye Selection Test Experiment

The Eye Selection Test demonstrates how a pattern-based approach can improve speed and reliability in an eye tracking interface in the task of identifying user attention. An experiment is performed to evaluate the pattern-based InVision interface in comparison to a fixation-based interface. The objective of this experiment is to address the first part of this work's hypothesis: to quantitatively investigate whether a pattern-based analysis can improve the reliability and speed of an eye tracking interface. Object size, while not the only measurable independent variable, is one of the biggest factors influencing selection performance. For this reason, selection speed and accuracy is measured for each interface over the size of the objects being selected. This provides a level means of comparison across different interfaces. The following sections outline the experiment performed, present the experiment results, and finally discusses the analysis of the results.

This experiment displays a sequence of trials each consisting of circular targets on the subject's screen. Targets appear three at a time in random locations on the screen (see Figure 3). Target size is randomized across trials but all the objects in the same trial are of equal size. The subject is instructed to select each of the three targets as rapidly as possible when the targets appear at the beginning of the trial. Selection, defined in the context of this interface, is equivalent to target acquisition. When an individual target has been selected, it disappears, and after the three targets in the trial have all been selected, a new trial is displayed. If a trial is not completed in a designated time, it is skipped. The trial begins when the user selects the first target and ends when the last target selection in a trial is completed. The experiment records whether the targets have been successfully selected along with the time duration of the trial. The number of off-center fixations, or fixations that don't select a target, are recorded and are used to reflect the relative inaccuracy of the selection process. After the subject has completed the series of trials, data analysis is available. The data from each trial with the same object sizes is combined for the purposes of analysis.

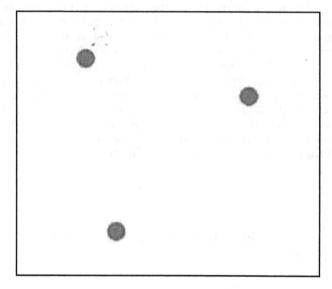

Fig. 3. The Eye Test Selection Experiment

The InVision system's pattern-based approach is compared to a system that uses simple fixation as a means of target acquisition, an approach that looks simply at whether a fixation falls within an object. While better fixation algorithms exist to recognize the intended location of off-center fixations (such as one that chooses the closest target to the fixation), this fixation-based approach is chosen for use as a base level comparison. For the actual experiment, 5 tests each composed of 500 trials were run on each interface. Each selection test used a random target object size between 5 and 150 pixels and placed the target at a random location on the screen. Through this experiment, selection accuracy is compared across object size between a fixation-based interface and the pattern-based InVision system.

4.2 Results, Speed Comparison

Data regarding trial times is collected from the experimental runs, combined and then summarized. In order to compare the two different sets of data, the time recorded for each trial is divided by three, the number of targets per trial. This gives a representation of the selection time per object for a certain object size using a particular interface. The selection times recorded per experimental run reflect an average of the selection times across all trials of a particular object size. The selection times for each experimental run is plotted across object size for both interfaces and the results are summarized in Figure 4. A best-fit line is drawn through the two data samples.

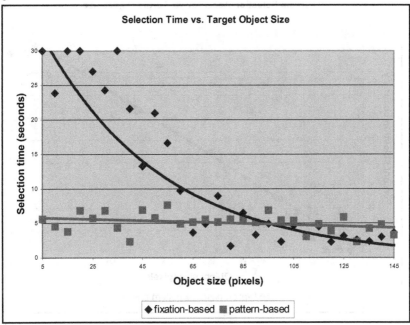

Fig. 4. Selection Time vs. Target Object Size for Fixation (blue) and Pattern-Based (red) Approaches

It is apparent that the data set representing the fixation-based approach requires a rather large number of fixations compared to the pattern-based approach. For the fixation-based technique, the number of fixations need to select an object is non-linear and reflects the calibration and inaccuracies in the eye tracking system. In a fixation-based approach, several fixations are required before a fixation falls on the target object. At small object sizes, the fixation-based approach requires a large selection time. This is due to the fact that as object sizes decrease, objects becomes harder to select. However as object sizes increase, the selection time approaches a constant. The significance of these results is that the pattern-based approach is able to remove the unpredictability and non-linearity of selection by not selecting through fixation but through pattern.

4.3 Results, Accuracy Comparison

Selection accuracy is used as a measure for system reliability. Data is taken from the same experimental runs used in the speed comparison analysis performed above. Selection accuracy for a particular object size is measured by dividing the number of target objects within the trial by the total number of fixations recorded in the trial. Similar to the speed comparison analysis performed above, the data collected from each experiment for each object size is averaged across trials. The percent selection accuracy for each experimental run is plotted across object size for both interfaces and is displayed in Figure 5. A best-fit line is drawn through the two data samples.

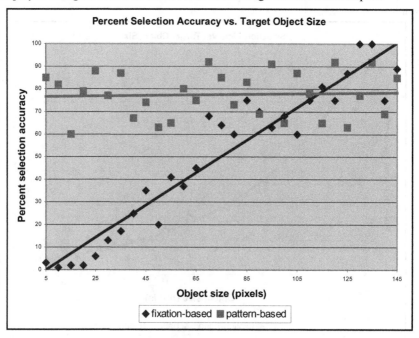

Fig. 5. Percent Selection Accuracy vs. Target Object Size for Fixation (blue) and Pattern-Based (red) Approaches

The results for the accuracy comparison show that the InVision interface performs at a much higher selection accuracy than the fixation-based interface that is used for the experiment. Figure 5 shows a graph of the selection accuracy of the interfaces while object size varies. This graph shows that InVision performs better across all object sizes and performs significantly better when the object size is small, maintaining a high level of selection accuracy where the fixation-based system becomes very inaccurate.

The InVision system is also more adept at distinguishing between close objects than other systems. InVision correctly distinguishes the target object from two objects that are relatively close on the screen at a higher frequency than does the fixation-based technique that is examined.

4.4 Kitchen InVision

The Kitchen InVision is an intelligent virtual agent that can interact with a user by *listening* to patterns of eye fixation. An image of a kitchen is displayed along with several items commonly found in a kitchen. Interaction in this non-command (Nielson 1990) interface is achieved by watching a user's eye motion, interpreting patterns of eye fixation and delivering a visual response reflecting a change in the state of the kitchen or one of the items.

The interaction across this interface from user to system is not necessarily a direct one. Eye movements reflect thought process, and indeed a person's thought may be followed to some extent from eye movement analysis (Yarbus, 1967). The project described does not employ direct control and manipulation but rather builds a non-command interface in which the system *responds* to the interpreted eye pattern rather than being controlled. Therefore, few command instructions need to be provided on how to use the system. Providing instructions specific to the interface control implies a direct control mode of interaction between user and system, which as stated earlier, is not the intent of the project.

The system can recognize the following tasks: cooking a turkey, washing dishes, and unpacking food from a grocery bag. Each task is made up of a sequence of independent actions. For example, the task of cooking a turkey involves opening a cabinet, putting a tray on the counter, taking the turkey out of the fridge, putting it on the tray, sticking the turkey in the oven, cooking the turkey and taking it out at the appropriate time. Active objects in the kitchen function in much the same way as one would expect them to in real life; the fridge, oven, and cabinets can open, food items can be cooked or be placed in the fridge, dishes can be washed, etc (see Figure 6).

Fig. 6. The Kitchen InVision Project

The Kitchen project depends on InVision to recognize several types of fixation patterns. Simple patterns such as detecting user attention on one or more objects are recognized by the system, as well as complex patterns involving higher-level analysis and interpretation of aggregate patterns. Simple algorithms determine the weight of the user attention on an object, or a set of objects by using the number of fixations on particular active objects in the image over a specified length of time. Inherent within the system is a flexible logic that is used to determine matches between user eye motion and user task and intent.

The Kitchen InVision project demonstrates how eye patterns can be used to interpret high-level user attention. The success of this demonstration is not entirely unexpected; it is logical that patterns of eye movement preserve data relating to a user's intention and attention. Where the eye comes from, what the eye has seen and when the eyes have moved all are factors that help understand user attention on more than just a localized scope. It should be stated that the concept of attention is a complicated idea that cannot be adequately identified by the eyes alone. However, as defined earlier, the scope of this work focuses on the eye's contribution to the state of user attention and attempts to better understand what user attention is, and how to help identify it using data collected from eye motion.

The Kitchen InVision project is a preliminary step into understanding how a pattern-based eye tracking technique can help an intelligent agent. It is both an experiment in a new type of human computer interaction as well as an intelligent virtual agent. It serves as an example of an interface that uses a combination of eye fixation pattern and contextual information as the means of identifying user task and intention. Previous endeavors to understand patterns of eye motion have emphasized the use of patterns of selected objects to make inferences about user intention, rather than patterns of fixations. A pattern-based approach can offer speed and reliability in the research of using patterns to explain cognitive intent, especially in the area of non-command interfaces and context-sensitive environments.

5 Conclusion

This work has proposed the use of interpreting eye motion data through patterns of aggregate eye movement and has discussed how the field of intelligent virtual agents can benefit from eye pattern analysis. A system called InVision is built which adopts a pattern-based approach to eye motion interpretation. InVision provides a platform on which interfaces using eye pattern analysis can be built. The abilities of a pattern-based approach are tested and evaluated by using the interface structure provided by InVision. Next, comparison benchmarking is performed between a pattern-based and a fixation-based approach. Finally an intelligent virtual agent, called Kitchen InVision, is created to demonstrate how patterns of eye fixation can be used to infer context-specific user intent. Results point to several advantages gained through the use of patterns, confirming the benefits of a pattern-based approach proposed earlier in this paper. The three benefits that are demonstrated by this research to be gained from the use of eye pattern analysis are:

1. Speed through pattern identification
2. Reliability through pattern correlation
3. Understanding through pattern interpretation

To conclude, the analysis of fixations on the pattern-level has been identified as a new approach for understanding the human user that can offer both better ability as well as new capability to eye tracking interfaces. It is hoped that the research outlined in this paper will give encouragement to future research and development of eye fixation patterns within the space of intelligent virtual agents.

References

1. Babsky, E., Khodorov, B., Kositsky, G., & Zubkov, A. (1975). Human physiology. Moscow: Mir Publishers, 182-214.
2. Blue eyes: Suitor [WWW Document]. URL http://www.almaden.ibm.com/cs/blueeyes/ suitor.html (visited 2001, February 2).
3. Edwards, G. (1998). A tool for creating eye-aware applications that adapt to changes in User Behaviors. International ACM Conference on Assitive Technologies 1998. 67- 74.
4. Goldberg, J. H. & Schryver, J. C. (1995). Eye-gaze determination of user intent at the computer interface. In J. M. Findlay, R. Walker, & R. W. Kentridge (Eds.), Eye movement research: Mechanisms, processes, and applications (491-502). New York: Elsevier Science Publishing.
5. Jacob, R. J. K. (1995). Eye tracking in advanced interface design, in W. Barfield & T. Furness, eds, 'Advanced Interface Design and Virtual Environments'. Oxford: Oxford University Press, 258-288.
6. Nielsen, J. (1993, April). Noncommand user interfaces [Communications of the ACM, volume 36, no. 4]. 83-99.
7. Salvucci, D. D. (1999). Inferring intent in eye-based interfaces: Tracing eye movements with process models. Proc. CHI '99, 254-261.
8. Starker, I. & Bolt, R. A. (1990). A gaze-responsive self-disclosing display. Proc. ACM CHI '90 Human Factors in Computing Systems Conference, Addison-Wesley/ACM Press, 1990. 3-9.
9. Yarbus, A. L. (1967). Eye movements during perception of complex objects, in L. A. Riggs, ed., `Eye Movements and Vision'. New York: Plenum Press, chapter 7, 171-196.
10. Ware, C. & Mikaelian, H. T. (1987). An evaluation of an eye tracker as a device for computer input. Proc. ACM CHI, GI '87 Human Factors in Computing Systems Conference. 183-188.
11. Zhai, S., Morimoto, C. & Ihde, S. (1999). Manual and gaze input cascaded (MAGIC) pointing. Proc. ACM CHI '99 Human Factors in Computing Systems Conference, Addison-Wesley/ACM Press, 1999. 15-20.

---

[i] In this research we look at patterns of fixation points, although eye movement patterns are not necessarily limited to fixation points alone.

Communicating Emotion in Virtual Environments through Artificial Scents

Carlos Delgado-Mata and Ruth Aylett

Centre for Virtual Environments, The University of Salford, Business House,
University Road, Salford, M5 4WT, United Kingdom
C.Delgado@pgr.salford.ac.uk, R.S.Aylett@salford.ac.uk

Abstract. In this paper we describe an emotional- behavioural architecture. The emotional engine is a higher layer than the behaviour system, and it can alter behaviour patterns, the engine is designed to simulate Emotionally-Intelligent Agents in a Virtual Environment, where each agent senses its own emotions, and other creature emotions through a virtual smell sensor; senses obstacles and other moving creatures in the environment and reacts to them. The architecture consists of an emotion engine, behaviour synthesis system, a motor layer and a library of sensors.

Keywords: autonomous agents, multiple agents, emotion, virtual environment, behavioural architecture, virtual sensors, virtual smell.

1 Introduction

This paper discusses work-in-progress in the use of emotion as a form of interaction between (pseudo-)embodied agents in a virtual environment (VE). It attempts to integrate emotions at the pseudo-physiological level into an existing behavioural architecture which will be briefly described. It then seeks mechanisms for the transmission of emotion between agents, and for the perceived emotion of one agent to influence the emotion and thence the behaviour of another. One branch of this work confines itself to the behavioural level, taking sheep as exemplar agents, we will discuss it here. The other branch considers how a planning system might be integrated into the architecture and takes the idea of the Holodeck, a soap-opera type drama played out by virtual pseudo-human agents, as its test-bed.

While emotional interaction between agents naturally requires an internal emotional architecture, this architecture has to be linked both to transmission and reception mechanisms. Thus the focus is somewhat different from much existing work which either concentrates on the internal agent architecture or considers the agent-human user relationship. As discussed below, transmission and reception are asymmetric: transmission is the sole step in communicating emotion to another agent, but reception may also involve an interaction between the sensed emotion and the existing emotional state of the agent before feeding

A. de Antonio, R. Aylett, and D. Ballin (Eds.): IVA 2001, LNAI 2190, pp. 36–46, 2001.

into its behaviour. Note that we do not include intentionality in this system - emotional interaction is being modelled as essentially involuntary.

This paper starts by introducing previous work, namely the Behaviour Synthesis Architecture. Then a description on how the Behaviour Synthesis Architecture can be extended to include emotions and communicate emotion through virtual scents is presented. This paper finishes by giving the status quo on the project.

2   Behavioural Architecture - Previous Work

Previous work had taken a behavioural architecture developed for multiple cooperating robots - the Behavioural Synthesis Architecture or BSA [4] - and reapplied it to agents in a virtual environment (VE) in the Virtual Teletubbies project [2]. We here give an overview of this architecture. The BSA incorporated three structures at increasing levels of abstraction: behaviour patterns, behaviour packets, and behaviour scripts.

2.1   Behaviour Patterns

At the most primitive level, a behaviour pattern, (**bp**) as illustrated in figure 1, was defined as a pair of functional mappings, one from incoming sensory stimulus to outgoing desired motor response, and the other from sensory stimulus to utility, a mapping defining the importance of the motor response for the given level of stimulus. An agent possesses a repertoire of behaviour patterns, with each active pattern at any given time proposing its desired motor response according to its current sensory input. These responses were weighted by their utility values and synthesised together to produce an emergent response, which was the actual behaviour of the agent. Thus second-to-second variation in emergent behaviour was dealt with via weighted synthesis on a continuous basis, unlike the time-sliced Brooksian architecture.

Consider the situation where the sensory stimulus relates to an agent's forward facing distance-to-obstacle measuring sensor and the associated motion response relates to the forward translate velocity for that agent. From Figure 1 it can be seen that as the agent gets nearer to the object then its forward translate velocity will be reduced to zero. At the same time, the associated utility for this motion response increases. A similar pair of functions for rotation produces an increasing rotation away from the obstacle, also with increasing utility, as its distance from it diminishes. Thus as the agent gets nearer to an object in its path, it becomes more important for the agent to slow down and turn away from it.

In the BSA four behaviour levels (often known as strategy levels) were identified, originally for purely conceptual convenience [3]. A Self level contains those **bps** concerned with the maximisation and replenishment of internal resources, e.g. making sure an agent does not go hungry, or not walking up hills when

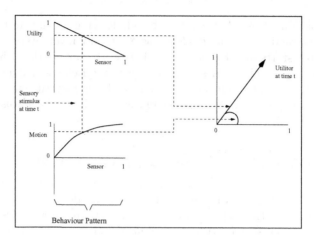

Fig. 1. Behaviour pattern example

energy is low. An Environment level contains **bps** associated with activities involving objects within the agent's environment, e.g. collision avoidance, collision detection, playing with a toy.

A Species level contains those **bps** associated with co-operant activities e.g. two agents carrying an object together, two agents hugging each other. A Universe level contains **bps** specific to a particular task, e.g. navigating to the initial location of an object to be relocated (such as the location of a slice of bread for example), then subsequent navigation to the desired goal location (the toaster in this case).

These strategy levels became an implementational feature as discussed below when the architecture was moved from robots to virtual agents.

2.2   Behaviour Packets

If all the **bps** in an agent's repertoire were active at the same time then the overall emergent behaviour of the agent might be of little value. For example patterns designed to produce obstacle avoidance as described above are not useful if you want an agent to sit down on a chair or hug another one of its species. The **bp** designer must always bear in mind that the low-level architecture is sensor-driven, and not task or even sub-task dependent. What is needed in this case is an automatic mechanism for deactivating the 'obstacle avoidance' **bps** when the 'sit' **bps** or 'hugging' **bps** are active. Associated therefore with every **bp** within an agent is an 'active flag', which enables or disables it. Thus obstacle avoidance **bps** for example can be turned off and on when required. A **bp** is 'deactivated' in the BSA by forcing the respective utility to zero. The action effectively produces a **bp** of zero importance and hence one which does not contribute to the overall emergent behaviour of the agent.

This mechanism is applied by grouping together **bps** in goal-achieving sets known as behaviour packets. A behaviour packet is a small data structure which includes a sensory pre-condition for activating the **bps** it references, and a sensory post-condition which controls deactivation of the named **bps**. Behaviour packets show some similarity with AI production rules [8], though they work at the sub-symbolic level and are driven by incoming sensor data rather than by an inferencing system. They support behavioural sequencing for agents performing at a task (universe) behaviour level. Thus a sensory pre-condition of 'being near the chair' could be used to move from a behaviour packet in which obstacle avoidance **bps** were active to one in which they are not.

Thus behaviour packets provide a mechanism for contextually sensitive behaviour switching, which is seen as a more flexible mechanism than the finite-state machine definition of inhibition and excitation between behaviours of the subsumption architecture.

2.3 Behaviour Script: High-Level Sequencing and Agent Drives

A behaviour script is simply a set of behaviour packets assembled for the achievement of a particular task, using the sensory pre-and post-conditions. The original approach was to generate behaviour scripts on the fly using a reflective agent incorporating a symbolic AI planner, and then send the individual scripts to behavioural-based agents. This hybrid approach was taken with the co-operative robots in MACTA [1] and is appropriate where the domain is predominantly task-based. However, while the lower levels of the architecture were moved from robots to virtual agents with no change, virtual agents are less likely to live in a task-oriented environment. It was at this point that the issue of incorporating emotion into the architecture came to the fore since if behaviour is not task-directed then drives or emotions are required instead. Broadly, if an agent is not being told what to do, then it does 'what it likes'.

The default script executes a single packet containing **bps** that effectively lets the low-level module handle wandering in the environment while avoiding obstacles. In the case of sheep this might be modified to grazing behaviour. The default script is changed when another sensory precondition from another set of packets is met.

Based on what has been described above, we believe that emotions are important for an agent. In the next section we describe how emotions, drives and moods can be used to to modify agent behaviour and how they can communicate their emotions using a virtual smell sensor.

3 Emotion as a Behaviour Pattern or Pattern Modifier

This section will start by defining emotions in action-selection and later it will address how the agents can communicate emotions through a virtual environment using virtual scents.

3.1   Emotions, Drives, and Moods

We all know by experience that too much emotion can impair decision, but recent studies in neuro-science [7] [12] found that too little emotion was the cause of flawed decision-making, as it has been evidenced by Damasio's studies of patients with damage to the prefrontal cortex and the amygdala. Further, LeDoux [12]has shown that that the amygdala plays a role in emotion.

Until recently the field of Artificial Intelligence, AI, had largely ignored the use of emotions and intuition to guide reasoning and decision-making.

Minski was one of the first to emphasize the importance of emotion for Artificial Intelligence, Cañamero [6] used Minski's concept of mind as a society of agents to develop her emotion architecture saying "An emotion is an agent that amplifies (or modifies) the motivational state of a creature and its perceived bodily state. It is characterized by: an incentive stimulus; an intensity proportional to its level of activation; a list of hormones it releases when activated; a list of physiological symptoms; a list of physiological variables it can affect."

Other models of emotion have been proposed; Picard focuses on in recognizing emotions [17], Bates [3] and Blumberg [5] synthesised emotion in their architectures as the primary means to create believable synthetic agents, and Velásquez [23] synthesised emotions and some of their influences on behaviour and learning.

The concept of drive is used in Cañamero [6] saying "These states or drives constitute urges to action based on bodily needs related to self-sufficiency and survival.

A mood will be used to refer to a long-term emotional state, Picard [17]says "a mood may arise when an emotion is repeatedly activated, for example a bad mood may arise during a half hour of reinforced negative thoughts or actions, or may be induced by taking drugs or medication".

Based on the description given above we decided to define emotions as reflective autonomic responses, that is primary emotions [7], triggered by particular stimulus, and the strength of these emotions can be influenced by the mood of the creature.

3.2   Emotions to Influence Behaviour

The use of emotion/drives to switch behavioural mode is however only one way of dealing with the relationship between emotion and behaviour. In other words in order to influence behaviour, emotions can be linked to internal virtual sensors, and so they can act as preconditions to behaviour packets –thus when fear rises past a certain level it will activate a fleeing packet behaviour.

The architecture also supports a much lower level relationship at the level of the synthesis mechanism. Two approaches are possible here. One is to consider a drive or emotion as a behaviour pattern in its own right, driven by a particular sensor input.

Its output is an actuator response which is synthesised into that of the other bps, thus having an effect upon the global emergent behaviour. Thus if an unfamiliar smell is sensed on the prevailing wind, a grazing sheep might slowly graze in the opposite direction to it so as to move away from it, with its fear behaviour. Or alternatively it might graze closer to other sheep, producing a more compact flock.

Alternatively, one could view it as an extra input into the stimulus-utility function component of a behaviour pattern. By affecting the utility component of more than one pattern, an emotion/drive in effect couples utilities together, reintroducing the idea of inhibition/excitation between patterns but in a flexible functionally defined manner. This would not only allow new behaviour to be added, but would allow existing behaviour to be suppressed via a flattening of its utility function. It would also allow for a emotional behaviour to gradually become more dominant - for example a grazing sheep becoming more and more jumpy in the face of a threatening stimulus. These approaches are not mutually exclusive, since a free-standing emotional behaviour could be different from other behaviour patterns precisely through its ability to cross-couple with utilities. Analysis of real sheep behaviour is needed to constrain the design of this emotional system.

A sheep subject to an alarming sensory stimulus may become 'restless' - fidgeting while it grazes, twitching its ears. As its level of fear rises, it may break off grazing to look around, before resuming; at a higher level still it may stop grazing and enter a state of alert, before finally panicking and running. With several drives/emotions acting concurrently, possibly with some modelled as a temporal cycle, it ought to be possible to model the characteristics put forward by Neary [15]. He notes that sheep will move more sluggishly on hot days and during the middle part of the day. This is simulated in our architecture by affecting the moods, as illustrated in figure 2. The mood can act as a filter for the activation of emotions patterns. Thus if the sheep is in a bad mood it could get angrier fast, or if the sheep is sluggish it could react (the sensing sensitivity could be affected) slowly and move awkwardly. The sheep are creatures of habit and they usually graze, drink and are more active in the morning and during the evening. Thus, if you are running (i.e. herding them) in the middle part of the day, the sheep may flock tighter, move slower, and spend more time looking at and fighting a dog. This suggests that careful analysis is needed in order to establish the most appropriate set of drives/emotions - Neary also points out that for sheep to be sheep, there needs to be a minimum number of five in the group. Less than five and their behaviour is not as predictable, suggesting a drive/emotion one might describe as 'group security' acting as a behavioural modifier.

3.3 Communicating Emotion

Because agents exist in a VE and not in the real world, in principle the transmission of emotion between agents could just be carried out by 'cheating', that is by allowing agents to read each other's internal state directly. We choose not to do this however, since we see advantages in re-usability and in matching real-world behaviour (that is in real sheep for example) by trying to model emotional

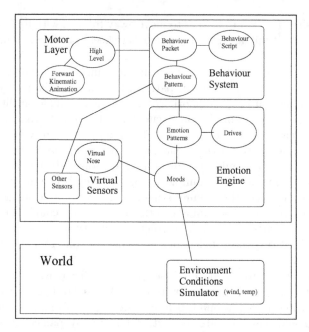

Fig. 2. Architecture Block diagram

interaction in a slightly more principled way. In the real-world however, emotional transmission may well be multi-modal, with certain modes such as the perception of motion (or in the general case 'body language') being particularly difficult to model. Thus we have limited ourselves for now to a single mode, and the one we have chosen is scent, to be perceived by a virtual nose sensor.

In our emotional architecture we use a virtual nose sensor, because the nose has been linked with emotional responses and intelligence. Goleman [11] states "The most ancient root of our emotional life is the sense of smell, or, more precisely, in the olfactory lobe, the cells that take in and analyse smell. Every living entity, be it nutritious, poisonous, sexual partner, predator or prey, has a distinctive molecular signature that can be carried in the wind." Neary [15]points out that sheep, particularly range sheep, will usually move more readily into the wind than with the wind, allowing them to utilise their sense of smell.

There is ongoing research in the field of electronic noses, Gardner [10] but we are not aware of the use of virtual noses in a virtual environment, so important issues arise like modelling molecules and wind flow, and how the wind moves them in the environment. The structure of a particular molecule is important in determining odour. This requires sensors which are responsive to the shapes or structural features of the organic molecules being modelled.

In real animals chemoreceptors (exteroceptors and interocetors) are used to identify chemical substances and detect their concentration. Smell exists even among very primitive forms of life . In our architecture we intend to model the exteroceptors which detect the presence of chemicals in the external environment.

To sense smell in the virtual environment, the molecules must be distributed in the environment; this is modelled by setting the density of each of the molecules within the environment represented as a grid. To simplify the computation the current grid is 2D, but we plan to use a voxel-based grid in the future.

The smell sensor and the virtual molecules used to represent the signature of different smells, is an important feature of our architecture, because it can be used to communicate emotions between agents through the environment. For example if a sheep panics it could exude a distinctive odour, or molecular signature, to the environment using a density function, and through time the molecules would disperse depending on several artificial environment factors like wind, rain, season and time of day. Other sheep will sense the panic smell and they will panic themselves and also exude the distinctive odour for panic so that the odour will propagate through the flock in few simulation steps.

To simulate volatile particles, i.e. scent which can be detected with the virtual olfactory system, we use particle systems theory [19], in which each particle represents a concentration of molecules with a different primary odour or other chemical signal, like panicking sheep. The particles behaviour depend on emitter properties.

The number or particles at a particular time can be derived from the following formula.

$$N(t) = M(t) + I(t)$$

Where M(t) is the mean number of particles perturbed by the intensity of the scent I(t) in the case of sheep panic.

The position of the particles will be influenced by weather condition, in particular wind and time of day.

$$P_i(t) = P_i(t-1) + W(t)$$

Where $P_i(t)$ is the Position of the particle at time t and W(t) is the weather vector at time t.

Molecule properties are encoded using an abstract binary mask, that is 1 for fear, 2 for food, 4 water. In this way we can give a special signature for different odours, and even an individual signature can be used for each sheep, in that way more complex behaviour as imprinting of baby sheep to their mother can be implemented. For show purposes the molecules will be shown if desired with different shapes and colours for each particle.

Through each simulation step the virtual molecules (particles) will be updated depending on the weather conditions and their properties, enumerated above. Only the particles near the head will be smelled (recognised by the virtual nose) and depending on the number of particles the intensity of the corresponding chemoreceptor will be triggered.

The next section presents the design of the implementation of the Behaviour Synthesis Architecture with virtual sensors as a mean to integrate an emotion mechanism to influence behaviour of virtual agents.

4   Implementation

To simulate the "emotional" virtual sheep in a virtual environment we are using the architecture described in Delgado [9], see figure 3.

The creature body is stored in a file containing data on the limbs and their relation to the parent joint. The hips are always the root joint.

A further file is used to store the animation which is carried out using forward kinematics, that is we first define the position of the hip and then we calculate the orientation of the thigh (and knee joint). And the with the orientation of the knee we can compute the position of the shin (and ankle). With this approach is quite straight forward to incorporate new movements or even change the bodily form of the agent, without having to start from scratch.

The sensors which drive the architecture produce data from both the external environment and the internal state of the agent. Virtual Sensors have been used in Virtual Actors [21], like the seminal work from Daniel Thalmann. They have also been used to simulate artificial fish, Tu and Terzopoulos fish controller[22], an object is only considered to be seen if any part of it enters the fish s view volume and if it is not fully occluded by another object.

Currently sensors include a distance sensor, a beacon sensor and a hunger sensor. Sensor abstraction has been implemented, so that the developer has a common interface in the architecture for all sensors and he could expand the library of sensors with more as needed, the virtual nose sensor (which we are currently developing use this sensor abstraction).

One example is the beacon sensor which is computed with the following formula, where B is a point in the facing vector of the creature and C is the position of the beacon. Agents moving towards a beacon using the beacon sensor and avoiding obstacles is shown in figure 3.

$$\theta = cos^{-1} \left(\frac{A_x B_x + A_y B_y}{\sqrt{A_x^2 + A_y^2} + \sqrt{B_x^2 + B_y^2}} \right)$$

And to know if the beacon on the left or the right of the creature

$$left = \begin{vmatrix} A_x & A_y \\ B_x & B_y \end{vmatrix}$$

If determinant is positive then beacon is θ degrees left of the agent, if negative beacon is θ degrees right of th agent.

Rendering of the virtual environment is done using SGI Performer, the sample applications have been successfully tested on Silicon Graphics Works stations,

Personal Computers with Linux and on the CAVE, The CAVE is a surround-screen, surround-sound, projection-based virtual reality (VR) system. The illusion of immersion is created by projecting 3D computer graphics into a cube composed of 4 solid screens 3m (width) x 2.8m (height) per screen that completely surround the viewer.

We are currently developing the emotion engine that will influence behaviour patterns and hence the behaviour performed by sheep. We hope to be able to show further advance in the workshop.

Fig. 3. Agents in the virtual environment moving toward a beacon

5   Conclusion

In this brief paper we have tried to explain the behavioural architecture being used for virtual agents and to look at how drives/emotions can be integrated into it in a more sophisticated manner than the existing use of a meter representation. We believe that by modelling transmitted emotion as a smell and using a virtual nose for reception, we are employing a biologically plausible mechanism. Work will continue both to produce hopefully accurate collective sheep behaviour as well as to investigate the more varied interaction between emotion received and induced in more human-like agents.

Acknowledgments. Funding for this research is provided by CoNACyT under grant 155753.

References

1. Aylett, R.S., *Communicating goals to behavioural agents - A hybrid approach*, Proceedings of the Third World Congress on Expert Systems, Seoul, Feb 1996
2. Aylett, R.S et al., *Virtual teletubbies: reapplying a robot architecture to virtual agents* Proceedings, 3rd International Conference on Autonomous Agents, 1999.
3. Barnes, D.P., *A behaviour synthesis architecture for cooperant mobile robots*, Advanced Robotics and Intelligent Machines, eds. J.O.Gray and D.G.Caldwell, IEE Control Engineering Series 51.295-314, 1996.
4. Barnes, D.P., Ghanea-Hercock, R.A, Aylett, R.S. and Coddington, A.M. *Many hands make light work? An investigation into behaviourally controlled cooperant autonomous mobile robots*, in: Proceedings of the first International Conference on Autonomous Agents, 413-20, Johnson, L. eds., Marina del-Rey, Calif.: ACM Press, 1997.
5. Blumberg, B., *Old Tricks, New Dogs: Ethology and Interactive Creatures*, Ph.D. diss. Massachusetts Institute of Technology, 1996.
6. Cañamero, D. *Modeling Motivations and Emotions as a Basis for Intelligent Behaviour*, Proceeding of the First International Conference on Autonomous Agents, 1997.
7. Damasio, A. *Descartes' Error:Emotion, Reason and the Human Brain*, Papermac, Oxford, U.K., 1996.
8. Davis, R., and King, J.*An overview of Production Systems, in Machine Intelligence*, E.W. Elcock and D. Michie (Eds.), Wiley and Sons, 300-332, 1977.
9. Delgado, C. and Aylett, R. *From Robots to Creatures: Extending a Robot Behaviour Based Architecture to Create Virtual Creatures*. In ISRA 2000, Monterrey Mexico, 2000.
10. Gardner, J. and Bartlett, P., *Electronic Noses:Principles and Practice*, Oxford University Press, United Kingdom, 1999.
11. Goleman, D., *Emotional Intelligence*, Bloomsbury, United Kingdom, 1996.
12. LeDoux, J., *The Emotional Brain*, Simon & Schuster, United Kingdom, 1998.
13. McFarland, D., *Animal Behaviour*, Addison Wesley Longman, 1999.
14. Minski, M., *The Society of Mind*, Simon and Schuster, New York, 1985.
15. Neary, M, *Sheep Sense*, http://www.working-border-collie.com/article3.html.
16. Ortony, A., Clore, G, Collins, A., *The cognitive Structure of Emotions*, Cambdrigde University Press, 1988.
17. Picard, R., *Affective Computing*, The MIT Press, 1997.
18. Pines, M., *Seeing, Hearing and Smelling the World: New findings help Scientists make sense of our senses*, Report from the Howard Hughes Medical Institute, 1997.
19. Reeves, W.T., *Particle Systems –A Technique for modeling a Class of Fuzzy Objects*, SIGGRAPH 83, 1983.
20. Reilly, S. and Bates, J., *Building Emotional Agents*, Technical Report CMU-CS-92-143, School of Computer Science, Carnegie Mellon University, May 1992.
21. Thalmann, D.,*Virtual Sensors: A Key Tool for the Artificial Life of Virtual Actors*, Proc. Pacific Graphics '95, Seoul, Korea, August 1995.
22. Tu, X. and Terzopoulos, D., *Artificial Fishes: Physics, Locomotion, Perception, Behavior*. Computer Graphics, 28:43–50, 1994.
23. Velásquez, J., *When Robots Weep: Emotional Memories and Decision-Making*, In: Proceedings of the Fifteenth National Conference on Artificial Intelligence (AAAI-98). Madison, WI: MIT/AAAI Press, 1998.

A Framework for Reasoning about Animation Systems

Eric Aaron, Dimitris Metaxas, Franjo Ivančić, and Oleg Sokolsky

Department of Computer and Information Science
University Of Pennsylvania
200 South 33rd Street
Philadelphia, PA USA 19104-6389
{eaaron, dnm}@graphics.cis.upenn.edu,
{ivancic, sokolsky}@saul.cis.upenn.edu

Abstract. In this paper, we consider the potential for reasoning about animations in the language of hybrid dynamical systems (i.e., systems with both continuous and discrete dynamics). We begin by directly applying hybrid systems theory to animation, using a general-purpose hybrid system specification tool to generate multi-agent animations; this application also illustrates that hybrid system models can provide systematic, modular ways to incorporate low-level behavior into a design for higher-level behavioral modeling. We then apply the logical framework of hybrid systems to animation: We formally state properties of animation systems that may not be readily expressed in other frameworks; and we mechanically check a collision-avoidance property for a simple race-like game. This hybrid systems-oriented approach could improve our ability to reason about virtual worlds, thus improving our ability to create intelligent virtual agents.

Some properties of animation systems cannot be readily verified merely by watching a few graphical displays. As part of a motivating example, consider an animation like the following one, in which an agent's locomotion consists of three sequential segments. In the first segment, the agent tries to avoid obstacles; it is steered by a complex non-linear system of differential equations that has parameters to represent low-level attributes like aggression (how near an agent will get to an obstacle before starting to swerve around it). In the second segment, the agent is in no danger of colliding with obstacles, so it instantaneously switches to a simpler, linear course that takes it to a final target. The third segment begins upon it reaching its target: No matter where in time and space that goal is achieved, the agent waits precisely one second before switching to another behavior, perhaps literally swelling up with pride for successfully completing its task. Given a set of parameter values for the non-linear steering in the first segment, that animation system is fully determined. For such a fully determined system, an absence of agent-obstacle collisions could be verified by viewing one animation.

Consider now the task of verifying collision-avoidance for *all* the animation systems that could result from different sets of parameter values. It might not be

A. de Antonio, R. Aylett, and D. Ballin (Eds.): IVA 2001, LNAI 2190, pp. 47–60, 2001.
© Springer-Verlag Berlin Heidelberg 2001

possible to check that property simply by viewing a small number of graphical displays, and we could certainly not watch every resulting animation. In cases such as this, where we want to reason about properties that we cannot easily see for ourselves, we might hope to ask for mechanical assistance. The first step toward that goal, however, is a major one: We must know how to model animation systems and state relevant properties formally and precisely. Once a linguistic framework for modeling and specification has been selected, we can investigate methods to assist us in reasoning.

To identify a candidate framework for reasoning about animation systems, we return to the animation described above. It is a *hybrid dynamical system* (*hybrid system*, for short), a combination of continuous and discrete dynamics; the agent's behavior is continuous in each segment, punctuated by instantaneous, discrete changes in behavior as it makes transitions between segments. There is a formal theory of hybrid systems [2,10,27], and although that theory has been employed in diverse application domains, animation is not typically considered in the hybrid systems literature. Nonetheless, some animation systems *are* hybrid systems, and hybrid system theory can be applied to animation.

In this paper, we explore the potential for reasoning about animations in the language of hybrid systems. We begin by directly applying hybrid system theory to animation, using the hybrid system specification and simulation tool CHARON [7,8] to generate several animations (including one similar to the one described in English above). This is a necessary preliminary; without demonstrating that animation systems could be modeled in the theoretical framework of hybrid systems, we could not use logics for hybrid systems to reason about animation. As part of this demonstration, we show that a hybrid system model can provide a systematic, modular way to incorporate sophisticated low-level behavior into a design for higher-level behavioral modeling.

We then consider how logics for hybrid systems might be applied to animations. We begin by expressing several properties that may interest animators, explicitly representing properties of time and reachability in space. Although many properties of complex hybrid systems are theoretically undecidable, there are many significant decidable cases, and we use the verification tool HYTECH [21] to mechanically check a result about a simple game-like animation.

We demonstrate our approach through a series of applications and experiments involving multi-agent animations with actors, targets, and obstacles [3].

1   Applying Hybrid Systems Theory to Multi-agent Animations

The presence of systems with both continuous and discrete dynamics is not new in animation, but it is not always clear how these systems relate to well-understood hybrid system models. In contrast, we make a strong connection to existing hybrid system theory by using the hybrid system tool CHARON [7,8] to implement multi-agent animation systems. Because of that connection, we are able to investigate the use of logics for hybrid systems (see section 3.1) as a framework for reasoning about animation.

We base our animations primarily on the agent-steering method presented in [17,18]. Below, we briefly review the tools we employed to create our animations and discuss some issues particular to implementing an animation system as a hybrid system in CHARON.

1.1   A Dynamical System for Agent Steering

There have been many approaches to guiding the behavior of autonomous agents. Logicist, artificial intelligence-based techniques have been successfully used for cognitively empowered agents [25] and animated actors [16]; perception and dynamics-based techniques [11,29,34] are often more readily able to adapt to dynamic environments. Our particular approach to low-level agent navigation —the continuous component of our hybrid animation system— is based on the method in [17,18], a scalable, adaptive approach to modeling autonomous agents in dynamic virtual environments. Like treatments of similar issues in the field of behavioral robotics [24], we consider only two-dimensional motion, although the mathematical foundations for three-dimensional navigation already exist [18].

Our animated worlds consist of three kinds of agents: *actors*, *targets* that represent actors' goals, and *obstacles* that actors attempt to avoid. All are graphically drawn as spheres; for our purposes, it suffices to represent an agent by its size, location, heading angle, and velocity.[1] There may be multiple actors, obstacles, and targets in an animation system. Further, obstacles and targets may be static and/or moving. These components provide a general conceptual palette that can be used to express a broad range of behaviors. For instance, an actor performing a multi-part task could be represented by its reaching a series of targets in sequence, each target corresponding to a component subtask.

At the core of the mathematics underlying our animated worlds are non-linear *attractor* and *repeller* functions that represent the targets and obstacles (respectively) in the system. Another non-linear system combines their weighted contributions in calculating an actor's angular velocity, dynamically adapting to real-time changes in the environment. Together, these non-linear systems generate natural-appearing motion, avoiding collisions and other undesirable behaviors. The agent heading angle ϕ is computed by a non-linear dynamical system of the form:

$$\dot{\phi} = f(\phi, \mathbf{env}) = |w_{tar}|f_{tar} + |w_{obs}|f_{obs} + n, \tag{1}$$

where f_{tar} and f_{obs} are the attractor and repeller functions for the system, and w_{tar} and w_{obs} are their respective weights on the agent. (n is a noise term, which helps avoid local minima in the system.)

---

[1] The mathematical treatment in [18] admits a more complex representation of actors than the one we use.

The weights themselves are determined by computing the fixed points of the following non-linear system:

$$\begin{cases} \dot{w}_{tar} = \alpha_1 w_{tar}(1 - w_{tar}^2) - \gamma_{12} w_{tar} w_{obs}^2 + n \\ \dot{w}_{obs} = \alpha_2 w_{obs}(1 - w_{obs}^2) - \gamma_{21} w_{obs} w_{tar}^2 + n \end{cases}, \qquad (2)$$

where the α and γ parameters are designed to reflect conditions for the stability of the system. Many other parameters are also concealed in the terms presented above. For instance, a repeller function f_{obs} depends on parameters that determine how much influence obstacles will have on an actor.

This is only an overview of one significant part of the agent steering system. There is considerably more detail to the system, including applications to three-dimensional environments, dynamic control of forward velocity, and modeling of low-level personality attributes such as aggression and agility. The above presentation, however, gives a feel for the kind of mathematics involved, suggesting the complexity involved in implementing it. Further, it introduces the role parameters may play in agent behavior, a notion to which we return in section 3 when discussing reasoning about a parameterized class of animation systems.

1.2   Hybrid Systems and CHARON

By definition, a hybrid system is one that combines continuous and discrete dynamics. Past domains of application for hybrid system models include descriptions of biological processes [4], air-traffic management systems [26,33], and manufacturing systems [31]. They occur frequently and naturally in many contexts and, because of this, they have received substantial attention by both computer scientists and control theorists [1,2,10,27]. From a general, intuitive perspective, any system characterized by discrete transitions between modes of continuous control is a hybrid system. This includes several kinds of systems that emerge in animation, from physical modeling of objects in a dynamic environment to agent-steering.

There are several different formal models for hybrid systems. Net-based models such as Constraint Nets [35], for instance, have been acknowledged in literature on cognitive agents. We focus in particular on automata-theoretic models such as hybrid automata [5,28]; the various kinds of automata differ in the behaviors they are capable of representing. As a brief, non-technical introduction to this perspective, we consider a hybrid automaton as having: a set of *discrete states* called *control modes*; a *continuous state space* (a subset of $\mathbb{R}^n$ for some n); and descriptions of how the system can evolve. There are constraints both on the continuous evolution of the system within a control mode and on the discrete transitions between control modes that the system might make. A state of the overall system is a pair (*control mode, continuous state*). (For more details on the mathematics and applications of hybrid automata, see [5,9,13,19].) Research and analysis of hybrid automata underlies practical tools such as CHARON [7,8] and the model checker HyTech [21]. For this paper, we use Charon to implement animation systems and HyTech for verification.[2]

The architecture of a hybrid system in Charon is expressed as *hierarchical agents*, a model conceptually similar to hybrid automata and hierarchical reactive modules [6]. The key features of Charon are:

Hierarchy. The building block for describing the system architecture is an *agent* that communicates with its environment via shared variables. The building block for describing flow of control inside an atomic agent is a *mode*. A mode is basically a hierarchical state machine, i.e., it may have submodes and transitions connecting them. Charon allows *sharing* of modes so that the same mode definition can be instantiated in multiple contexts.

Discrete updates. Discrete updates are specified by *guarded actions* labeling transitions connecting the modes. Actions may call externally defined Java functions to perform complex data manipulations.

Continuous updates. Some of the variables in Charon can be declared *analog*, and they flow continuously during continuous updates that model passage of time. The evolution of analog variables can be constrained in three ways: *differential* constraints (e.g., by equations such as $\dot{x} = f(x, u)$), *algebraic* constraints (e.g., by equations such as $y = g(x, u)$), and *invariants* (e.g., $|x - y| \leq \varepsilon$) that limit the allowed durations of flows. Such constraints can be declared at different levels of the mode hierarchy.

Modular features of Charon allow succinct and structured description of complex systems. (Similar features are supported by the languages Shift [14] and Stateflow (see www.mathworks.com).) Among other benefits, this modularity provides a natural-seeming structure for developing animation systems with multiple levels of behavior.

2 Creating Animations as Hybrid Systems

Animation systems are implemented in Charon using the key concepts noted in section 2.[3] Modes are created to represent continuous behaviors; particular continuous dynamics (e.g., the non-linear system described in section 1.1) are represented as differential or algebraic constraints of a form such as `diff { d(angle) = AngleFunction(angle,...) }`. If constraints are necessary to limit the time in a particular mode, they are represented as invariants such as `inv {Cond && !Cond2 && distance(x,y)<=distance(x,z) }`. Guarded transitions between modes are presented in a straightforward `trans from Mode1 to Mode2 when Cond do Effect` syntax; when the guard `Cond` is true, the transition named `trans` is enabled, and if it is taken, statement `Effect` is executed along with the system's jump from `Mode1` to `Mode2`. The behavior of agents follows from

---

[2] We used HyTech for verification because, as of this writing, the model checking facilities for Charon are still under development.

[3] A more detailed description of the Charon language is presented in [32].

the systems described by modes. Each atomic agent is declared to begin in some mode, and it follows the behavior described there. The behavior of a hierarchical agent is, of course, determined by the behavior of its sub-agents. In this way, the underlying continuous mathematics and relations between modes of behavior are explicitly represented in a CHARON program. Further, the modularity of CHARON code makes it easy to change one aspect of a system while leaving others intact.

CHARON also generates numerical simulations of hybrid systems, which we exploited in creating animations from CHARON system specifications. We simply simulated our animation systems in CHARON, then used a small translation routine (like a Perl script) to format the output of those simulations so that a previously developed application (developed for research outside of the context of hybrid systems) could create graphical displays. Section 4 contains more details and sample images of the animations we generated.

The CHARON model of hybrid systems as hierarchical agents corresponded neatly to the high-level abstractions we considered when designing animations. In addition, the explicit representation of high-level (discrete) and low-level (continuous) processes made it straightforward to implement different kinds of cognitive behavior or intelligence in our agents. For instance, constraints on low-level perceptual capabilities (e.g., how far can an agent "see") or underlying behavioral attributes (e.g., aggression) were explicitly represented in the code that controls continuous behavior. Higher-level decisions to switch modes of behavior could be explicitly represented by adding to the discrete dynamics; new modes could represent new "states of mind."

3   Reasoning about Animation Systems

Some properties of games and other animation systems may not be verifiable by viewing a single animation. For example, one might want to verify properties of all possible executions of a parameterized or non-deterministic system. Even within a fully determined system, properties about agents' relative speed and precise distance may be too difficult to judge by eye. Indeed, merely finding a formal language to express interesting properties of such systems may be non-trivial.

This touches upon a motivating observation behind our research: Well-known logics for hybrid systems are capable of expressing properties of animation systems. In addition, there are practical *model checkers* —tools that can mechanically verify some properties of simple hybrid systems— that we might apply to animation systems. These model checkers have significant limitations; many properties are theoretically undecidable, and as a practical matter, even decidable properties may only be feasibly checked in simple cases. Still, as we discuss in section 5, there are approaches to reasoning about complex systems that allow us to circumvent some undecidability barriers.

In this section, we discuss more about logics for hybrid systems and how we might apply them to animation systems.

3.1 Modal Logic and Properties of Multi-agent Animations

There are many *modal* and *temporal* logics that can be used to reason about hybrid systems, such as **CTL**, **LTL**, and the μ-*calculus*; significant research has been devoted to the theory and applications of these logics ([13] and [9] are good surveys of recent work). For readers unfamiliar with fundamental modal logic operators, we provide a brief review.[4]

Modal logics are used to reason about *possible worlds* and properties of *possibility* and *necessity* such as "Proposition P is true in all possible worlds" or "Proposition P is false in some possible world." For our present application, we consider a "world" to be a "state of a hybrid system," and we consider a "possible world" to be a state reachable (under the constraints on system evolution) from the current state of the hybrid system.

A modal logic typically contains the standard propositional logic operators (negation, implication, etc.) along with various modal or temporal operators. For this paper, we introduce two common modal operators:

- **possibility**: $\Diamond P$ (intuitively, "It is possible that P")
- **necessity**: $\Box P$ (intuitively, "It is necessary that P")

As expected, they are duals: $\neg\Box\neg P \equiv \Diamond P$. In the context of a system execution, possibility and necessity also correspond to the intuitive readings of *eventually* and *always* (respectively). That is, $\Box P$ means that P is necessarily true of every state of the entire execution; it is always true. As its dual, $\Diamond P$ means that P is not always false; it is true at some state of the execution, i.e., eventually true. (From a rigorous logical standpoint, these explanations are overly simplistic, but they convey basic intuitions necessary for this paper.)

Logics for hybrid systems are powerfully expressive. In addition to modal operators such as $\Box$ and $\Diamond$, they explicitly represent time, and we may specify that a condition be true at some particular time in an animation. We can also express properties of non-deterministic animation systems or parameterized classes of animations. We illustrate these points by presenting several example properties below. In each case, we formally express that the system execution E satisfies property P by writing $E \models P$, and we use the notation $loc(A)$ to refer to the location of an agent A.

- The velocity of actor a_1 is never greater than that of actor a_2:
  $E \models \Box(velocity(a_1) \leq velocity(a_2))$

There are several ways to reason about parameterized or non-deterministic systems. In the logical formulas below, we do so by quantifying over all possible executions of a system.

---

[4] By no means does this section constitute a thorough introduction. There are many noteworthy modal logic texts available, providing differently oriented introductions to the basic concepts; for example, a classic general introduction such as [23] may supply substantially different insights than more-directed texts such as [15]. The paper [13] from Davoren and Nerode may be of particular interest to readers who seek an overview of logics for hybrid systems.

Fig. 1. An image from a crowd simulation animation. The crowd of actors (light spheres) on the bottom half of the image are moving to a target (darker sphere) on the top, crossing through actors that are moving from the top of the image to a target on the bottom.

- If the aggression parameter of actor a is set within the range $[2, 4]$, actor a reaches target t:
  $(\forall E)E \models (aggression \in [2, 4]) \Rightarrow \Diamond(loc(a) = loc(t))$

- No matter what non-deterministic choices are made, at 5 seconds into the animation, agent a_2 is at least 100 units from agent a_1:
  $(\forall E)E \models \Box((clock = 5) \Rightarrow distance(a_1, a_2) \geq 100)$

- No matter what non-deterministic choices are made, agent a_1 is at target t when agent a_2 is not, but agent a_2 eventually reaches target t:
  $(\forall E)E \models \Diamond(loc(a_1) = loc(t) \wedge loc(a_2) \neq loc(t) \wedge \Diamond(loc(a_2) = loc(t)))$

4   Experiments and Applications

4.1   Multi-agent Animations

Figures 1-4 contain images from our multi-agent animations. In this paper, actors are the lightest objects, obstacles are the darkest objects, and targets are an intermediate gray. In the actual animations, actors, obstacles, and targets are distinguished by color. (CHARON-generated animations, including ones from which these Figures were taken, may be found at [3].)

Figure 1 shows a frame from a crowd simulation animation in which several actors need to navigate around other actors to reach distant targets. Figures 2

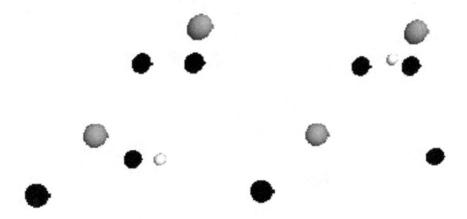

Fig. 2. An actor (lightest object) has already swerved around a stationary obstacle (darkest) and is now reacting to avoid a moving obstacle.

Fig. 3. The same actor as in Figure 2, later in the same animation, having switched to simpler behavior and passing between two obstacles.

and 3 show frames from a CHARON animation similar to the one described at the beginning of this paper, in which the actor's behavior is described in three segments. In the first segment (Figure 2), the actor avoids a static obstacle and a moving obstacle on the way to a first target. It need not engage in complex evasive behavior as it progresses to the second target in the second segment (Figure 3); it will fit between the two remaining obstacles by simply traveling in a straight line, so it may intelligently switch to a simpler system for navigation. That resulting animation system thus contains a discrete transition between continuous dynamics and is straightforwardly represented as a hybrid system. Note also that if the actor did not switch to a simpler behavior for segment two, it would perform unnecessary obstacle avoidance, as shown in Figure 4. Further, the CHARON specification of the actor's behavior is on the intuitive level of "reach target one, avoiding obstacles; reach target two, simply going straight; wait one second, then celebrate." It does not require details about the location in space (or time) of targets or obstacles.

4.2   Verifying Properties

Although there are significant undecidability barriers when reasoning about hybrid systems in general, property verification is decidable for restricted classes of hybrid systems [9,22]. Consider, for example, systems in which each mode constrains every variable to constant velocity; changes in direction or velocity require transitions between modes. Some animation systems can be specified

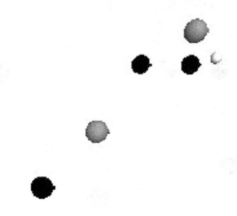

Fig. 4. Contrast with Figure 3: Here, the actor maintains the complex, obstacle-avoidant behavior, and winds up taking a longer route to the target. (Note that the moving obstacle has moved off-screen.)

within this restricted framework, and many properties expressible in the modal logic framework described in section 3.1 are decidable for such systems.

To demonstrate this, we specified the rudiments of a race-like game in the model checker HYTECH [21] and mechanically checked a collision-avoidance property. Our animation system contains three agents, two racing actors and one obstacle, each moving at constant speed around a square, two-lane track. The rules of the race encode that each actor (naturally) prefers to race on the inside lane, and must do so whenever possible. Because one racer is slower than the other and the obstacle is slower than both, racers may move to the outside lane to pass slower agents, moving promptly back to the inside lane when they are done passing.

Consider an infinite race, an endless execution of this animation system. Will the two racers ever collide? Although we thought we had specified collision-avoidant behavior, we were mistaken. By checking the states reachable by this animation system, HYTECH discovered a scenario in which a collision would occur: when the faster racer is changing lanes in front of the slower racer *at the corner of the track*, as graphically represented in Figure 5. (HYTECH output, which is too lengthy and cumbersome to include in this paper, may be found among the supplementary material at [3].) Note that Figure 5 is not a frame from an actual animation; we did not use HYTECH to generate animations. A simple animation of a similar race-like game implemented in CHARON can be found at [3].

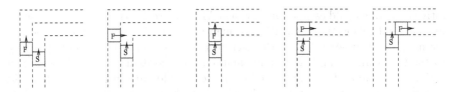

Fig. 5. A block diagram of unexpected collision behavior in a simple race game, as detected by HYTECH. The faster racer (marked with "F") has passed the slower one (marked with "S"), but the slower one catches up on a corner.

5 Conclusions and Extensions

Hybrid continuous/discrete dynamics are commonly utilized in animations without regard for underlying hybrid system theory. We took a different approach, directly applying general-purpose hybrid system theory to generate multi-agent animations, explicitly linking the normally disparate disciplines by demonstrating that some animation systems may be modeled by hybrid automata. Models of hybrid systems can simultaneously integrate and distinguish high-level and low-level behavior; thus, they may be natural tools for modeling intelligent virtual agents.

Because we were within the theoretical framework of hybrid systems, we were also able to specify and reason about properties of animation systems using expressive modal logics for hybrid systems. Although automatic verification of complex properties is infeasible in many cases, we did mechanically check a property about collisions in a race-like game animation.

Furthermore, we need not simply abandon hope of verifying complex properties of complex systems: There are *approximation* techniques for verification that might be applicable to animation systems. Properties such as those discussed in this paper are *reachability* properties of animation systems, fundamentally about whether some proposition holds in the states reachable by an animation system. It is often impossible to effectively reason about the exact set of reachable states of a complex system, but we may be able to verify properties on an approximation of that set. That is, if S is the actual set of states reachable by a system, and we cannot decide property P on S, we might instead be able to overestimate S by a computationally simpler set $S' \supset S$ on which P is decidable. Then, if we prove that P holds on all states in S', we know P also holds on all states in S. This kind of reasoning by approximation is an active area of research in the hybrid systems community [12,20,30], but it has not yet been explored in the context of animation systems.

There is an understood connection between logic and animation: Our ability to reason about virtual worlds is essential to our ability to create intelligent virtual agents. This observation underlies the groundbreaking, artificial intelligence-based approach to cognitive modeling taken by Funge [16], which permits animated characters to simulate cognitive abilities such as perception, inference, and planning. Potentially, a hybrid systems-oriented approach to cognitive modeling could escape some typical AI-based restrictions. Such a cognitive model could follow the delineation of high-level and low-level cognitive behavior mentioned in section 3, with discrete hybrid system modes corresponding to "states of mind" and continuous mathematical systems representing mental activity; mental states of animated characters could vary in real time. It could also enable characters to reason directly about time, not just about endpoints of previously determined discrete events. In addition, it could allow the characters' cognitive and physical systems to be cleanly integrated and expressed in the same mathematical language. It is an open question, however, whether an implementation of this approach to cognitive modeling might enjoy the same virtues of practical applicability as Funge's system.

Despite the clear relationship between hybrid system theory and animation systems, this natural interdisciplinary interface has not been well explored. We do not know what models of hybrid systems might reveal about the mathematical structure of animation systems, or if there is any mathematical structure to be exploited for effective reasoning with modal logics. We do believe, however, that further exploration can improve human inference about animation systems, extending our perspective on and vocabulary of animation.

Acknowledgments. We thank Siome Goldenstein for his advice and technical assistance. We also thank Thao Dang, Jan Allbeck, and Norm Badler for helpful discussions, and we appreciate the helpful suggestions made by anonymous reviewers of this paper. This research was supported in part by NSF grant NSF-SBR 8920230.

References

1. *IEEE Transactions on Automatic Control, Special Issue on Hybrid Systems*, 43(4), April 1998.
2. *Proceedings of the IEEE*, 88, July 2000.
3. E. Aaron, F. Ivančić, and S. Goldenstein. CHARON-generated animations. Available at http://www.cis.upenn.edu/~eaaron/IVA01_animations.html.
4. R. Alur, C. Belta, F. Ivančić, V. Kumar, M. Mintz, G.J. Pappas, H. Rubin, and J. Schug. Hybrid modeling and simulation of biomolecular networks. In *Hybrid Systems: Computation and Control*, volume 2034 of *Lecture Notes In Computer Science*. Springer Verlag, April 2001.
5. R. Alur, C. Courcoubetis, N. Halbwachs, T.A. Henzinger, P.H. Ho, X. Nicolin, A. Olivero, J. Sifakis, and S. Yovine. The algorithmic analysis of hybrid systems. *Theoretical Computer Science*, 138:3–34, 1995.
6. R. Alur and R. Grosu. Modular refinement of hierarchic reactive machines. In *Proceedings of the 27th Annual ACM Symposium on Principles of Programming Languages*, 2000.
7. R. Alur, R. Grosu, Y. Hur, V. Kumar, and I. Lee. Modular specification of hybrid systems in CHARON. In N. Lynch and B. H. Krogh, editors, *Hybrid Systems : Computation and Control*, volume 1790 of *Lecture Notes in Computer Science*. Springer Verlag, 2000.

8. R. Alur, R. Grosu, I. Lee, and O. Sokolsky. Compositional refinement for hierarchical hybrid systems. In *Hybrid Systems : Computation and Control*, volume 2034 of *Lecture Notes in Computer Science*, pages 33–48. Springer Verlag, 2001.

9. R. Alur, T. Henzinger, G. Lafferriere, and G. Pappas. Discrete abstractions of hybrid systems. *Proceedings of the IEEE*, 88:971–984, July 2000.

10. R. Alur, T.A. Henzinger, and E.D. Sontag, editors. *Hybrid Systems III*, volume 1066 of *Lecture Notes in Computer Science*. Springer-Verlag, 1996.

11. David Brogan, Ronald Metoyer, and Jessica Hodgins. Dynamically simulated characters in virtual environments. *IEEE Computer Graphics and Applications*, 18(5):59–69, Sep/Oct 1998.

12. T. Dang and O. Maler. Reachability analysis via face lifting. In T. Henzinger and S. Sastry, editors, *Hybrid Systems : Computation and Control*, volume 1386 of *Lecture Notes in Computer Science*, pages 96–109. Springer Verlag, Berlin, 1998.

13. J. Davoren and A. Nerode. Logics for hybrid systems. *Proceedings of the IEEE*, 88:985–1010, July 2000.

14. A. Deshpande, A. Göllu, and L. Semenzato. Shift programming language and run-time systems for dynamic networks of hybrid automata. Technical report, University of California at Berkeley, 1997.

15. R. Fagin, J. Y. Halpern, Y. Moses, and M. Y. Vardi. *Reasoning about Knowledge*. MIT Press, 1995.

16. J. Funge. *AI for Games and Animation*. A K Peters, 1999.

17. S. Goldenstein, E. Large, and D. Metaxas. Non-linear dynamical system approach to behavior modeling. *The Visual Computer*, 15:349–369, 1999.

18. Siome Goldenstein, Menelaos Karavelas, Dimitris Metaxas, Leonidas Guibas, and Ambarish Goswami. Scalable dynamical systems for multi-agent steering and simulation. In *Proceedings of the IEEE Conference in Robotics and Automation*, May 2001. to appear.

19. T.A. Henzinger. The theory of hybrid automata. In *Proceedings of the 11th Annual Symposium on Logic in Computer Science*, pages 278–292. IEEE Computer Society Press, 1996.

20. T.A. Henzinger and P.-H. Ho. A note on abstract-interpretation strategies for hybrid automata. In P. Antsaklis, A. Nerode, W. Kohn, and S. Sastry, editors, *Hybrid Systems II*, Lecture Notes in Computer Science 999, pages 252–264. Springer-Verlag, 1995.

21. T.A. Henzinger, P.-H. Ho, and H. Wong-Toi. A user guide to HYTECH. In E. Brinksma, W.R. Cleaveland, K.G. Larsen, T. Margaria, and B. Steffen, editors, *TACAS 95: Tools and Algorithms for the Construction and Analysis of Systems*, volume 1019 of *Lecture Notes in Computer Science 1019*, pages 41–71. Springer-Verlag, 1995.

22. T.A. Henzinger, P.W. Kopke, A. Puri, and P. Varaiya. What's decidable about hybrid automata? *Journal of Computer and System Sciences*, 57:94–124, 1998.

23. G.E. Hughes and M.J. Cresswell. *An Introduction to Modal Logic*. Mehuen and Co., New York, 1968.

24. E. Large, H. Christensen, and R. Bajcsy. Scaling the dynamic approach to path planning and control: Competition among behavioral constraints. *International Journal of Robotics Research*, 18(1):37–58, 1999.

25. H. Levesque and F. Pirri, editors. *Logical Foundations for Cognitive Agents: Contributions in Honor of Ray Reiter*. Springer, 1999.

26. J. Lygeros, G. J. Pappas, and S. Sastry. An approach to the verification of the Center-TRACON Automation System. In T. Henzinger and S. Sastry, editors, *Hybrid Systems : Computation and Control*, volume 1386 of *Lecture Notes in Computer Science*, pages 289–304. Springer Verlag, Berlin, 1998.
27. N. Lynch and B. H. Krogh, editors. *Hybrid Systems : Computation and Control*, volume 1790 of *Lecture Notes in Computer Science*. Springer-Verlag, 2000.
28. N. Lynch, R. Segala, F. Vaandrager, and H.B. Weinberg. Hybrid I/O automata. In *Hybrid Systems III*, volume 1066 of *Lecture Notes in Computer Science*, pages 496–510. Springer-Verlag, 1996.
29. H. Noser, O. Renault, D. Thalmann, and N. Thalmann. Navigation for digital actors based on synthetic vision, memory and learning. *Computer and Graphics*, 1995.
30. G. J. Pappas and S. Sastry. Towards continuous abstractions of dynamical and control systems. In P. Antsaklis, W. Kohn, A. Nerode, and S. Sastry, editors, *Hybrid Systems IV*, volume 1273 of *Lecture Notes in Computer Science*, pages 329–341. Springer Verlag, Berlin, Germany, 1997.
31. D. Pepyne and C. Cassandras. Hybrid systems in manufacturing. *Proceedings of the IEEE*, 88:1108–1123, July 2000.
32. O. Sokolsky, Y. Hur, R. Grosu, and E. Aaron. *CHARON Language Manual, Version 0.6*. University of Pennsylvania, 2000. Available at http://www.cis.upenn.edu/mobies/charon/CHARONmanual.ps.
33. C. Tomlin, G. J. Pappas, and S. Sastry. Conflict resolution for air traffic management : A study in muti-agent hybrid systems. *IEEE Transactions on Automatic Control*, 43(4):509–521, April 1998.
34. X. Tu and D. Terzopoulos. Artificial fishes: Physics, locomotion, perception, behavior. In *Proc. of SIGGRAPH '94*, pages 43–50, 1994.
35. Y. Zhang and A. Mackworth. Constraint nets: A semantic model for hybrid dynamic systems. *Theoretical Computer Science*, 138(1):211–239, 1995.

Autonomous Avatars?
From Users to Agents and Back

Matthias Scheutz[1] and Brigitte Römmer[2]

[1] University of Notre Dame, Notre Dame, IN 46556, USA
[2] Universität Wien, Vienna, A-1010, Austria

Abstract. We describe the architecture of an interactive, "believable" agent with personality, called *user agent*, which can act on behalf of a user in various multi-user game contexts, when she is not online. In a first step, information about the personality of the user is obtained from a questionnaire and then, in a second step, integrated in the reactive system of the user agent, part of which implements a primitive affective system. User agents can interact with their users through a simple affective natural language generation system (SARGS), which is integrated in the deliberative system of the user agent and can recount what happened to the user agent in the game while the user was not present.

1   Introduction

Recently, agents *with personality* have become a new area of interest in AI research (e.g., [17,10,8] and others). The rapid increase of multi-user dungeons (MUDs) and other kinds of online multi-user games provides novel territory for the application of agent technology: in virtual worlds autonomous agents can take on roles, which usually are of little to no interest to human players, either because the role is boring or short-lived (e.g., "the shoemaker down the corner" or "the soldier in the first row of the formation"). Agents may also function as "tour guides" and "sources of information" within the simulation (e.g., see [6]). To make games with agents exciting and entertaining, the "believability" of computer controlled characters [2] is crucial. Synthetic characters that always behave in a repetitive, clearly predictable way, are typically perceived as boring and users might not only loose interest in them, but *mutatis mutandis* in the whole game.

In MUDs, which are not solely text oriented, but based on 2D or 3D simulations of some virtual world (that may or may not have a graphical representation), users need to be present (or online) to control their *avatar*, i.e., their representation in the simulated world. However, since it is not possible for users to play the game all the time, the user's character will not be able to take part in all events. While this does not matter in some contexts, a continuation of the character's interactions can or may be possible and desirable in certain game contexts (e.g., when several players have to cooperate and coordinate their moves to attain a goal).

A. de Antonio, R. Aylett, and D. Ballin (Eds.): IVA 2001, LNAI 2190, pp. 61–71, 2001.

In this paper, we describe an approach to cope with this difficulty. Instead of classical avatars (which are completely controlled by users), we propose a special kind of *autonomous agents* to represent users within a game simulation. These agents, call them *user agents*, are really hermaphrodites between avatars and autonomous agents in that they live an autonomous life, if their users are offline, acting their behalf, but can be controlled by users, who are online. The availability of such agents will allow game designers to create a variety of different games, in which users can join in and participate at their leisure (without becoming marginalized within or excluded from the game if they cannot play very frequently).

We start out by placing our agent model in the context of a particular game and discussing the difficulties that arise out of integrating user personalities in agent architectures. We then briefly review different models of human personality and describe the hybrid reactive-deliberative architecture of the proposed user agent. In particular, we present the simple affective language generation system (SARGS), which is part of the deliberative system and allows user agents to report in an entertaining story-like manner what happened while their users were offline. Finally, we summarize the advantages and disadvantages of our agent architecture, briefly discussing immediate as well as possible applications and extensions.

2   From Users to Avatars

The user agent is intended to be used in massive multi-user online games with a strong community building character, where agents have to represent and act on behalf of their users. The game context, in which the user agent has been developed, is a *dating game*[1], where agents are "sent out" in a virtual world on behalf of their users to find a flirt partner (as represented by another agent). When users log on, a report of their agents' "experiences" (e.g., how many "dates" their agents had) is dynamically generated using text templates, while a (minimally animated) 2D graphical representation depicts their agent in a cartoon-like fashion in a particular part of the game environment (e.g., a bar).[2] A much simpler, predecessor version of the user agent has already been used successfully in this game environment.

2.1   How to Model Users in Game Contexts

Since user agents need to act on behalf of their users, certain user characteristics (in particular, aspects of the user's personality and character traits) need to be modeled insofar as they determine basic decision making and behavior of

---

[1] For commerical and legal reasons we are not permitted to reveal any details about the game beyond what is presented here.

[2] The main reason for such a reduced graphic realization is that user should be able to play the game over the internet with standard web browsers, i.e., without having to download and install simulation software.

the agent. However, modeling users is not trivial, as their limited patience, and willingness to reveal large amounts of personal data severely constrains the kinds and quality of applicable models. Consequently, one needs to be pragmatic in finding a compromise between the accuracy of the personality model and the information available, which is usually obtained from some sort of questionnaire. The questionnaire typically contains one or more questions for each relevant (psychological) dimension, from which a *user profile* is generated.

There are two ways of incorporating the user profile in the game, which differ with respect to the degree to which the user profile is integrated in the agent: the first option keeps the user profile separate from the agent architecture and only derives general action tendencies for the user agent from it, which serve the role of "meta-knowledge" about how to act in certain situations. It is by following behavioral guidelines determined by such meta-knowledge about the user's action tendencies that the agent reflects the user's personality to some degree.

The alternative, which we pursue in this paper, is to integrate the user profile directly into the agent architecture, i.e., to "recreate" to some (in our case very limited) extent the user's personality in the agent. Obviously, this is a much harder problem, but will in the end contribute significantly to the believability of the agent. While some projects have integrated human personality models in agents [14], they have not attempted to model human players in agents participating in the game.

2.2 A Brief Overview of Models of Human Personality

A commercially popular model of human personality is based on the works of C.G. Jung.[3] Keirsey and Bates [9] suggest to analyze human personality along four dimensions, which they experess in terms of binary categories yielding 16 types of personality. The model does not only make detailed assumptions as to what the interests and behaviors of each individual type are (in public and in private life), but also suggests whether and how well each type gets along with any other type. The definition and implementation of such a model, however, would be rather complex if not practically infeasible, since for each possible situation all possible actions of all 16 personality types would have to be determined in advance and explicitly represented within the game simulation (e.g., in the form of condition-action rules). How such a model could be embedded in an agent architecture is unclear.

A different analysis of human personality, the Eysenk PEN-model [1] proposes three dimensions of personality, namely *psychoticism* (with the extremes "troublesome" - "socialized"), *extraversion* ("sociable" - "quiet"), and *neuroticism* ("anxious" - "calm"), the extremes of the dimensions being pathological. While Eysenk's suggestion that all three dimensions are ultimately linked to physiological states seems to make the model applicable (at least for *embodied* agents), the details of this relation are not clear (e.g., see [3]). And, furthermore,

---

[3] Such models are typically used in consulting (e.g., for the management of teams).

given the model's origin in clinical research, some of the questions used in the *Eysenck Personality Questionnaire* [5] are not suitable for a game context.

In psychological research, the dominant model of personality is the 5-factor-model, or "Big 5" [7]. It is based on a factor analysis yielding *extroversion, neuroticism, openness, agreeableness*, and *conscientiousness* as the basic dimensions of human personality, and has also been used as venture point for attempting to equip agents with human personality [14]. The problem with "Big 5" (as with the other above-mentioned models), however, is that it is silent about the relation between personality and affective states. There is one model, which claims to provide some of this information–Mehrabian's three dimensional PAD model [12] (whith dimensions "pleasure" - "displeasure", "arousal" - "nonarousal" and "dominance" - "submissiveness"). The PAD model is intended as a model of human temperament as well as human emotions [13], where the influence of personality on emotional states is given by the very fact that the basic dimensions of personality and emotions coincide (different emotions and personality types are viewed as variations along these three dimensions).

2.3   Integrating Aspects of User Personalities in Agent Architectures

Given the difficulties of obtaining an accurate user profile in game context,[4] we decided to use a hybrid model of personality and emotion, which is inspired by the PAD Model: the dimensions which represent emotions (or, more generally, affective states), are also taken to be basic to personality. To the three dimensions *pleasure, arousal*, and *dominance* we have added a fourth dimension, which determines the general attitude towards anything new, as well as the agent's expressivity.[5]

This affective system can be thought of a four-dimensional dynamic system, whose state space corresponds to the personality of the agent. Different regions in this four- dimensional space correspond to different emotions (in analogy to the PAD model), and we say that if the system is in a state, which is part of one of those regions, that the system is in the *affective state* (or, put metaphorically, "has the emotion") associated with this part of the space. In analogy to the PAD Model, low pleasure, high arousal, and high dominance, for example, may define "anger", whereas low pleasure, high arousal and low dominance may define "fear". Through external input the system will be able to change states and traverse the space on trajectories that are determined by the original setup (i.e., personality) and current input.

---

[4] The psychological models ofq the previous section all rely on questionnaires of around 50 questions to yield reliable personality measures. However, the type of game we refer to is aimed at the casual player, who tends to loose interest quickly. From experience with previous questionnaires (used to "personalize" the predecessor version of the user agent) we learned that the upper limit of an acceptable number of questions is about 12.

[5] Note that we do not claim that this fourth dimensions is basic to a model of human personality, but rather we introduce it because of its usefulness for generating behavior which is comprehensible for the user.

Since the "personalization procedure" needs to be as brief and efficient as possible, we choose questions directly corresponding to the four dimensions.

Example. You think you did a fine job writing a summary report of last week's meeting, but your boss rips it to pieces, because he does not like the format. How do you react?

(a) I apologize and offer to reformat the report immediately.
(b) I tell him not to be ridiculous.

The example corresponds to the dimension of dominance, where answering (a) leads to a more submissive, (b) to a more dominant personality of the user agent.

Another type question, employed to make the actions of the agent transparent to the user, asks for preferences regarding actions which are of importance in the context of the game. Whether an agent in the dating game will tend to ignore hunger if excited, for example, may depend on whether the user provides a particular answer to a question like the following:

Example. Suppose you have been craving a juicy steak all day long. As you finally sit down to order, this gorgeous, foreign-looking babe walks up to you and asks you whether you could recommend any sights for her to see. What would you do?

(a) Tell her that you are busy and call the waiter.
(b) Smile at her and ask her if she wants to join you.
(c) Immediately get up and show her around the city.

The user's answers are then used to adapt the affective system of the agent. Depending on the representation of this dynamic space, different adaptations methods can be used. E.g., for affective systems realized in trainable neural networks, where affective states are represented by the degree of activations of various units, question-answer pairs can become part of the training set.

This affective model is a pragmatic solution, which allows for great flexibility, since the agent can be easily adjusted to various game contexts and even modified during a game. For example, it is possible to start a game with a user agent (based on inital questionnaires with only a few questions) and then retrain the agent as more information about the user becomes available (e.g., because users are asked more questions in the course of the game).

3   The Architecture of User Agents

We use a hybrid architecture for user agents, which consists of a reactive and a deliberative system. The former controls inputs to, outputs from, and bodily functions of the agent, and implements a primitive affective system. The latter is concerned with planning, reasoning, and in particular the communication with the user. Since user agents should also be applicable in mere text-based games (e.g., games played using wireless devices such as cellular phones with SMS or WAP, etc.) and not limited to games with graphical interaction, it is crucial to provide a natural language generation (NLG) system, which updates users on past and current events, and, furthermore, allows them to learn about the experiences of their agent (its motivations, feelings, etc.).

3.1   The Reactive System

The reactive system integrates external and internal sensory information to produce the basic behaviors needed for the "survival" of the agent. In particular, it is in charge of satisfying two basic bodily needs: "hunger" and "thirst" (which can be satisfied in various ways depending on the game contexts), and also implements the rudimentary affective personality model described above.

In our current implementation, the reactive system is realized as a three-layer neural network, where the input layer is divided into two classes: inputs from exteroceptive sensors or perceptual systems *Extinput* (e.g., vision) and inputs from proprioceptive sensors *Intinput* (e.g., the level of energy). Similarly, the output layer is divided into units representing "inner states", called *Context* (such as curiosity or arousal), and units representing actions *Action* (such as drinking or moving in various directions). A probability-based action selection mechanism is employed: the activation of the *Action* is taken as the probability that the action associated with the unit will be *attempted* by the agent–whether it can actually be executed will depend on various additional factors (i.e., energy level, constraints of the current environment, etc.).

The mapping from sensory input and internal states to action and internal states is learned using a slightly modified, faster version of the backpropagation algorithm. The training set for supervised learning contains some general rules, vital to the agent's survival (e.g., the rule "if you see food and hunger is high, attempt to eat it"), but also rules derived from the results of the user questionnaire. Note that even for identical answers on the questionnaire the trained neural nets will vary slightly because their weights are initalized at random (such variations are quite welcome as experience suggests that monotonicity and similarity of agent behavior is a major cause of "boring games").

After successful training, which takes place every time a new agent is created (i.e., when a new user joins the game), the network is partly rewired: the connections from the *Intinput* units to the hidden units are connected to the *Context* units, which now constitute a "context layer"–it still receives input from the proprioceptive sensors, yet the previous activations of its units are also taken into account (which, strictly speaking, augments the reactive system by "inner states"). Furthermore, the update rule for those "context" units is altered to implement the personality model: while all other units use a sigmoid activation function to compute their activation and output values, these units use an IAC update rule [11]. For all four dimensions of the affective system, rest levels and decay rates are set in accordance to the basic personality type as determined by the user questionnaire (e.g., an agent for a user with "high dominance" will have a high positive rest level of the "dominance" context unit).

3.2   The Deliberative System

The deliberative system provides the basic natural language interface for user interaction and, furthermore, allows for additional planning and reasoning components, which permit game designers to extend the agents' capacities and adapt them to specific game environments. The natural language interface uses an additional "text sensor" to read in commands from the user and responds through an additional "text effector" using the *simple affective report generation system* (SARGS), to be described below. SARGS is a rudimentary NLG system, which is fully integrated in the deliberative layer (thus amenable to changes in the deliberative rule system, although these possibilites are not taken advantage of at present). It can be embedded in a lager hybrid NLG system of the game simulation, which in the dating game uses text templates [15] to provide background information about the current state of the game.

The deliberative system also provides short-term and long-term memories, which can be accessed by components extending the deliberative capabilities. The former is standardly used for the storage of perceptions and recent experiences, while the latter typcially contains knowledge about the simulation environment, the agent's past experiences together their "affective evaluation" (see the next section), and rules about what to do (and how to do it). Depending on the particular game, different rules will be part of the agent's memory (e.g., in the dating game there is a calendar for the agent to enter dates and schedule appointments, and a global directory of the simulated world, which the agent can use to plan its moves, meetings, etc.).

Currently, the deliberative system is implemented in POPLOG (which implements a PROLOG virtual machine among others). The databases for short and long term memory is mapped onto the built-in database (available in PROLOG). Any kind of *factual knowledge*, past experience, etc. is stored similar to a PROLOG *fact* (with a time stamp to avoid inconsistencies of the database). For example, if the agent meets another agent at time 145, the following facts about this meeting might be stored: $meet(a12, 145)$, $woman(a12)$, $hair(a12, brown)$, etc. Furthermore, the agent also stores its affective status, e.g., $arousal(0.8, 145)$, $hunger(-0.7, 145)$, etc.[6] *Condition-action rules* can be applied to those facts (similar to PROLOG *clauses*), where antecedents may contain a default conjunct to allow for non-monotonic extensions [16]. Planning can be achieved using forward chaining (or, if the PROLOG virtual machine is used, unification on a particular goal clause with a free variable [18]). While no particular planning (or reasoning) mechanism is part of the agent architecture, an interface to the action selection mechanism is provided for a planner to pass a sequence of actions with corresponding probablilities that the action will be attempted (a probability of 1.0 means that the action will be attempted with certainty). It is also possible

---

[6] Note that a new constant is automatically generated for each perceived entity, and if the encountered entity can identified (e.g., as a previously known agent by virtue of a name), then the constant will be automatically replaced by that identification (e.g., if $a12$ turns out to be the same agent as $a3$, never mind how, then all occurrences of "$a12$" will be replaced by "$a3$").

to "override" the reactive system completely by substituting the plan actions for whatever action the reactive system may have selected in a subsumption style manner.

3.3 The Simple Affective Report Generation System (SARGS)

SARGS was conceived as a tool to allow users to learn about the "inner lifes" of their agents and to be able to understand better, why their agent chose a particular action and not another. The idea is that agents describe what they "perceived" and how they "felt" at a given time, what action(s) they chose in response to their perceptions and inner states and what actions were actually executed. Call such a tuple $\langle P_t, F_t, I_t, A_t, \rangle$ (consisting of a set of perceptions $P_t = \{p_{t,1}, p_{t,2}, ..., p_{t,n}\}$, a set of "feelings" or "inner states" $F_t = \{f_{t,1}, f_{t,2}, ..., f_{t,k}\}$, a set of action intentions $I_t = \{i_{t,1}, i_{t,2}, ..., i_{t,m}\}$, and a set of performed actions $A_t = \{a_{t,1}, a_{t,2}, ..., a_{t,j}\}$) an *event* E_t at time t. A *story* of length l starting at time t, then, is a sequence $S(t, l) = \langle E_t, E_{t+1}, ..., E_{t+l} \rangle$ of events.

To create a report, SARGS first retrieves all events from short term memory that are part of the story $S(t, l)$, where t was the last time the user inquired about the agent's *status quo* and $t + l$ is the current point in time. From this story SARGS produces a sequences of natural language sentences, which describe the story to the user in an *entertaining* way. To be entertaining, the story should at least

1. have an appropriate beginning and ending (i.e., set up the context for users to get into the right mind frame to see things from their agents' perspective– e.g., "Hi. Haven't seen you in a while. Last time you checked in I was not doing all that well..." or "So, that's where we are right now.")
2. have an element of non-determinism (i.e., if the same story is recounted twice, word choice and sentence structures should be somewhat different and vary from time to time)
3. use affective language to evoke emotions (such as sympathy, empathy, etc.) and express the degree of activation of the reported affective states (e.g., "...quite excited...")
4. either omit states that have not changed over a pre-determined interval of time or report them as such (e.g., "Still hungry, ...")

SARGS is an affective NLG [4], which uses the agent's affective states for content planning, i.e., for deciding, which aspects of the description of perceptions, inner states, and actions (intended and performed) of an event to describe to the user based on its current affective states: the higher the activation of a state, the more likely that the corresponding aspect will be part of a description. Furthermore, depending on the length l of the time frame to be described, events will be ignored and erased from short-term memory if their affective evaluation is below a certain threshold to avoid long-winded and boring stories (the remaining events will be transferred to long-term memory).

For sentence planning and realization, it uses a *grammar database* of schemas of different sentence types (declartive sentences, questions, etc.). For each event, a schema is selected at random (also taking into account the schema used to describe the previous event). For example, a schema for perceptions could look like this: S → TAdv N V NP (where S is a sentence, TAdv a temporal adverb, N a noun, V a verb, and NP a noun phrase, which itself can be decomposed into a definite or indefinite article, possible adjectives, and a noun).

To describe a particular event, the grammatical categories in the sentence schemas are filled in with words from a *word database*, which contains a variety of different applicaple words (or expressions) for every sensory modality and possible percept, every inner state, and every possible action. The perception of a bar in the dating scenario, for example, could then be mapped onto the above schema: "Then I saw a cool bar". Furthermore, the database contains various adjectives, adverbs and conjunctions, which can be used to connect sentences and to describe properties of perceived entities (e.g., "cool") as well as degrees of "feelings".

Special rules are used to deal with "aggregation" [15] within and across events. By keeping track of what changes and what stays the same between two events, SARGS determines which inner states to talk about: only those are chosen that have actually changed within some predetermined time interval (as users are not interested in learning every time that their agent is "hungry", for example). It then uses adverbs such as "still", "again", "not yet", etc. to describe the developments of parts of events (perceptions, inner states, intentions, and performed actions) over sequences of events. Furthermore, it uses other adverbs such as "very", "not much", etc. to describe the intensity of a "feeling" (i.e., the degree of activation of an inner state) [4]. For example, if an agent has an arousal level of 0.8 (where 1.0 means "maximally aroused"), which was at only 0.3 at the previous event, SARGS might add the following phrase to its description of the current event: "...even more excited...".

4   Discussion and Future Work

We have proposed an architecture for agents, which can represent users to a certain degree in game environments. A simple characterization of the user's personality is obtained from a user questionnaire and used to adjust parameters in the agent's control system, which model (in a simplistic way) these personality traits. The main advantages of our design are:

- The agent's sensors, effectors, and inner states can be easily extended by adding units to the neural network and new rules to the training set.
- User characteristics beyond the simple personality model are modeled (e.g., concrete decisions in particular circumstances).
- SARGS is a first attempt to recount a story according to the user's own preferences (insofar as they are determined by personality and affective states), while at the same being quite adaptive (i.e., it can be used in different game contexts with only minor modifications of names of objects, locations, actions, etc.).

- By virtue of using neural networks, somewhat inconsistent user profiles–users sometimes seem to contradict themselves on questionnaires–can be used to define agents (although the compromise found by the learning algorithm may not be always be appropriate).

The present version, however, has also some disadvantages:

- If the update interval is high, running many agents on one system becomes infeasible. Furthermore, if users rarely check on their agents, huge amounts of data will accumulate in each agent's short-term memory.
- Depending on coding, number and nature of the rules, the backpropagation algorithm might not be able to learn a sufficiently adequate mapping within a reasonable timespan (or, in the worst case, not at all)–general constraining factors are needed to guarantee that backpropagation will not fail (e.g., estimates on the number of required hidden units, etc.).
- SARGS does not easily extend to a genuine NLP/NLG system, where users can "chat" freely with their agent.
- The affective system only implements a so-called "shallow model of emotions" and higher affective states (such as "frustration", "disappointment", etc.), which essentially depend on a deliberative layer, are not supported [19].

Ideally, at some point, we would like to have agents with personalities *very similar* to those of the users, especially if they are to be used in "social games", where personality and social interaction are the crucial features. Unfortunately, we are still far from achieving this goal and would only deceive ourselves if we took labels such as "surprise", "disappointment", "anxiety", etc. (which too often are prematurely assigned to rather simple control states these days) at face value.

In the current project, we have restricted ourselved to a shallow model of affective states and personality, given the constraint of producing a functional system for multi-user games rather than a tenable computational model of affect in a reasonable amount of time. As of now, our model is implemented in POP11 and currently being tested in the context of the dating game. Once the tests are concluded, the code will be transcribed in JAVA and the model will become part of a new commercial multi-user game, which is played over the internet.

While user agents may find rather immediate application in certain game environments, we see this project, however, as a first step in a long term investigation, which attempts to capture and implement in much more detail the properties and processes involved in human personality and emotions.

References

1. Amelang, M., Bartusek, D.: Differentielle Psychologie und Persoenlichkeitsforschung, Stuttgart, Kohlhammer (1997) 324–335
2. Bates, J.: The role of emotion in believable agents, Communication of the ACM, Special Issue on Agents (1994)

3. Brody, N.: Personality: In Search of Individuality, San Diego: Academic Press (1988)
4. de Rosis, F., Grasso, F.: Affective Natural Language Generation, Proceedings of the IWAI (1999) 204–218
5. Eysenck, H.J., Eysenck, S.B.G.: Manual of the Eysenck Personality Questionnaire London, Hodder and Stoughton (1975)
6. Foner, L.N.: Entertaining Agents: A Sociological Case Study, The First International Conference of Autonomous Agents (1997)
7. Goldberg, L.R.: Language and inividual differences: the search for universals in personality lexicons, Review of Personality and Social Psychology **2** (1981) 141–165
8. Hayes-Roth, B., van Gent, R., Huber, D.: Acting in Character, Proceedings of AAAI Workshop on AI and Entertainment (1996)
9. Keirsey, D., Bates, M.: Please Understand Me. Character and Temperament Types, Prometheus Nemesis Books Company (1984)
10. Loyall, B., Bates, J.: Personality-Rich Believable Agents That Use Language, Proceedings of the 1st International Conference on Autonomous Agents (Agents97), ACM Press (1997)
11. McClelland, J.L., Rumelhart, D.E.: Parallel Distributed Processing, Vol. 1 and 2, MIT Press, Cambridge (1988)
12. Mehrabian, A.: Framework for a comprehensive description and measurement of emotional states, Genetic, Social, and General Psychology Monographs **121** (1995) 339–361
13. Mehrabian, A.: Pleasure-arousal-dominance: A general framework for describing and measuring individual differences in temperament, Current Psychology **14** (1996) 261-292
14. Nicholson, A., Dutta, A.: Intelligent agents for an interactive multi-media game, Proceedings of the International Conference on Computational Intelligence and Multimedia Applications (1997) 76–80
15. Reiter., E.: NLG vs. Templates, Proceedings of the 5th European Workshop on Natural Language Generation, Leiden, Netherlands (1995)
16. Reiter., R.: A logic for default reasoning, Artificial Intelligence **13** (1980) 81–132
17. Rizzo, P., Veloso, M., Miceli, M., Cesta, A.: Personality-driven social behaviors in believable agents, Proceedings of the AAAI Fall Symposium on Socially Intelligent Agents (1997)
18. Russell, S., Norvig, N.: Artificial Intelligence: A Modern Approach Prentice Hall (1995)
19. Scheutz, M., Sloman, A., Logan, B.: Emotional States and Realistic Agent Behaviour, Proceedings of GameOn2000 (2000)

Equipping a Lifelike Animated Agent with a Mind

L. Chen, K. Bechkoum, and G. Clapworthy

Department of Computer and Information Sciences
De Montfort University
Hammerwood Gate, Kents Hill
Milton Keynes, MK7 6HP, U.K.
Tel: 0044 – 1908 – 695511 – 4145
{lchen, kbechkoum, gc}@dmu.ac.uk

Abstract. This paper presents a computational mind model for lifelike animated agents. It consists of a motivational system and an emotional system. The motivational system guides an agent's behaviour by generating goals. The emotional system exerts further control over the agent's behaviour by regulating and modulating the way that behaviour is undertaken. The mind model is embedded in a layered hierarchical agent architecture that provides a framework and flexible way of modelling these system's influence on each other, and ultimately on the behaviour of lifelike agents. The mind model together with the agent architecture is implemented using a logical formalism, i.e. the Event Calculus. We have followed this approach to develop and control an animated lifelike agent operating in a virtual campus.

1   Introduction

Recently there is an increasingly growing interest in building animated lifelike agents (also known as synthetic characters or creatures) in both academia and industry. Research work has been done in various labs around the world. While the earlier empirical studies have been very encouraging, they also suggest that simply embodying and animating an agent is insufficient. To come across as being lifelike, an agent needs to incorporate a deeper model of motivations and emotions, and in particular, to connect this model to agent's behaviour-generating process.

Motivations and emotions are essential parts of our lives. They determine what we are going to do and how to do it. They also influence how we communicate or interact with others. Several researchers have acknowledged their importance in human thinking and behaviour [1], [2], [3], and recent neurological evidence seems to support these idea [4], [5]. However, the field of artificial intelligence has generally ignored the important role that motivations and emotions play in cognitive process. Only more recently, computational approaches to motivation and emotion modelling have received increased attention. For example, [6], [7], [8], [9], [10] have integrated models of motivations and emotions into synthetic agents to create lifelike qualities and personalities. [11], [12] have developed agent architectures that model the influences of emotions in behaviour and learning. [13], [14] implemented systems that can recognise the affective state of people. Even though models and architectures

A. de Antonio, R. Aylett, and D. Ballin (Eds.): IVA 2001, LNAI 2190, pp. 72-85, 2001.

have been proposed, most of these models concentrate on the modelling of one specific aspect of motivation or/and emotion. The depth and extent to which these models address different mental phenomena vary widely, and so do the theories and taxonomies upon which they are based.

Our research is to build animated lifelike agents. The Holy Grail is to endow an agent with not only a believable appearance but also the natural intelligence that human beings possess. To achieve this goal, we try to equip an animated lifelike agent with a mind. In this paper, we first propose a computational mind model that consists of a motivational system and an emotional system. We describe a motivation model and introduce an algorithm for motivation arbitration that finally result in an active goal for agents. In emotional system, we adopt a commonly accepted emotion model and apply a highly developed logical formalism to reason about emotional elicitors and emotions. In section 3, we present a layered hierarchical agent architecture where the mind model is a core component. By means of the architecture we discuss in details on how the mind model, i.e. motivations and emotions, influences an agent's behaviour. Finally, we partially implement an animated lifelike agent with the proposed model and architecture.

2   Mind Model

Human minds are incredibly complex systems. Different scientific disciplines such as neurology, psychology and philosophy take different approaches to the problem of studying the mind. Our solution is to treat a mind as a control system and take a computational approach to model its mental phenomena. To simulate human problem-solving processes, we propose a computational mind model as shown in Figure 1. The mind model is composed of a motivational system and an emotional system, which emulates the two main cognitive processes that happen in human mind. The motivational system consists of a Motivation Synthesizer and a Goal Generator while the emotional system contains an Emotion Reasoner and an Emotion Synthesizer. They are described in details below.

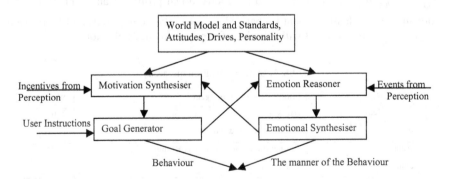

Fig. 1. Mind model

2.1   Motivational System

A motivation is anything that can influence the focus of attention of an agent. The motivational system serves several purposes. First, it evaluates all currently available motivations, then activates the most important and situation-relevant motivation that in turn determines an agent's active goal. Second, it provides goals for the emotional system where these goals are used as criteria for emotion appraisal. Finally, it provides a learning context – an agent learns skills that serve to satisfy its motivations.

The Motivation Synthesiser accomplishes motivation modelling, calculation and arbitration. It produces a dominant motivation as the top control point of the whole agent architecture. At any time point an agent is controlled by one single motivation. In the Goal Generator, motivations are mapped to corresponding goals. These generated goals, on one hand, will be passed on to the Emotion Reasoner of the emotional system for emotion appraisal in related to events. On the other hand, the active goal is used as an input to the behavioural layer of the architecture to drive the whole system into operation.

Motivation Synthesizer. We develop computational mechanisms for motivation modelling, representation and arbitration. The Motivation Synthesizer generates the motivational state of an agent, i.e. a set of currently existent motivations and further determines an active motivation through these mechanisms.

Motivation Model. Drawing ideas from motivation theory [15], [16] and other works, we develop a motivation model that subsumes a static motivation hierarchy and a dynamic component. The static motivation hierarchy as shown in Table 1 provides motivations with static priorities empirically found in human beings. In this model the low-level needs have higher priority than the higher-level needs, and that the former must be satisfied before a human starts satisfying the latter. The relative importance of each motivation category is characterized with a list of weights: W_{phys}, W_{safe}, W_{aff}, W_{ach}, W_{learn}, which is called the motivational profile of an agent. When the motivational profile of an agent is changed, i.e., the relative importance of motivation category changes, the agent will exhibit differently motivated behavior.

Table 1. Static motivation hierarchy

Motivation Category	Interpretation for an agent	Weights
Physiological	Drinking	W_{phys}
Safety	Avoid collision & hostile agents	W_{safe}
Affiliation	Cooperation, social activity, Helping others	W_{aff}
Achievement	Achieve its own goals	W_{ach}
Self-Actualisation	Learning & creative activity	W_{learn}

The dynamic component of the motivation model determines the varying intensity of agents' motivations. Determinants of a motivation include internal needs and external stimuli. The internal needs, also known as drives, represent the urgency for an agent to perform a specific behavior. The external stimuli, also refer to as incentives, can be anything happened in an agent's situated environment, which is related to an agent's drives in one or another way. We introduce an algorithm for calculating the intensity of a motivation as follows:

$$\text{SoM}_{it} = \sum_k D_{kt} W_k + \sum_j I_{jt} W_j \, . \tag{1}$$

Where SoM_{it} is the strength of motivation i at time t; D_{kt} is the intensity of drive k at time t; I_{jt} is the intensity of incentive j at time t; W_k and W_j are the weights corresponding to drive k and incentive j; both the drive k and the incentive j range over the drives and incentives that directly effect the strength of motivation i. Since both D_{kt} and I_{jt} change over time, the strength SoM_{it} is a time-varying variable. Taking into consideration the static priorities of motivations, we obtain the revised equation as follows:

$$\text{SoM}_{it} = W_{catei} \left(\sum_k D_{kt} W_k + \sum_j I_{jt} W_j \right). \tag{2}$$

Here W_{cate} is the priority weight of the static motivation category to which the motivation SoM_i belongs.

By incorporating the static priority hierarchy into the calculation of motivation strength, lower-level motivations, in general, are more likely to be chosen than higher-level motivations. However, if a higher-level motivation has a high relative importance, it may be preferred to a lower-level motivation.

Motivation Representation. We use a frame-like structure to represent a motivation as shown in Figure 2.

```
name <motiName>
static prio < one of the five category weights>
participants  <names of participants>
incentives  <set of (first-order) formula or variables>
drives  <set of drive formula or variables>
drive change   <temporal function >
motivation strength < a calculation function based on Equation (2)>
```

Fig. 2. Abstract description of a motivation

Each slot of the structure denotes an attribute of a motivation. The advantage of the representation is that more attributes can be added later if necessary and logical formulae can be used to specify the attributes. *Different motivations may have different drives, incentives and corresponding weights. Therefore, each motivation will have a unique function for computing its strength.*

Motivation Arbitration. An agent may have a bulk of possible motivations with respect to its current situational and mental context. Motivations have to compete with each other. Only the motivation with the strongest strength will be allowed to control the agent. This does not mean that all other motivations are simply discarded. They are dormant and their strengths change over time. Once the current motivation is satisfied or its strength is lower that others, another motivation (or goal) will be activated. The algorithms for motivation arbitration can be summarized as follows.

1) Set the motivational profile of the agent.
2) Specify the initial situation such as internal drives, incentives, goals and objects.
    Then at each time step:
3) Compute the strength of all motivations and rank them according to their magnitudes.
4) Choose the first motivation Fm.
5) Compare the Fm with the current active motivation. Make the motivation with bigger magnitude active.
6) Map the active motivation to its corresponding goal g. (in Goal Generation module)
7a) Pursue the active goal (in the Behavior Engine)
7b) Continue the loop from the step 3 while the agent proceeds to step 6 and 7a.

Using the above motivation selection mechanism, it is natural to realize opportunistic goals. For example, during the process that an agent pursues its current active goal, it may find some new objects nearby that serve as an incentive for a secondary goal. This emerged incentive may cause the motivation for the secondary goal to become the strongest motivation, and thus leads to activation of a new goal. After finishing this goal the agent will continue the original goal.

Goal Generator. The Goal Generator is responsible for generating goals in accordance with the motivational state of an agent. If the newly generated goal is different from the current goal that an agent is pursuing, the agent will suspend its current behavior and adopt the new goal. Otherwise it will continue its effort for achieving the current goal.

Goal Representation. A goal can be conceptualized as a representation of a possible state-of-affairs towards which an agent has a motivation to realize. Like motivations, goals are represented as frame-like structures with each slot denoting one of their attributes as shown in Figure 3.

> goal_name < goalName>
> goal_descr < a set of formula >
> participants <name of involved objects or agents>
> importance < integer >
> preconditions <a set of formula>
> commitment status < one of active, successful, rejected and failure>
> plan < controller>

Fig. 3. Goal specification

Some properties of a goal will be inherited from its motivation attributes. Note that the plan slot may be empty. That means the planning module of the architecture has to make a plan for this goal from scratch.

Goal Generation. We design a motivation-goal structure that provides a one-to-one mapping relationship between a motivation and a top-level goal. If a motivation takes control of an agent, then a top goal will be generated automatically from the motivation-goal structure. Once a motivation is mapped to a goal, the goal will use some of the motivation properties to construct its own properties. For example, in our implementation we use the intensity of a motivation to designate the importance of its corresponding goal.

Goal Persistence. One problem with the above motivation arbitration algorithm is that oscillations can easily occur, i.e., an agent can't commit itself to one goal. To sort out this problem, we always use the original strength of an adopted motivation for later motivation arbitration. When an agent starts to pursue a goal, the strength of the motivation will decrease. We do not use this new strength for competition with other motivations but still the original strength of the motivation. Other motivations can suppress an adopted motivation only when their strength is larger than the original strength of an active motivation or the currently active goal has been achieved. This will provide an agent some persistence while keeping it flexible to dynamic events.

2.2   Emotional System

The emotional system generates affective responses to events and objects with regard to goals, standards and attitudes, i.e. emotions. Emotions of an agent serve three functions. First, it influences goal generation in the motivational system. Second, it biases action selection during planning process, and finally it modulates the manners that actions are performed. In the following we will briefly discuss the emotion theory on which the emotional system is based. Then we present a mechanism for emotion generation. In the next section we will describe the influences that emotions have on an agent's behavior.

Emotion Theory. Emotions form a powerful, but ill-defined class of mental phenomena that have spawned a wealth of competing definitions and theory [17], [18], [5], [4]. Several models or taxonomies for analyzing the conditions leading to emotions have been proposed [19] [20]. Since our research concentrates on developing a computational emotion model, i.e. emotion representation and generation rather than on emotion itself. We adopt the OCC model [19] as the basis of our work.

The OCC model classifies emotions to 24 emotion types according to the valenced reaction of an agent to events, actions and objects. Each emotion belongs to one emotion type. An emotion type can have many variations. All members of an emotion type share certain mechanism and characteristics, including similarities in antecedent events, expression and likely behavioral responses. These characteristics differ between emotion types and distinguish one from another.

Emotion Representation. We use a frame-like structure to represent an emotion as shown in Figure 4. Each slot of the structure denotes an attribute of an emotion.

emotion_name < emName>
type <one of the 24 types>
intensity < integer >
causes < set of formula>
directional <the bearer of the emotion effect>

Fig. 4. Emotion representation

Emotion Generation. It is commonly accepted that what determines whether an emotion will be felt and what emotion it will be depends on the evaluation and interpretation of events, rather than on the events per se. The basic idea of the OCC model is that any emotion is generated based on the valence reaction to events and objects in the light of agent's goal, standards and attitudes. Even though both cognitive and non-cognitive elicitors of emotions exist, in this paper we focus on the mechanism of emotion generation that concerns with cognitive elicitors.

Emotion generation takes place in the Emotion Reasoner where an agent appraises events or/and object according to its goal, standards and attitude. In [21], we have developed a logical approach to modelling agent's behavior based on a highly developed logical theory for reasoning about actions and effects, i.e. the Event Calculus (EC) [22]. We extend the current EC in two aspects to take into consideration the emotion issues. The first extension is that events include not only the actions that an agent can take, but also the exogenous events happened in the world in which the agent situates (including other agents' actions, environmental events such as object or agent appearance). The second is that events will affect not only the external world that an agent situates but also the internal world of the agent itself, i.e. the motivational and emotional state.

We use the extended EC formalism to formalize emotion generation processes. We introduce three Appraisal actions to evaluate various events and objects with respect to goals, standards and attitudes, three fluents that denote the effects of appraisal actions on an agent's internal world and an emotional fluent representing the generated emotion. Using the predicates in the extended Event Calculus, we can produce a set of emotion generation formulae, each of them will have the following form.

Initiates(AppraiseEvent(agent_ag, event_e, goal_y), emotion(agent_ag, Joy, emInt, emDir, emCau), t) ← HoldAt(vrteDesirability(agent_ag, event_e)> 0, t) ∧ emotion(agent_ag, Joy, emInt, emDir, emCau) = calc_joyEmotion(vrteDesirability(agent_ag, event_e), prevEmotionState())

Here AppraiseEvent(agent_ag, event_e, goal_y) is the appraisal action; emotion(agent_ag, Joy, emInt, emDir, emCau) is the emotional fluent, and vrteDesirability(agent_ag, event_e) is the effect of the appraisal action.

This formula means that Joy emotion is generated when an event is appraised as being pleasant with respect to the agent's goals. The desirability is the only variable affecting the intensity of the emotion.

Emotion Synthesizer. Emotion Synthesizer concerns with emotion storage, combination and decay. It generates the emotional state of an agent by maintaining, updating emotions that an agent has. An agent may have many emotions with different intensity at the same time. When different emotions of the same type are stored together, they can be combined in some manners. We use two methods for emotion combination. One is the winner-takes-all policy, i.e. the emotion with the strongest intensity serves as the active dominant emotion of an agent. The other is to add all the intensities of these sub-emotions together. If different types of emotions occur simultaneously, a new emotion will generate based on emotion blend. These compound emotions have been included in the OCC model.

Emotion decay is a thorny problem that receives very little attention. What we are concerned about here is not why emotions decay but how, i.e., the mechanism involved in the decay process. In Emotion Synthesizer, each type of emotion is provided a built-in decay function that controls the evolution of the emotion. This function is specific to each type of emotion and can have different models of emotion decay. In each update cycle, the Emotion Synthesizer will evaluate all emotions in the storage according to decay functions. Together with the newly added emotions, it determines the current emotional state of an agent.

3   Emotion-Based Behavior

Emotions motivate and bias behavior but they do not completely determine it. When an agent has a strong emotion, it may provoke emotional behavior, adding a goal, but most of the time emotions just regulate or modulate an agent's behavior. We have found that emotions can influence agent's behavior at motivational level, action planning level and motor level. The influence of an emotion can take effect at any level or/and at all three levels at the same time. An agent reacts to emotions' influence differently at different levels of control.

To facilitate the modelling of emotion influences on agent's behavior, we develop an agent architecture as shown in Figure 5. The architecture consists of three hierarchical layers. The lowest layer is the Animation Engine that provides agents with primitive expressive or non-expressive actions. The Behavior Engine is to generate and execute plans to achieve agents' goals. On the top of the Behavior Engine lies the mind model that produces goals and emotions dynamically for agents.

3.1   Emotional Influence on Goal Generation

We agree with Tomkins' view that the affect system is the primary innate biological motivating mechanism because without its amplification, nothing else matters, and with its amplification anything else can matter. Based on this stance, it is natural and straightforward to incorporate emotional influence into motivation system by multiplying the intensity of a drive variable with an emotional amplification factor. The revised equation is as follows:

$$\text{SoM}_{it} = W_{catei} \left(\sum_k D_{kt} F_{ek} W_k + \sum_j I_{jt} W_j \right). \qquad (3)$$

Here F_{ek} is the emotional factor representing emotion's effect towards drive k. it can be positive or negative. Other parameters are the same as Equation 2.

It is apparent from Equation 3 that the change of an agent's emotional state may cause the rearrangement of the current motivations. Some may go down or be discarded; others may go up or be topped. Whether an emotion triggers a motivation or not depends on the intensity of the emotion. Only when the motivation reinforced by an emotion wins the arbitration competition, the goal can be activated. An agent can have many types of emotion. How each type of motion affects different motivation depends on application scenario and the situational context.

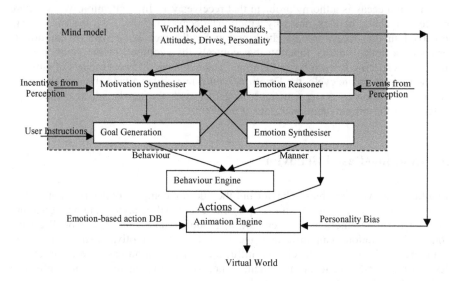

Fig. 5. Agent architecture

To take into account emotions' influence in goal generation, the algorithm for motivation arbitration is as follows.

1) Set the motivational profile of an agent.
2) Specify the initial situation such as internal drives, goals and objects.
   At each time step:
3) Implement cognitive appraisal and generate the current emotional state.
4) Compute the strength of all motivations taking into account emotion influence and rank them according to their magnitudes.
5) Choose the first motivation Fm.
6) Compare the Fm with the current active motivation. Make the motivation with bigger magnitude active.
7) Map the active motivation to its corresponding goal g. (in Goal Generation module)
8a) Pursue the active goal (in the Behavior Engine)
8b) Continue the loop from the step 3 while the agent proceeds to step 7 and 8a.

Using the above algorithm and mechanism we can create emotional or rational agent by adjusting the emotional factors. If we designate emotional factors with large values, then motivations of an agent will be more sensitive to its emotional state. Thus it is easily controlled by emotion-dominated motivations. In this case, the agent can be said to be an emotional agent. On the other hand, if the values of emotional factors are very small, this will lead to an agent to ignore its emotions. Thus a rational agent is created. By fine-tuning the magnitude of emotional factors, we can create agents that behave both rationally and emotionally, i.e., intelligently.

3.2   Emotional Influence on Planning

Emotions have three functions at the middle layer of the architecture, i.e., the Behavior Engine. First of all, emotions can influence the choice of strategies and mechanisms that an agent chooses for a particular given goal. It is common that multiple plans or controllers are feasible for a goal. Emotions can make some controllers potential candidates that would otherwise not be chosen; they can increase or decrease the likelihood of a controller being chosen. They can also make a potential candidate no longer an option. Second, even when a controller has been chosen to realize a given goal, an emotional state can bias the choice of actions, thus lead to different action sequences. This emotional modulation is particularly useful for implementation of controller [21]. The EC-based controllers are high-level action sketches that need to be filled in during run-time execution. Dynamic emotional modulation helps controllers determine which action to select to achieve its goal. Finally emotions can affect how many times behavior is attempted before giving up a goal or taking another goal.

We have developed an approach to realizing emotion-based decision-making. It is based on the event calculus and the behavior specification language [21]. We incorporate emotion information into the construction of controllers or plans by modifying the preconditions of actions. During plan decomposition, an agent's emotion will bias the choice of sub-level actions. Therefore, an agent with the same goal can have different action sequence according to its emotional state. In the following we show an emotion-based controller comact_greet that controls an agent's behavior of greeting.

```
proc comact_greet(anAgent)
act_sensingEntity(iag);
ifπ theAgent(theAgent⊂fl_sensingEntity(iag)∧emotionalState(iag)= liking(theAgent))
then
act_seningPos(theAgent);
comact_moveTo(fl_position(theAgent);
act_waving(iag, theAgent);
else
ifπ   theAgent(theAgent⊂fl_sensingEntity(iag)∧emotionalState(iag)≠liking(theAgent))
then
act_seningPos(theAgent);
comact_moveTo(fl_position(theAgent);
act_waving(iag, theAgent);
endif
act_resetAgent(iag)
endproc
```

With the embedded emotional information, an agent iag first chooses an agent theAgent it likes and engage a greeting or talk. If there is no such agent available, then it will choose the ones it does not dislike and engages a talk or greeting. Therefore, the emotional state of the agent iag plays a role of biasing the agent's choice about which agent to greet first rather than indiscriminately. The emotion can be further used to make a choice about how the greeting is conducted, i.e., by kiss, hug, nod or waving.

3.3   Emotional Influence on Performing Actions

An agent can express its emotions through facial expression, voice, body posture and the manner it conducts an action. If we view an action as a verb, then emotions can be viewed as the way the actions are performed, similar to the adverbs. What we expect is that an agent can take the same action differently in terms of its emotional state.

To achieve the above objective, first we need a list of primitive actions that an agent can take and a set of primitive emotions that an agent is able to generate. Second a mechanism is required to combine the agent's action with its emotional state and produce a particular emotion-expressive action. As a first approximation, we can view the emotion types as all possible emotional states. This can lead to a two-dimension matrix with each row as a primitive action, each column as an emotion and each element as a specific emotion-expressive action. If we would like to model the subtle differences that different emotional states within the same type of emotion have, we can extend each emotion type to a third dimension representing the sub-emotion type under one emotion type. This will result in a three-dimension matrix with the third dimension representing sub-emotions. Figure 6 shows the full structure of the emotion-expressive action selection mechanism.

With this model, it is flexible to model expressive actions at different granularities according to application scenario. The difficulty lies on the practical implementation of various actions with subtle animation differences.

4   Implementation

The mind model and the architecture in which it is embedded have been used to develop and control an animated lifelike interface agent. The agent operates in a virtual environment as shown in Figure 7.

The motivations and corresponding goals of the animated lifelike interface agent, which will act as a human user to participate virtual activities in the virtual environment, are modeled as in Table 2.

With the methodology described in 2.2 we produce a set of emotion generation formulae. At each time step the interface agent will appraise events occurred or objects (including agents) appeared. By means of the unification of appraisal actions and the formulae the interface agent can generate different emotions. For example, unsatisfied goals produce *Distress* and *Anger*; successful interaction with other agent or users incurs *Happiness* or *Joy*.

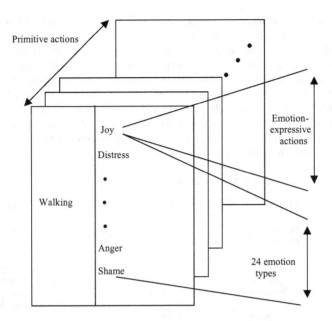

Fig. 6. Structure of emotion-expressive actions

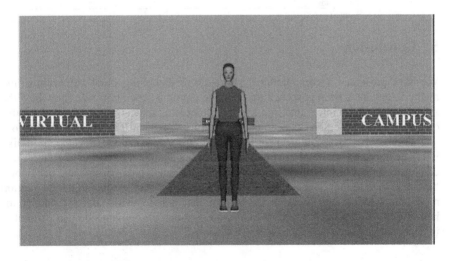

Fig. 7. The interface agent in virtual environment

Given a goal, the behavior engine generates a sequence of actions. It is implemented based on a logical formalism, the Event Calculus and a high-level behavior specification language [21]. The plan generation or action selection is accomplished through hierarchical planning via compound action decomposition. Each compound action serves as a sketch plan or a part of a plan. Actual actions for the plan are selected depending on agents' emotional state and situational conditions.

Examples of such behavior include *Approach-Position, Avoid-Obstacle, Greet-person, Navigation and Express-Emotion.*

We introduce a notation eeAction(priAction(), emType(), emVar(), matchConditions) to denote an expressive action. Here the first three arguments represent a primitive action, an emotion type and the variation type of the emotion type respectively. The forth argument matchConditions tests all the match conditions for the combination of the primitive action and the emotion. Through the expressive action structure in 3.3 it is straightforward to access and select correct expressive actions according to agents' current action and emotional state. Currently the interface agent has *Joy* and *Sad* expressive actions.

Table 2. Motivation modelling of interface agents

Motivation category	Motivations	Drives	Stimuli	Goals
Physiological	Drinking	Thirst	Water	Godrinking
Safety	Collision avoidance	Security	Obstacles	CollisionAvoidance
Affiliation	Greeting	Sociability	Agents	Greeting
	Provide information	cooperation	Upon request	ForwardInfo
Achievement	Achieving its own tasks	Accomplish tasks	Task-oriented	Goto(pos) or Do(thing)
Self-Actualisation	Self-amusing	Boring	None	Selfamusing
	Navigation & exploration	Curiosity	Unknown area	Navigation
	Learning, creative activity			

5   Conclusion

We have presented a computational approach to modelling mind. Algorithms and methodology have been proposed for goal and emotion generation. We show how the mind model can be integrated into agent architecture, serving as a high-level control centre. We are particularly concerned about how emotions affect an agent's behaviour and discuss this issue in details. Following this approach we develop a lifelike interface agent for a virtual environment. With the equipped mind the interface agent demonstrates not only rational behaviour - goal-oriented and opportunistic behaviour, but also emotional behaviour – emotion-based decision-making and action modulation. While the research has shown that a computational mind model for building lifelike agents is practical, it also suggest more work is needed, in particular, in the construction of various expressive actions.

References

1. Clark, F. C., (1958), "The effect of deprivation and frequency of reinforcement on variable-interval responding", Journal of the Experimental Analysis of Behavior, 1, 211-227.
2. Minsky, M. 1986. The Society of Mind. New York: Simon & Schuster
3. Toda, M. 1993. Emotions and Urges. Technical Report, No. 93-1-01, School of Computer and Cognitive Sciences, Chukyo University

4. LeDoux, J. E. (1996). *The Emotional Brain: The Mysterious Underpinnings of Emotional Life*. New York: Simon and Schuster.
5. Damasio, A. R. 1994. Descartes' Error: Emotion, Reason and the Human Brain. New York: Gosset/Putman.
6. Bates, J. 1994. The Role of Emotion in Believable Agents. Communications of the ACM 37(7):122-125
7. Reilly S. 1996. Believable Social and Emotional Agents. Technical Report, CMU-CS-96-138, Schools of Computer Science, Carnegie Mellon University
8. Elliott, C., et al. 1998. Story-morphing in the Affective Reasoning Paradigm: Generating Stories semi-automatically for use with „emotionally intelligent" agents. In Proceedings of AutonomousAgents'98
9. Andre E., Klesen M., Gebhard P., Allen S. and Rist T. 1999. Integrating Models of Personality and Emotioins into Lifelike Characters. In Proceedings of the workshop on Affect in Interactions - Towards a new Generation of Interfaces in conjunction with the 3rd i3 Annual Conference, pp. 136-149, Siena, Italy.
10. Kline, C. and Blumberg, B. 1999. The Art and Science of Synthetic Character Design. In AISB 1999 Symposium on AI and Creativity in Entermainment and Visual Art. Edinburgh, Scotland.
11. Canamero D. 1997. Modelling Motivations and Emotions as a Basis for Intelligent Behaviour. In Proceedings of AGENTS'97. New York: ACM Press.
12. Velásquez, J. (1998). Modeling Emotion-Based Decision-Making. In Proceedings of the 1998 AAAI Fall Symposium Emotional and Intelligent: The Tangled Knot of Cognition. AAAI Press.
13. Vyzas, E. and Picard, R. 1998. Affective Pattern Classification. In Proceedings of AAAIFS98, Emotional and Intelligent: The Tangled Knot of Cognition. AAAI Press
14. Tosa, N. and Nakatsu, R. 1996. Lifelike Communication Agent – Emotion Sensing Character MIC and Feeling Sension Character MUSE. In Proceedings of International Conference on Multimedia Computing and Systems
15. Maslow, A. 1954. Motivation and Personality. Harper Row, New York.
16. Hull, C. L. 1943. Principles of Behavior, New York: Appleton-Century-Crofts.
17. Tomkins, S. S. (1984). Affect Theory. In K. R. Scherer and P. Ekman (Eds.), *Approaches to Emotion*. Hillsdale, NJ: Lawrence Erlbaum Associates.
18. Frijda, N. H. 1986. *The Emotions*. Cambridge: Cambridge University Press.
19. Ortony, A., Clore, G. L., and Collins, A. (1988). *The Cognitive Structure of Emotions*. Cambridge: Cambridge University Press.
20. Roseman, I. J., Jose, P. E. and Spindel, M. S. 1990. Appraisals of Emotion-Eliciting Events: Testing a Theory of Discrete Emotions. Journal of Personality and Social Psychology 59(5):899-915.
21. Chen L., Bechkoum K and Clapworhty G. 2001. A Logical Approach to High-Level Agent Control. The 5th International Conference on Autonomous Agents. Montreal, Canada. (to appear)
22. Shanahan, M. P., 1997. Solving the Frame Problem, MIT Press.

Intelligent Agents Who Wear Your Face: Users' Reactions to the Virtual Self

Jeremy N. Bailenson, Andrew C. Beall, Jim Blascovich, Mike Raimundo, and Max Weisbuch

Research Center for Virtual Environments and Behavior, Department of Psychology, University of California, Santa Barbara, CA, 93101, USA
bailenson@psych.ucsb.edu

Abstract. The three-dimensional models used to embody intelligent agents are becoming increasingly realistic. We discuss two studies in which we embodied intelligently behaving virtual agents with photographically realistic models of human subjects' heads and faces. We then immersed those subjects with agents embodied with their <u>virtual selves</u> and compared their interactions and nonverbal behaviors to separate subjects who were immersed with agents embodied with <u>virtual others</u>. Subjects treated agents embodied with their virtual selves fundamentally differently than agents embodied with virtual others in regards to both measured nonverbal behaviors and questionnaire ratings. Implications for systems incorporating realistic embodied agents are discussed.

1   Introduction

About twenty years ago, William Gibson [6] described an outrageous world in which an intelligent agent masqueraded through virtual space by embodying the faces, bodies, and personalities of real people. Veritable human beings who interacted with this agent had great difficulty discriminating the agent from their fellow humans. While his brilliant work, *Neuromancer,* was fiction, as the decades pass by certain aspects of his visions begin to ring true. Embodied agents are becoming increasingly common in business applications, communications systems, and entertainment.

How intelligent would a virtual agent have to be in order to fool a reasonable human in the manner described above? Not surprisingly, this depends on how one defines intelligence. From a traditional artificial intelligence perspective, one might look to the agent's ability to solve specific problems such as machine vision or language understanding. For these tasks and many others, no agent (i.e., algorithm) exists today that competes favorably with human capabilities, so when comparing agents to humans in an objective sense, agents are not likely to fool a human. While this certainly may change in the future, we believe in many situations today it is not the actual intelligence that matters but rather the <u>perceived state</u> (i.e., intelligence, intention, identity, etc.) of the agent that matters. As philosophers and psychologists have argued for over a century, what matters in human-human interaction are the interactants' subjec-

A. de Antonio, R. Aylett, and D. Ballin (Eds.): IVA 2001, LNAI 2190, pp. 86-99, 2001.

tive beliefs about one another, not the objective truth of the interaction. Since one of the many important applications of virtual agent technology is interaction with humans, understanding how an agent can fool or otherwise impact human-agent interaction will be crucial to development and future success of agent technology.

The question becomes: What drives the perception of an agent's intelligence, intention, and identity? There are many likely variables that interact in complex ways; some of which are photo-realism, non-verbal behavior, autonomy, and interactivity [4]. However, extremely realistic digital humans are now making their debut in the public arena and may have a dramatic impact on the manner in which these variables interact. As a case in point, we cite both Eve Solal, a new and popular personality on the World Wide Web who models clothing, DJ's parties, and even has her own "agent" (i.e., a human being who is responsible for managing her contracts); and a current film, "Final Fantasy," whose cast consists exclusively of realistic three-dimensional agents (in contrast to previous full-length animated films that used the cartoon mechanism as a way of suspending disbelief).

In the research community, there is a growing body of research using experimental methods to carefully test human-agent interactions. This research shows that humans respond to virtual agents in ways that are very similar to their responses to other humans. A remarkable finding of this work is that this is true even for non-photorealistic agents that have very basic levels of behavior or interactivity [10]. It appears that built-in mechanisms in the human mind engage and respond in social manners to certain low-level stimuli, including agents. As such, we propose that in many instances it may be possible to generate meaningful human-agent interactions by evoking these built-in mechanisms, while at the same time relieving the agent developer from the burden of programming sophisticated algorithms of cognitive abilities. In these ways, we believe agents can use low-level influences to 'fool' humans in a social arena. In fact, it may be nearly impossible to avoid being fooled in cases in which an agent evokes certain basic characteristics or behaviors.

In the current paper, we discuss what we believe to be an extremely serious and substantial issue. How do people react when exposed to agents embodied with their virtual selves?

What is the virtual self? The answer to this question may in fact be more appropriate for philosophers than for social or computer scientists. However, in this discussion, we operationally define the virtual self as a virtual entity that resembles a given human along a certain dimensions (e.g., face, body, behavior, personality, etc.). The middle and right panels of Figure 1 show an example of a virtual self that has facial resemblance to a particular individual (as shown in the left panel). We contrast the term "virtual self" to the term "avatar," which has recently been adopted to describe a virtual entity that serves as one's proxy, because an avatar need not resemble the self along any particular dimension.

According to our definition, the virtual self can be conceptually framed in ways quite different from one's actual self. Consider an Internet-based chat room, or perhaps an immersive virtual environment (IVE) in which there are many virtual representations of people walking around. A given user can traverse that environment, and the virtual self, the representation that looks just like the user, can be used as her avatar. In other words, the movements and actions of that virtual representation can be completely tied to and controlled by the user. The user does not see her own face (unless she looks into a virtual mirror), and when the user looks down, she sees her

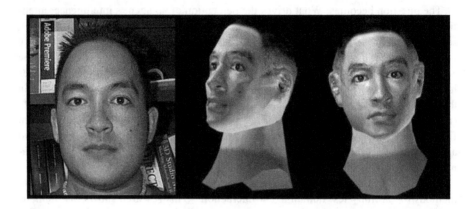

Fig. 1. The leftmost image is a photograph of the user while the center and rightmost images are different views of the three-dimensional model of the user

own torso and feet. In this type of a situation, the virtual self is most closely tied with the actual self.

However, consider the following situation. A given user has her virtual self in the chatroom, and then decides to get up and abandon whatever interface device she was using to control it. While she is gone, her little brother meanders into the room and plugs into the chatroom, commandeering the user's virtual self to traverse the environment. The little brother tours the chatroom, guiding the visual analog of his older sister through the environment. In this sense, a virtual self can be used by anyone to masquerade through virtual space. Virtual identity is not necessarily tied to physical identity.

More provocatively, a virtual self can be driven by an intelligent agent, some kind of algorithm that controls the representation. Virtual environments are increasingly becoming popular for both communications and commerce. One can conceivably design a computer program that is capable of guiding his virtual self through these different types of environments. In other words, if a user wants to send his virtual self to a chatroom, and to have his virtual self personally give every user in that environment his home phone number, the user does not necessarily have to be physically attached to his virtual self in order to accomplish that goal. He can simply use his virtual self to embody an intelligent agent who can easily run such an errand.

If we examine this last case more closely, some potentially unsettling questions arise. Assume that a person uses his virtual self to embody an agent and sends that embodied agent into a virtual environment. Then that user himself enters the virtual environment, and while traversing the environment encounters the agent driving his virtual self. In other words, he discovers another entity that resembles him along various dimensions and yet is in no way respondent to his movements or actions (as would be if he were looking in a mirror). Does he treat that virtual entity like himself, or like someone else entirely? Is this like running into a long lost twin, or is the resemblance between the user and the agent irrelevant to their interaction? In other words, can the virtual self be defined by a user's visual representation or behavioral personality, even if that visual representation is not at all tied to a user's actions or behaviors?

It is possible to take this hypothetical situation a bit further. Suppose that the user always uses his virtual self to embody a given agent, and on a daily basis he shares virtual space with the agent and interacts often with the virtual representation. How attached does he become with the embodied agent? If there was a database failure or a computer crash, and the virtual self was destroyed, is the user upset? Does he mourn for the death of his virtual representation? Is it like losing a best friend, or like losing a faithful dog? Or is it more akin to losing a goldfish? Is the representation of the virtual self completely replaceable, or will the old one be sorely missed?

The notion of a detachable virtual self opens up a plethora of mind-boggling questions; moreover every question raised tends to hint at dozens of others. For this reason, social science research concerning embodied and intelligent agents is uniquely exciting. In the following paper we describe two studies which barely scratch the surface of the research which will become absolutely necessary as humans begin to rely more and more on visual analogs of themselves.

The remainder of this paper will be structured as follows. First, we briefly discuss previous work that has measured human behavior in the presence of agents. Next, we describe the technique we use to produce realistic virtual representations of people in a single experimental session. Finally, we report data from two experiments in which subjects came to the lab, waited while we built their virtual selves, and then interacted in a number of novel situations with agents that were embodied with their virtual selves.

1.1 Behavioral Measures of Social Influence

There has been substantial research on interactions between intelligent agents and humans. For the sake of brevity, we limit discussion here to work on measuring the degree of social influence that humans exhibit during an interaction with an embodied agent.

We define social influence as the degree to which users of a virtual environment behave as if a virtual agent is in fact a real human being. Previous work suggests that the true litmus test for social influence lies in the behavioral experience of the user [3,4,7,8,9,12,13] . In other words, asking the user to explicitly discuss the humanity of the agent may be somewhat informative, but the surefire way to determine a user's regard for an agent's humanlike characteristics is to measure that user's behavior.

In our previous work [3], we have focused on a specific nonverbal behavior called proxemics, the amount of interpersonal distance that a user leaves between himself and an embodied agent in an IVE, as a gauge for social influence. We manipulated the realism of virtual agents' behavior and appearance. In regards to personal space, subjects in those studies treated embodied agents in a manner similar to real humans. Our users traversed the virtual environment attempting to memorize incidental features of the agent, such as the agent's name, hair color, and shirt color. Even though they were unaware of our measuring their personal space, the average minimum distance between them and the virtual agent was close to a half-meter away, indicating that users avoided direct contact with the agents. In addition, the shape of the personal space bubble around the embodied agents closely resembled the shape of the bubble that people typically leave around real humans, with the front distance being larger than the back distance [1]. This study also included a control condition in which subjects walked around a pylon of similar shape and size of a virtual human. They went much closer to the pylon than to the embodied agent.

Furthermore, the personal space bubble changed as a function of our realism manipulations. Previous research has demonstrated that interpersonal distance is higher between people who are maintaining eye contact than between those who are not [1]. Consequently, we also manipulated gaze in our studies. In conditions where the virtual agent exhibited realistic mutual gaze behavior by turning their heads to maintain eye contact with the users, the users left more personal space between themselves and the virtual agent than in conditions where the agent did not maintain mutual gaze.

In the first study described in this paper, we again measure the user's proxemic behavior, this time while they are immersed with an agent embodied with their virtual self in an IVE. We also gauge their explicit reactions through post-experimental interviews and questionnaires. In the following section we discuss the manner in which we build the virtual self.

2   Virtual Self Construction

Building the virtual self involves three main stages: creating the texture mask of the user's head and face, applying that texture of the user to a three dimensional template model, and then animating behaviors of the agent embodied with the user's texture map. We describe those processes in turn.

When the user arrives at our laboratory, we use a digital camera to take four photographs of the user's head and face: one profile, one head-on shot with the user's eyes closed, one with the user's eyes open, and one with the user's mouth open. Using a technique similar to that described by Sannier and Thalmann [11], we then stitch the profile and one of the front views together in order to create a texture mask that wraps around a three-dimensional model. Next, we use an image editor to create an additional texture mask with the user's eyes closed (to be used in a blinking animation).

We used two three-dimensional mesh models as templates: one for women and one for men. To apply a user's mask texture onto the appropriate three-dimensional model, we stretched the texture mask to ensure that the user's eyes, nose, mouth, and ears were in the correct locations on the model. We then used 3D modeling software to wrap the texture mask onto the model.

The embodied agent exhibited two separate nonverbal behaviors in order to create the perception of at least low-level intelligence. The first was blinking. At random intervals between two and five seconds, we swapped the texture map with the user's eyes closed onto the mesh model. The eyes remained closed for 200 ms before we switched back to the original texture mask.

The second behavior was head-turning. The embodied agent continually turned its head so that it constantly gazed at the user's face as he or she traversed the environment. The agent's head turned 85 degrees about the vertical axis in either direction. When the user walked beyond that point, the agent's head slowly turned back to looking straight ahead, until the user walked back within the 85 degree range. At that point the agent again maintained eye contact with the user.

3   Experiments

We now describe two studies we have conducted that measure the different responses people make to virtual agents. In both studies, we designed our agents to exhibit behaviors such as mutual gaze and blinking that create the perception of at least rudi-

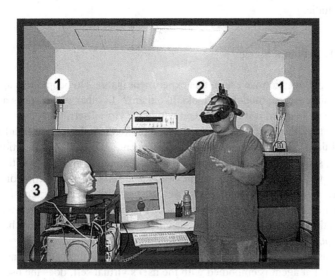

Fig. 2. The IVE being used in a 3m x 3m workspace. The components are: *1*) position tracking cameras. *2*) HMD, orientation tracking sensor, and microphone, and *3*) image generator

mentary intelligence. The key distinction we addressed with the current research is whether or not the agents visually resembled our subjects. The first study draws on the previous findings (as discussed in section 1.1) that people are unwilling to approach behaviorally realistic agents closer than they would a real human being, and tests further how this behavior may change when one uses self-identity to manipulate the perceived level of intimacy with an agent. Study two again uses identity to manipulate agent intimacy and tests whether perceived agent mortality affects peoples' emotions and self esteem.

In these studies, we sought to maximize a) social influence from the virtual agents and b) the ecological validity of walking behavior and personal space tendencies. As a result we chose to use IVE rather than desktop simulations. The technology for the current studies has been described in detail elsewhere [3], but is described briefly here. The head mounted displays (HMDs) were Virtual Research V8 HMDs with 680 by 480 resolution stereoscopic LCD devices running at 72 Hz refresh rates. Visual rendering was stereoscopic with a 60 degrees diagonal field of view. The display updated on average at a frame rate of 36 Hz with a latency of less than 65 ms between subjects' head or body movements and the concomitant update in the visual display. We tracked the subjects' orientation with inertial tracking and their position with passive optical tracking. Graphics were generated on a 450 MHz dual-processor, Intel Pentium III based-PC using an Evans & Sutherland Tornado 3000 video adapter. The real-time rendering software is OpenGL-based and has been developed internally. Figure 2 shows a photograph of the different components of the system we employed to run both studies.

3.1 Study 1: Personal Space

The fundamental question we ask in this experiment is this: Do people feel special ties with a three-dimensional model that looks like them? In other words, does a user pay special regard to an agent if it is embodied with their virtual self?

To answer this question, we examined users' proxemic behavior. We had the users walk around the IVE and examine an embodied agent. We had two conditions in this study. In the self condition, people walked around an agent embodied with their virtual self. In the other condition, people walked around an agent embodied with a virtual other. Unbeknownst to the user, we constantly recorded their position in the room in order to measure the amount of personal space they left between their physical body and the agent embodied with their virtual self. Previous research has demonstrated that people traversing an IVE leave appropriate amounts of personal space between themselves an unfamiliar agent [3]. However, if the agent is familiar to a user, if in fact that agent is embodied with the user's virtual self, does the user still feel the need to maintain the appropriate amount of personal space? This question, one which never had the mechanism or the motivation to be studied before the advent agent technology, was our focus here.

Subjects arrived at the lab one at a time for a one-hour session. We immediately took their pictures and began stitching their photographs together. During the stitching process (which took approximately 20 minutes to complete), subjects completed a biographical questionnaire.

We then immersed the subjects in a virtual environment that contained a floor and a virtual agent. Figure 3 illustrates the setup; here we have inserted a photograph of an actual participant into the rendered scene in order to illustrate the scale of the room. However, the subjects could not see themselves wearing the HMD; they could only see virtual agent.

Fig. 3. The virtual environment with an agent embodied by a virtual other as seen by the user

The virtual eyeheight of the participant was set to 1.7 m, which was also the exact height of the agent's eyes. We used the same generic body for all subjects. As Figure 3 illustrates, the body was always covered by a loosely fitting robe. We focus on the head and face because we believe that a majority of a person's identity is captured in that region. Furthermore, modeling the entire body would be too time consuming and difficult to do in a single experimental session using our current methods.

The usable tracking space in the physical room was approximately 3m x 3m. When the subjects entered the virtual room, they were approximately 1.5m away but facing the agent, who was also initially facing the subjects. We instructed subjects to walk to the left side of the agent, then to the right side of the agent, and then to the front of the agent.

There were 16 subjects in the study; eight of whom walked up to their virtual selves and eight of whom walked up to a virtual other (a control condition). The model used to embody the agent in the virtual other condition was always the same gender as the subject, and was chosen from a pool of models of people unfamiliar to the subjects. As a further control, subjects in the virtual other condition also had their

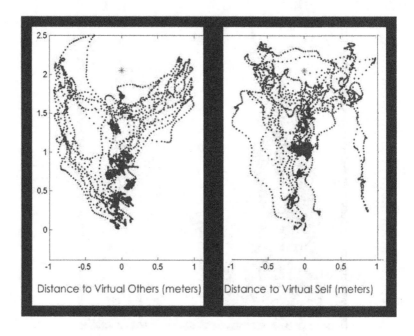

Fig. 4. Position points from all 16 subjects in our study. The graph on the left plots all the data points from the 8 subjects in the virtual other condition. The graph on the right plots all the data points from the 8 subjects in the virtual self condition. On each graph, small *dots* indicate individual position points and the *star* denotes the location of the agent. The starting point for subjects was at *(0,0)*

pictures taken and their faces made into virtual models. Both types of agents—self or other—exhibited the same behaviors, namely blinking and head-turning. All subjects received partial course credit for an introductory psychology course for participation.

The computer system sampled the subjects' position at a rate of approximately 8 hertz. Each sample measured the subjects' position in the virtual room, and we computed the distance obtained between the participant and the center-point of the virtual agent's head during each trial. Subjects had no problems navigating (i.e., physically walking) through the virtual space and none experienced any significant simulator-sickness. After the study, none of the subjects indicated that he or she had guessed their proxemic behavior was under scrutiny.

We measured personal space, our index of social influence, by using minimum distance, the shortest distance that a given participant maintained between themselves and the agent across trials. Our previous studies on proxemics in IVEs also utilized this measure.

We hypothesized that virtual selves would be perceived as more intimate and therefore subjects would not feel the need to maintain as high a level of personal space between their virtual selves as between virtual others. This is exactly what we found. Subjects went much closer to their virtual selves ($\underline{M}$ = .23 m, $\underline{SD}$ = .15) than to the virtual others ($\underline{M}$ = .51 m, $\underline{SD}$ = .19), $\underline{F}(1,14)$=11.23, $\underline{p}$<.005. Figure 4 shows plots of the position samples in the two conditions. Clearly, the bubble of personal space is much larger around the agent embodied with the virtual other than around the agent embodied with the virtual self.

Importantly, the current study replicates the size of the personal space bubble (about half a meter) that has been established in previous research on agents in virtual environments with respect to virtual others. The current data provide a notable exception in the case of virtual selves; here subjects do not leave a large personal space bubble between their physical bodies and their virtual selves.

This result makes sense given the past research on personal space. The size of the personal space bubble between two people gets is inversely proportional to the level of intimacy [1]. When people identify aspects of themselves in an otherwise autonomously behaving agent, we conclude they experience increased levels intimacy with the agent and are therefore willing to reduce the personal space bubble.

In addition to measuring their personal space, we also verbally administered a ratings questionnaire while they were immersed with the agent. The questionnaire is shown in the Appendix, and measures self reported social presence (i.e., the degree to which people report being in the presence of a veritable human being), affect towards the agent, and finally, how willing they would be to perform a series of embarrassing acts in front of the agent.

To measure affect, we averaged questions seven and eight from the Appendix. There was a trend for people to show positive affect towards the agent embodied with their virtual self ($\underline{M}$ = .50, $\underline{SD}$ = 1.40) and negative affect towards the agent embodied with the virtual other ($\underline{M}$ = -.37, $\underline{SD}$ = 1.18), however, due to the small number of subjects in this study, this difference was not statistically reliable. To measure social presence, we took a summation score of the first six questions from the Appendix. Positive numbers indicate high social presence while negative numbers indicate low social presence. According to their verbal report, people experienced no reliable difference in social presence in the two conditions, with a mean score of -1.95 ($\underline{SD}$ = 6.00) for the virtual self and -2.04 ($\underline{SD}$ = 6.85) for the virtual other.

Perhaps the most interesting data from the questionnaires is the willingness to perform an embarrassing act. We took a summation score of the last four questions from the Appendix; positive numbers indicate willingness to commit an embarrassing act (i.e., change clothes or tell secrets to the agent) while negative numbers indicate unwillingness to commit an embarrassing act. Subjects were more willing to commit an embarrassing act in front of an agent embodied with their virtual self ($\underline{M}$ = 4.25, $\underline{SD}$ = 3.11) than in front of an agent embodied with a virtual other ($\underline{M}$ = .13, $\underline{SD}$ = 5.11), $\underline{F}$(1,15)=3.80, $\underline{p}$<.07. Clearly, our subjects were experiencing a unique relation with the agent embodied with their own representation if they were willing to change their clothes in front of it! In other words, the subjects experienced a lesser degree of self-consciousness in front of their virtual self than in front of the virtual other.

3.2   Study 2: Agent Mortality

In the first study, we demonstrated that people exhibit unique nonverbal behavioral affinities towards an agent embodied with their virtual self. In the second study, we sought to answer the following question: Are the ties that people form with their virtual selves strong enough to elicit negative responses when those virtual selves are destroyed?

In the second experiment, we recruited people from the community and embodied agents with their virtual selves. As a cover story, we told them we were creating a permanent archive to store three-dimensional versions of people. We then had two conditions: a mortality and a control condition. In the mortality condition, we feigned a computer crash and deceived subjects by convincing them we had lost their virtual selves. In the control condition, we kept the version of their virtual selves. We then compared the two groups on a number of measures to gauge their reaction to the "loss" of their virtual selves.

We recruited subjects from our second study by putting an advertisement in the local newspaper, offering to pay subjects to put themselves into our virtual three-dimensional database. The purpose of doing this was to ensure that our subjects were highly motivated to have their virtual selves created. In other words, if someone was willing to answer an advertisement in the newspaper and drive out to campus, then we could assume that they were at least moderately excited at the prospect of having a virtual self. An unanticipated benefit of this recruitment strategy was that we had large amounts of diversity in age ($\underline{M}$ = 35, Min =21, Max =58) and occupation.

This study was very similar to the first one, in that subjects came into the lab, posed for photographs, and waited while we built virtual versions of them. We constructed the virtual self and animated the embodied agent in exactly the same way as in the first study. In the mortality condition, while the subjects were navigating about the IVE and interacting with their virtual self, we feigned a computer failure and convinced the subjects that we had not only crashed our system, but also had lost all traces of their virtual selves. We then administered a number of questionnaire-based measures of attitude change and self-esteem. In the control condition, subjects traversed through the IVE with the agent embodied with their virtual selves and then filled out the same attitude and esteem measures (without being led to believe their representation had been destroyed). There were 30 subjects in the study, 15 in each of the two conditions.

The results demonstrated no difference between the two conditions. In other words, subjects were not upset by the loss of their virtual self. First, there was no difference between attitude ratings concerning virtual people or virtual environments. Second there was no change on self-esteem scales between the two conditions. Third, anecdotally, subjects in the virtual mortality condition did not display any strong reactions or regret to the loss of their virtual representation.

Certainly there are limitations to this study. One problem is that our subjects only became acquainted with their virtual selves for about an hour before the virtual mortality occurred. In order to understand the relationship between a person and her virtual self, a study needs to allow subjects to become more attached to their three-dimensional representations. Future studies should examine users' interaction with their virtual selves in more detail. Nonetheless, the current study provides a worthy starting point for examining the nature of one's regard for her personal self. The current data suggest that the loss of such a representation is not a particularly devastating event.

4   Conclusions

In the current set of studies, we begin to examine the nature of human behaviors in the presence of agents, specifically ones embodied with the head and face of the users. Study 1 shows that people do exhibit a unique relationship with agents embodied with their virtual selves. First, we demonstrated nonverbal behavioral evidence: users were willing to violate those agents' personal space (but not other agents' personal space). Second, we demonstrated evidence from questionnaires: on ratings scales, users indicated that they would be more willing to commit embarrassing acts in front of an agent that resembles themselves than in front of an unfamiliar agent. In Study 2 we qualified this effect, saying the ties that users created between themselves and their virtual selves were not so strong to suggest that the loss of the virtual self was in any way traumatic.

These studies are only an initial foray towards understanding the virtual self. In the future, we would like to model the virtual self behaviorally, as opposed to photographically. There is a growing body of work that describes techniques to tailor the behaviors and gestures of agents [2,5]. Future endeavors along the lines of the current studies should examine embodied agents whose gesture sets and behavioral personalities are tailored towards specific users.

The personal space findings from the current study replicate a number of previous studies described in the Introduction. In previous studies, we featured a number of different experimental tasks in attempt to induce our subjects to violate the personal space of an agent. For example, we tried putting small labels on the agents' shirts that the subjects had to memorize. However, subjects consistently left a bubble of about half a meter around the agent, despite the realization that they may perform poorly on the task. But in the current study, subjects had absolutely no problem violating the personal space of agents when those agents looked like themselves. We hypothesize that the reason subjects were willing to come so close to their virtual self stemmed from some kind of implicit familiarity or intimacy. In the same way one does not necessarily feel the need to respect the personal space of his significant other, he doesn't feel the need to respect the space of his virtual self.

These findings certainly have implications towards both educational and commercial systems employing embodied intelligent agents. Agents who are trying to forge some kind of a relationship with the user may be more successful if they look like the user. Along the same lines, users should be wary of agents who wear their face, as these agents may unwittingly elicit preferential treatment from a user.

References

1. Argyle, M. (1988). *Bodily communication* (2nd ed.). London, England UK: Methuen.
2. Badler, N. I., Chi, D. & Chopra, S. (1999). Virtual human animation based on movement observations and cognitive behavior models. In *Proceedings of SIGGRAPH'99*: p. 1-17.
3. Bailenson, J.N., Blascovich, J., Beall, A.C. & Loomis, J. (In Press). Equilibrium revisited: Mutual gaze and personal space in virtual environments. *PRESENCE*.
4. Blascovich, J., Loomis, J., Beall, A., Swinth, K., Hoyt, C., & Bailenson, J.N. (In Press). Immersive virtual environment technology as a methodological tool for social psychology. *Psychological Inquiry*.
5. Cassell, J. & Vilhjalmsson, H. (1999). Fully embodied conversational avatars: Making communicative behaviors autonomous. *Autonomous Agents and Multi-Agent Systems, 2, 45-64*.
6. Gibson, W. (1984). *Neuromancer*. New York : Ace Books.
7. Heeter, C. (1992). Being there: The subjective experience of presence. *PRESENCE ,1(2),* 262-271.
8. Isbister, K., Nakanishi, H., Ishida, T. & Nass, C. (2000). Helper agent: Designing an assistant for human-human interaction in a virtual meeting space. *Proceedings of ACM CHI 2000 , v.1*, 57-6
9. Rickenberg, R. & Reeves, B. (2000). The effects of animated characters on anxiety, task performance, and evaluations of user interfaces. *Proceedings of ACM CHI 2000, v.1*, 49-56
10. Reeves, B. & Nass, C. (1996). *The Media Equation: How People Treat Computers, Television, and New Media Like Real People and Places*. Cambridge: Cambridge University Press.
11. Sannier G. & Thalmann, M. N. (1998). A user friendly texture-fitting methodology for virtual humans. *Computer Graphics International '97*, 1997
12. Swinth, K. R., & Blascovich, J. (2001, June). Conformity to group norms in an immersive virtual environment. Hot Topic Paper presented at the annual meeting of the American Psychological Society (APS), Toronto, Ontario.
13. Zahorik, P., & Jenison, R. L. (1998). Presence as Being-in-the-World. *Presence, 7*, 78-89

Appendix

Strongly Disagree	Disagree	Somewhat Disagree	Neither Agree nor Disagree	Somewhat Agree	Agree	Strongly Agree
□	□	□	□	□	□	□
-3	-2	-1	0	1	2	3

How Much Do You Agree with Each of These Statements?

_____ 1.   I perceive that I am in the presence of another person in the virtual room with me.

_____ 2.   I feel that the person in the virtual room is watching me and is aware of my presence.

_____ 3.   The thought that he (or she) is not a real person crosses my mind often.

_____ 4.   The person appears to be sentient (conscious and alive) to me.

_____ 5.   I perceive the person as being only a computerized image, not as a real person.

_____ 6.   I feel that the person in the virtual room would be able to experience pain.

_____ 7.   I like the virtual person.

_____ 8.   I think the virtual person is attractive.

_____ 9.   If nobody else was in the physical room, I would be willing to sing the national anthem in front of this virtual person.

_____ 10.   If nobody else was in the physical room, I would be willing to change clothes in front of this virtual person.

_____ 11.   If nobody else was in the physical room, I would have no problem telling personal secrets to the virtual person.

_____ 12.   If nobody else was in the physical room, I would be upset if the virtual person noticed something stuck in my teeth.

Intelligent Virtual Agent Societies on the Internet

F. Alonso Amo, F. Fernández Velasco, G. López Gómez, J.P. Rojas Jiménez,
and F.J. Soriano Camino

DLSIIS, Facultad de Informática, U.P.M., Madrid, Spain
{falonso, glopez, jsoriano}@fi.upm.es
{fvelasco, rojas}@pegaso.ls.fi.upm.es

Abstract. The principal advances in the research field of IVAs within virtual environments have taken place in the area of agent architectures. However, very few papers have addressed the development of metamodels to conceptualize this kind of systems from an organizational and social point of view, despite their intrinsic sociability and their close relationship to life-like virtual words. Likewise, no platform has been yet developed that contributes to the development of virtual environments and looks at all these concepts. This paper introduces a taxonomy containing all the agent types that would take part in a virtual environment, considered as a whole society. On the basis of this taxonomy, we put forward a metamodel, which can be used to define how this society would be organised. An agent platform, known as PIVAS, has also been developed to support the described metamodel, while providing the necessary services for the creation of Virtual Agent Societies, such as migration, location, etc.

1 Introduction

All virtual agents within a virtual environment must be capable of orderly relating to one another, without compromising their autonomy, in order to overcome their general lack of self-sufficiency. Top priority must, therefore, be given to a social conception of the environment they inhabit. At least two different levels of abstraction must be taken into account when developing a Virtual Agent Society [1]:

- An **Agent's Internal Level**, which defines the agent's architecture, respecting relevant issues such as user embodiment and believability, as well as all the features traditionally associated with these agents as individual entities [2]. These include their autonomy, which means their ability to control their own actions and state; their reactivity, which denotes their ability to perceive their environment and react properly to changes in this environment; their pro-activity, that is, their ability to take the initiative in target-oriented behaviour; and intelligence, encompassing their reasoning and learning abilities, their self-motivation and adaptation to the environment.

A. de Antonio, R. Aylett, and D. Ballin (Eds.): IVA 2001, LNAI 2190, pp. 100–111, 2001.

– An **Agent's Social Level**, which defines the agent's social structure, e-nabling it to recognize, identify and relate to other agents that form the virtual society it inhabits. Sociability is not just a prerequisite for achieving co-operative behaviours that will contribute to problem-solving, it will also make it possible to model the social features of a human being thanks to new tools such as virtual environments.

Obviously, no clear dividing line can be traced between the agent's internal and social levels. For the purposes of this paper, however, this rather artificial distinction proves to be very useful, since it means the modelling of society -roles, relationships, organization, social laws, services, etc.- can be separated from the internal architecture of the agents of which it is composed.

Research into agent architectures has engendered three different and well-defined types of architectures for the design of autonomous agents, and in parti-cular, intelligent virtual agents: **The Deliberative or Symbolic architectu-re**, considers agents as knowledge-based systems with learning -planning para-digm in AI [3]. In the **Reactive or behaviour based architecture**, an agent is modelled according to a group of behavioural, level-layered tasks, which must be carried out by the agent. Each behaviour task is implemented as a finite-state machine, which directly maps inputs from a sensor to certain outputs [4]. And there is also the **Hybrid architecture**, of which the Procedural Reasoning System (PRS) is the most popular; it was developed by Georgeff [5] according to the BDI *Belief- Desire- Intention* paradigm.

The first research into social structure was carried out in the field of Dis-tributed Artificial Intelligence [6], as a result of the advent of Multi-Agent Sys-tems (MAS). These systems focused on problem solving by a group of agents that co-operated, at a problem-division level, on finding a solution (Distributed Problem Solving-DPS). A lot of agent models (MAS) have been developed using this approach, initially from a *reductionist point of view* [7], in which agents were specifically devised for efficient problem-solving and, later on, from a *construc-tivist point of view* [8], which focused on determining what kind of social system will arise from the existing interdependence among already defined agents with a view to performing a task.

Neither the reductionist nor the constructivist viewpoints are sutied for buil-ding a *society of intelligent virtual agents*, in which a group of agents with their own goals and no shared objective participate. These agents are markedly independent and behave as autonomous entities that represent a user or an organization in performing a particular task. They accept the interest of the represented element as their own and act regardless of any sort of restriction. Here, therefore, there is a need, particulary in virtual environments to introduce a *social co-operative* component into the agent conceptualization in order to achieve a more efficient and orderly cooperation among agents. In this respect, several authors [9] suggest utilizing a Social Level, based on Newell's symbolic and knowledge levels [10], upon which to model all the social aspects of individual agents and MASes. However, their proposals amount to a mere a social extension of Newell's *Principle of Rationality*, by means of which individual needs and MAS needs can be balanced as a whole. It is, therefore, a co-operative rather than a truly social approach, which is, moreover, associated with the agent's internal level and is used at design time.

This paper, though, considers the concept of society in its broadest sense, which is essential to the development of virtual societies on the Internet. It, therefore, focuses on key concepts such as individual and social roles, social structures and relationships, reliance and interrelationships among agents, social rules, speech acts, coordination and negotiation, etc., which are associated with agent and, ultimately, social structure and behavior. It lays the foundations for a society model that preserves the autonomy of the individual agents that cohabit in the society. Additionally, the society models helps agents to attain their goals, offering them a means of cooperation, by means of which they can take advantage of their ability and resource interdependence, without having to give up watching over the benefit of society as a whole. It is essential that this architecture be conceived to include a level similar to the above-mentioned Social Level, which is, however, separate from the agent's internal level. This level must consider the social aspects of these systems and, consequently, dynamically influence agent behavior, thus contributing to achieving an efficient and well-regulated interrelation and cooperation among agents. The platform supporting this society of agents must provide the necessary infrastructure, ensuring that the agents using its services can relate to one another and attain their particular purposes, without harming the purposes of the others. Thus, what we are proposing here is an approach to *socially-responsible* virtual agents: autonomous agents, capable of benefiting from interactions with their environment and with other agents and, therefore, forced to observe certain social laws for the benefit of the rest of the system.

In this paper a taxonomy of the types of agents that take part in a virtual society and a social structure metamodel are defined, which can be used to represent how a specific agent society will be organized and behave. An agent software platform or agency, called PIVAS [24] (Platform for Intelligent Virtual Agent Societies), which supports this metamodel, is then presented.

2   Taxonomy of the Types of Agents That Take Part in a Virtual Society

The conception of virtual environments has evolved tremendously. These environments were originally composed of mere passive user representatives, termed *avatars*. They then evolved to avatar-agents that were reactive and communicative, also enjoying some autonomy and proactivity, but devoid of motivations. There is now a trend towards the concept of IVAs: intelligent autonomous agents guided by their own motivations, which live in a virtual world inhabited by other similar agents. This brings with it the need to characterize these IVAs [12].

In this context, any virtual agent society, as is the case with societies in the real world, is organized around individuals or *agents* (*IVA*). These are its basic organizational unit. IVAs are *active entities*: they have their own motivations driving them to attain a set of goals. There are also *passive entities* (or *objects*). These passive entities are characterized by functionality but there are neither motivated, nor pro-activity, nor autonomous. They can be used to model resources from a computational approach. They are used by active entities to attain their goals.

Not being generally self-sufficiency, an IVA cannot act exclusively on the basis of its individual needs and abilities. In order to attain its goals, it will have to relate to and cooperate with the other IVAs in the virtual society, and with the user who characterized the IVA. This engenders the concept of **cooperative agents**.

Traditionally, MASes were devised pursuant to the what is known as the assumption of benevolence [11], according to which the agents accept and try to respond to all the requests from other agents [13]. Later, the design of these systems leant on Newell's Principle of Rationality [10], according to which the agents may be selective and deliberately decide not to cooperate if they do not expect to benefit directly from such cooperation. Nowadays, what is known as the Principle of Social Rationality prevails. This principle, an extension of Newell's Principle of Rationality, was put forward by [9], and establishes that the agents selectively supply knowledge and resources according to a well-balanced consideration of individual and social interests, for the benefit of the system as a whole thus, they preserve their local autonomy and take advantage of interactions with other agents. These are the three design trends already discussed: the reductionist, the constructivist and the social-cooperative one. The coexistence of all this and other behavior models must be taken into consideration in order to be able to model the different parts of a society.

Additionally, two basic types of actors must be considered within a society: the *organic* and the *client* agent. These actors are classed as basic because their behavior is established during agent design, under no circumstance is it induced by the society. The behavior of the organic agent may be benevolent and cooperative, whereas the client's behavior is intrinsically individualistic. When these actor take part in a given society a new kind of behavior is induced in them by the society in execution time, and this is what is known as socially responsible behavior. A description of each type follows:

2.1   Organic Agent

If a multi-agent system is considered to be part of a superior social structure, it becomes an *organization*. Organic agents are cooperative and they carry out their function within the different organizations which are present in a society. They will cooperate differently depending on the design of the organization in which they are to act. A reductionist design of the organization will mean that this agents are conceived as benevolent, whereas a design guided by the Principle of Social Rationality will involve a social-cooperative conception of its agents. Finally, a constructivist design would imply that these agents are conceived as individualistic, which would make the coordination of the operation of the organization exceedingly troublesome and is, therfore, not considered for the present purposes. A virtual society includes a series of services carried out by organic agents that manage and control its operation. The organizations are modeled in this virtual society as IVOs (Intelligent Virtual Organizations).

2.2   Client Agent

The constructivist approach to a MAS adopts a bottom-up social interaction model, in which social interactions and organizations are a result of the agents' efforts to attain their own goals [15]. In the case of client agent, cooperation is not a prior assumption. On the contrary, it is assumed to be non-benevolent, that is, the agent does not necessarily have to help others to attain their goals, but to autonomously decide when to cooperate with such agents, depending on its own interests [9]. Client agents are, therefore, individualistic entities, and can choose to cooperate or not cooperate, if they do not see any direct benefit deriving from such cooperation. As mentioned above, the use of individualistic agents derived from a constructivist approach to MAS construction, leads to serious problems of coordination. It is, therefore, not considered for the present purposes. However, this constructivist approach to design is suited for modelling, by means of individualistic agents, the users of the services provided by the society through the MASes designed from a reductionist or social-cooperative viewpoint (i.e. by means of organic agents). These agents usually behave in the manner of autonomous entities, which represent a user or an organization in order to perform a particular task, considering the interests of the represented element as their own.

2.3   Socially Responsible Agent: Rules and Social Relationships

Through their interface agents, IVAs and IVOs are thought of as members of a society whose activities have to be considered. These activities must be governed by a set of conventions and both general and specific social laws that must be respected by both IVAs and IVOs. This means that they are socially responsible agents.

A feasible way to characterize a society is by identifying the potential social relationships that could take place among its members and, more specifically, among the different identified roles. As the society is open, these are dynamic relationships. The agents taking part in a specific relationship can behave in different ways (benevolently, individualistically or socially cooperatively), which leads to different kinds of relationships (control, peer-to-peer, benevolent, dependence or property relationships). The agent assumes complete responsibility for carrying out its individual tasks, behaving either benevolently, individualistically or socially cooperatively. This is not the case with its social responsibilities, however: the need to ensure that these social tasks are carried out means that both the social laws required for such actions to be completed and the social laws governing such relationships have to be identified. These laws have to be respected and/or enforced by the society, through its agency, if it is to work properly according to the generally expected behavior. It is these rules that govern social relationships and ensure a socially responsible behavior in agents with an individualistic design, that is, IVAs and organization interface agents. The idea of ensuring socially responsible behavior during agent design would not appear to be appropriate in a dynamic, heterogeneous environment like a society, where, just to give an example, interaction patterns are established dynamically. Coordination and negotiation models [16], as well as the social structure itself, make up the conceptual abstractions for establishing the laws that will govern both agent performance and their mutual relationships with the aim of attaining socially responsible behavior. As discussed further on, the coordination and negotiation means provided by the agency support such models and constitute the broker mechanism employed by the society to this end.

2.4   Passive Entities

Our model of a virtual society requires just one more entity class. This class can be used to model services, devices and similar resources from a computational viewpoint. These entities differ from IVAs primarily in that they lack autonomy, goals and motivations. These are, therefore, not agents, but of objects and software components.

3   The Agent's Conceptual Model

Figure 1 shows a diagram of an agent conceptual model, in which the following take part:

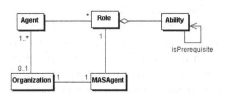

Fig. 1. Agent Model

3.1   The Agent

Active entity which may or may not adopt a series of roles. This definition of an agent is been made deliberately generic so that multi-agent system developers can employ the internal agent structure that best suits the application. An agent may or may not belong to an organization. As soon as the agent becomes a part of the organization, it is termed an organic agent. When the agent is not part of any organization, it is presented as an IVA.

3.2 The Organization

An organization is composed of a set of organic agents which cooperate with a view to providing a common purpose to all agents. From a client agent viewpoint, an organization is defined as an entity offering a number of services to its clients. Therefore, an organization represents a multi-agent system that is a-ggregated to a society. An organization is sought by the client agents in relation to the services it provides. The most important requirement for membership of an organization is to observe the organic conventions defined in that organization. A new client agent may apply to the organization for permission to enter (through the interface agent), which will be always granted, provided that the client agent abides by the rules of the organization in question, among other things. An organization may be distributed across different machines. However, unlike the *groups* in [17], an organic agent cannot belong to more than one organization at the same time. Nevertheless, agents may belong to more than one organization at different times.

As mentioned above, the organizations that participate in an intelligent virtual world are modeled as IVOs. A possible example of an IVO is a recreation room as part of the virtual environment. This recreation room would provide leisure activities, specifically games of cards, to its users. The room is made up of organic agents which cooperate to make the site work properly. Thus, the opponent agents, which represent the machine in the role of opponent, the agent responsible for the management of games tables and the other agents taking part in the organization, all cooperate to attain the goal of the IVO, which is the correct provision of its services.

Organic conventions. Every organization defines a set of interactions which could occur within the organization. That is, the room manager agent interacts with the client player agent, so as to sit it at a table according to its preferences. However, the IVO not only defines the interactions which could take place within its own organization, but it also defines the way of interaction of a IVA with the organization. In this way, the recreational organization does not allow to have two client agents representing the same user and playing at two different tables at a time. Both aspects define what has been termed as *organic conventions*.

3.3 The Role

One of the first attempts to incorporate the role concept into the description of multi-agent systems appeared [18], although this concept had already been mentioned back in 1977 in the field of DPS, in the description of the *Contract Net* protocol [19]. [20] takes a look at role modelling for multi-agent system analysis, design and implementation. Social relationships provide the conceptual framework in which each agent has its role or well-defined position within the society. This role motivates and structures all interactions between and assigns abilities to agents.

A role determines the following competence areas for the agent that assumes the role:

- *Services Provided.* The role is an abstract representation of the functionality or service provided by the agent.
- *Identification of services.* The interaction model could be described much more easily if an interaction scheme is identified among roles, rather than among specific agents. This also makes the location scheme more flexible and, thus, enables dynamic changes in the functionality and location of services by delegating all roles related to these services to new agents.
- *Responsibilities.* As mentioned in 2.3, the role assumed by an agent determines all the responsibilities assigned to the agent within the society. A distinction is made between individual and social responsibilities.
- *Patterns and protocols of interaction.* These are used to allow the agent to contact other agents and/or roles, get the information it needs from such agents and/or roles and provide agents with inferred information, as well as to coordinate agent activities. They are, therefore, based on role specification and information exchange.
- *Information requested and provided* for agents to fulfil their responsibilities.

As the environment is open and heterogeneous, it will be necessary for a virtual agent with a given role to dynamically discover all the role competence areas of the virtual agents with which it interacts (services, interaction protocols, requested and provided information, etc.) On the other hand, the process of assigning roles to agents is not automatic, it implies a process of negotiation during which an agent will have to satisfy certain conditions in order to acquire a specific role.

In the proposed model, an IVA can play several roles, and each IVO manages the roles of the organic agents located within the organization. In the above example of an IVO, there will, intuitively, be the *role of the player*, which could be carried out both by the agents belonging to the organization and the client agents that wish to play a game. On the other hand, there is the *role of the manager*, which is in charge of the table management.

Within an IVO there is also a special role referred to as **MASAgent** (or interface agent), whose responsibilities include handling organization access requests by client agents, as well as the management of any action application addressed to the organization it represents. No particular evaluation function is defined for the management of the use request made by a client agent wishing to use an organization, but support is given to implement any of the functions. The following are presented by way of an example of some of these evaluation functions for an access application to the IVO: automatically accept an use request to the organization by any agent, always deny use, restrict use if the agent does not possess a specific role, restrict use if the role does not include a series of abilities, etc. Nevertheless, once the client agent is interacting with the organization, it will have the opportunity to adopt a series of new roles as long as it remains there.

Going back to the above example, the IVO's interface agent limiting entry to the recreation room would be equivalent to an agent that permits or refuses entry to a client agent to the room, subject to acceptance of all the organic conventions of the organization.

3.4   The Ability

This is an abstract representation of a specific low-level function (i.e. service) associated with one or more specific roles. Abilities represent reusability and encapsulation at a fully detailed level of role behavior. Every role is formed by the addition of some specific abilities, and an ability may belong to more than one role. An important ability-related question is to define certain abilities as a prerequisite for others, i.e., the ability of multiplication within the 'Calculator' role must be preceded by the ability to add up.

Thus, an IVA with a card-player role will have the ability to make signs to its team mates, and it will be able to evaluate that game status, make suggestions about it, etc. However, the prerequisite ability for making suggestions would be to know how to evaluate the actual status of the game. Abilities are, therefore, low-level services associated with one or more roles; that is, an agent may have the ability to play cards, an ability that may also be shared by the role of student. Moreover, the model does not define that an agent having the ability to play cards must also have the role of card-player.

4   The Society's Conceptual Model

As stated above, the general lack of self-sufficiency of IVAs makes it necessary for them to relate to other IVAs and IVOs through their interface agents. They are, therefore, thought of as members of a society whose model must be taken into consideration. As shown in Figure 2, this model defines an IVE (Intelligent Virtual Environment) whose key concepts are the relationships between roles, the social laws which govern these relationships and the social structure that arises as a result. As the society is open, these relationships and social laws are dynamic. Therefore, the social structure will be determined by roles, social laws identified by these roles along with the social rules that govern these relationships.

As mentioned above, client agents (IVAs) need to make use of the organizations (IVOs) provided by the environment in order to achieve the goals for which they were designed. When a client agent joins the virtual environment, it is forced by the environment to abide by its social rules, thus becoming a socially responsible agent. The same applies to the IVOs that participate in the IVE. The mechanism employed to that end is the agency, since, being dynamic, these laws cannot be considered during internal agent design. Likewise, an agent belonging to an organization may act as a client agent in another organization, provided that both the social laws and the organic conventions of the latter allow for such interaction.

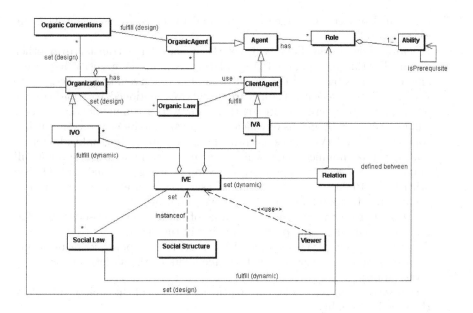

Fig. 2. Virtual Society Model

5 The Agency as the Basis for a Virtual Society

Over the last few years, different agent platforms have been developed, such as
Grasshopper [21], MOLE [22], MAP [23], MadKit [17], focused on a given characteristic of the agent: mobility, communication, location, and so on. As discussed
throughout this article, agent sociability is essential to heterogeneous and open
application environments and, specially to virtual environments. However, none
of these platforms, except, perhaps, Madkit, have taken into consideration how
to give development support at the proposed social level. From this viewpoint,
the Agency is proposed as an entity that controls the agents' life cycle and the
interactions among agents; as an entity which makes it possible to locate certain
agents with some specific features, to migrate one agent to a different agency,
etc. We suggest that the agency should serve as a basis for abstracting the virtual
society, thus being responsible for assigning the *Principle of Social Rationality*
[9].

PIVAS (Platform for Intelligent Virtual Agents Societies) is a platform that
supports the described metamodel and also provides all the basic services for the
creation of Virtual Agent Societies on the Internet [24]. PIVAS is not a graphic
tool for building virtual environments, like Active World or WorldUp, it is an
agent platform that supports all the activities proper to IVAs and IVOS, by
means of the following services:

- *Location service*: The IVAs will ask the agency to locate other agents. PIVAS
  includes a search for agents by role, in which an IVA will be able to ask the
  agency for an instance of the agent in charge of managing the locating service

(agentified service); this agent will be used to search for an agent with the requested role.

- *Mobility service*: The IVAs will ask the agency for a transfer to another agency. For this purpose, the PIVAS platform will need a negotiation process among agencies based on the social rules of the intervening agencies.
- *Communication service*: Thanks to the above-mentioned location service, one IVA will be able to locate another. However, a communication process will be necessary by means of which to establish communication, once it has contacted IVAs. PIVAS does not provide the possibility of graphically representing this communication, it will be the virtual world building tool that will graphically represent this process, for example, using a virtual chat. On the other hand, PIVAS does offer translation services in case two 'heterogeneous' agents want to communicate in their own languages.
- *Fault-tolerance service*: This is in charge of maintaining the society's coherence in the event of any problems arising in the agencies.
- *Information service*: An agentified PIVAS Service, responsible for recording all agents and organizations that are members of the societies to which it gives support.
- *Social service*: In charge of enforcing the social laws of the society, especially the social rationality laws.

6   Conclusions

This article has addressed the need to take advantage of the combined benefits of multi-agent systems and IVAs in a virtual environment.It addressed the need to examine the area of intelligent virtual agents from an organizational and social point of view, irrespective of their internal architecture. A taxonomy was proposed containing the types of agents that take part in a virtual environment, which is conceived as a society, a concept that introduces a new kind of behavior termed *socially responsible*, dynamically inferred from the environment. On the basis of this taxonomy, a metamodel was presented for defining how a specific virtual society environment will be organized. Our purpose is to be able to model how agents are going to relate to one another within the environment and how this environment will be organized. Finally, an agent platform known as PIVAS (Platform for Intelligent Virtual Agent Societies) was presented, which has been developed to support the described metamodel. It provides all the basic services for the creation of Intelligent Virtual Agent Societies on the Internet.

References

[1]   N. Gilbert: "Artificial Societies: The Computer Simulation of Social Life" pages 144-156. UCL Press: London, 1995.
[2]   Stan Franklin y Art Graesser: "Is it an Agent, or just a Program?: A Taxonomy for Autonomous Agents". proceedings of the Third International Workshop on Agent Theories, Architectures, and Languages, Springer-Verlag, 1996
[3]   M. P. Georgeff: "Emergence in Social Simulation". Annual Review of Computer Science, 2:359-400, 1987

[4] P. Maes: "Designing Autonomous Agents". The MIT Press: Cambridge, MA, 1990
[5] M. P. Georgeff y A. L. Lansky: "Reactive reasoning and planning". In Proceedings of the Sixth National Conference on Artificial Intelligence. 1987.
[6] A. H. Bond y L. Gasset, editors: Readings in Distributed Artificial Intelligence. Morgan Kaufmann Publishers: San Mateo, CA, 1988.
[7] V. R. Lesser and D. D. Corkill: "Distributed Problem Solving". Encyclopedia of Artificial Intelligence (ed. S. C. Shapiro) 245-251 John Wiley and Sons, 1987
[8] J. Ferber, and A. Drogul: "Using Reactive Multi-Agent Systems in Simulation and Problem Solving". In Distributed Artificial Intelligence: Theory and Praxis, (eds. N. M. Avouris and L. Gasser), 53-80, Kluwer Academic Publishers, (1992).
[9] N.R. Jennings y J. R. Campos: "Towards a Social Level Characterisation of Socially Responsible Agents". IEEE Proceedings on Software Engineering, pages 11-25, 1997
[10] A. Newell: "The Knowledge Level". Artificial Intelligence, (18), pages 87-127. 1982
[11] J. S. Rosenschein and M. R. Genesereth: "Deals Among Rational Agents". IJCAI-85, Aravind Joshi (eds.), pages 91-95, Morgan Kaufmann Publishers Inc., California, USA, 1985
[12] H. Vilhjálmsson and J. Cassell: "BodyChat: Autonomous Communicative Behaviors in Avatars". In Proceedings of the 2nd Annual ACM International Conference on Autonomous Agents. Minneapolis, 1998.
[13] M. Wooldridge and N. Jennings: "Agent Theories, Architecture and Languages: A Survey". Proceeding ECAI-94: Workshop on Agent Theories, Architecture and Languages, Springer-Verlag, Berlin, Germany, 1995
[14] M. Luck and M. d'Inverno: "Engagement and Cooperation in Motivated Agent Modeling". Proceedings of the First Australian Workshop on Distributed Artificial Intelligence, Zhang and Lukose (eds.), pages 70-84, Springer-Verlag, Berlin, Germany, 1996.
[15] R. Conte and J. Sichman: DEPNET: How to benefit from social dependence. Journal of Mathematical Sociology (20), pages 161-177, (1995).
[16] P. Ciancarini: "Coordination models and languages as software integrators". ACM Computing Surveys, 28(2), June 1996.
[17] O. Gutknecht and J. Ferber: "Madkit: Organizing heterogeneity with groups in a platform for multiple multi-agent systems". Technical Report 97188, LIRMM, 161, rue Ada - Montpellier - France, Dec 1997
[18] L. Gasser, C. Braganza, and N. Herman: "Mace: a flexible testbed for distributed ai research". In M. N. Huhns, editor, Distributed Artificial Intelligence, pages 119–152. 1987.
[19] R.G. Smith: "The Contract Net Protocol: High-Level Communication and Control in a Distributed Problem Solver". IEEE Transactionson Computers, C-29(12):1104-1113, (1980).
[20] E. A. Kendall: "Role Modelling for agent system analysis, design and implementation". In 1st International Symposium on Agent Systems and Applications. IEEE CS Press, October 1999.
[21] "Grasshopper Programmer's Guide". IKV++ Gmbh. July 2000.
[22] J. Baumann, F. Hohl, M. Straber, K. Rothermel: "Mole- Concepts of a Mobile Agent System" 1997.
[23] A. Puliafito, O. Tomarchio, and L. Vita: "Design and Implementation of a Mobile Agent Platform". Journal of System Architecture, 46(2): 145-162, 2000.
[24] F. Fernández, J. P. Rojas, F. J. Soriano, J. Velez: "PIVAS: A Platform for Intelligent Virtual Agent Societies". Technical Report, UPM, Madrid, 2001.

Virtual Agent Societies with the mVITAL Intelligent Agent System

George Anastassakis[1], Themis Panayiotopoulos[1], and Tim Ritchings[2]

[1] Knowledge Engineering Lab, Department of Informatics,
University of Piraeus, Piraeus, 185 34, Greece
{anastas, themisp}@unipi.gr
[2] School of Sciences, University of Salford,
Newton Building, University of Salford, Salford, M5 4WT
T.Ritchings@salford.ac.uk

Abstract. Intelligent multi-agent systems are currently used for a variety of purposes, both in research and for real-world applications. One of their most interesting, yet not fully explored uses, is as frameworks to support computer-based simulations of virtual worlds inhabited by life-like entities, that is, intelligent virtual environments, for purposes of education, demonstration and entertainment. This paper is a presentation of mVITAL, an intelligent multi-agent system aiming to serve most of the fields such systems are today used in, while being fully capable of supporting intelligent virtual environment applications, where issues such as sophisticated virtual reality representation, advanced reasoning, as well as user embodiment, intervention and interaction, are crucial. To justify this, a fully operational example of such an application, namely, the Vital Playground, is also presented.

1 Introduction

Intelligent agent systems have already been the subject of intense research over the past years. Their uses, still being explored, are numerous, and range from simple softbot applications to complex, industrial control systems. The term 'intelligent agent' has been extensively used to characterize a vast number of approaches. Despite the field's lack of standardization and co-ordinated research effort, it seems that intelligent agent technology is the ideal means to design and implement autonomous entities with advanced reasoning and environment interaction capabilities.

On the other hand, *intelligent virtual environments* (IVEs) are sophisticated simulations of virtual worlds inhabited by intelligent actors, where issues such as embodiment and believability are of crucial importance. Today, IVEs are employed in a variety of areas, mainly relating to simulation, entertainment, and education. Sophisticated simulated environments concerning open urban spaces, building interiors, and streets, can significantly aid in application areas such as architectural design, civil engineering, traffic and crowd control. In addition, precisely modelled simulations of real-world equipment as vehicles and aircrafts can be tested at reduced cost and risk.

A. de Antonio, R. Aylett, and D. Ballin (Eds.): IVA 2001, LNAI 2190, pp. 112-125, 2001.

Moreover, IVEs have set new standards in computer-aided entertainment, through outstanding examples of computer games involving large, life-like virtual worlds with imaginative scenarios to be challenged, active user participation in the plot of an interactive drama, virtual story-telling, and many other areas where immersion and believability are key factors.

Concluding, IVE-based educational systems incorporate believable tutoring characters and sophisticated data representation techniques, resulting in the stimulation of user interest and perceptual ability, thus providing a novel, effective and enjoyable learning experience.

Despite the fact that intelligent multi-agent systems seem to offer significant potential for producing intelligent virtual environment applications, a substantial number of issues still need to be addressed.

This paper is a presentation of our work in the field, in particular, the mVITAL system, an intelligent multi-agent system characterized by rich and expressive modelling, reasoning and visualisation capacity.

In the rest of this paper, a discussion of relevant research work is given in section two. Section three is a thorough presentation of the proposed system, while section four is a presentation of a fully functional platform available online for research and experimentation.

2 Related Work

The Beliefs-Desires-Intentions (BDI) model [4] is probably the most popular approach towards the design of intelligent agents, mainly due to its ability to trigger behaviours driven by conceptually modelled intentions and goals rather than explicit procedural information. In addition, it seems to be a functional abstraction for the higher-level reasoning processes of the human mind, those that are related to action selection and the focusing of intelligent reasoning processes on specific desired states. The BDI model has been adopted in a significant number of implementations:

IRMA, is an Intelligent Resource-bounded Machine Architecture presented by Bratman et al. in [5]. It is an architecture for resource-bounded (mainly in terms of computational power) deliberative agents, based on the BDI model. IRMA agents consist of four main modules: a means-end planner, an opportunity analyser, a filtering process and a deliberation procedure. In addition, they contain a plan library, and data structures to store beliefs, desires and intentions.

Jennings in [9] proposes GRATE, an architecture clearly focused on co-operative problem solving through agent collaboration. Central to the entire architecture is the notion of joint-intentions. In fact, even though GRATE is a deliberative architecture based on the BDI model, it is specifically referred to as a belief-desire-joint-intention architecture.

The BDI model has provided valuable theoretical grounds upon which the development of several other architectures and approaches, such as hybrid and layered agents, was based [8]:

The Procedural Reasoning System (PRS) [6] is a hybrid system, where beliefs are expressed in first-order predicate logic and desires represent system behaviours instead of fixed goals. PRS includes a plan library containing a set of partial plans, called knowledge areas, each associated with an invocation condition. Knowledge areas might be executed due to goal-driven reasoning or as a response to sensory data; this way, the agent is capable for both deliberative and reactive behaviours.

Muller in [10] proposes INTERRAP, a layered agent architecture focusing on the requirements of situated and goal-directed behaviour, efficiency and co-ordination. INTERRAP agents consist of a world interface, a behaviour-based, a plan-based and a co-operation component, each affecting agent behaviours at a different level of social and functional abstraction.

In [14], Sycara et al. present the Reusable Task Structure-based Intelligent Network Agents (RETSINA) architecture. The architecture consists of three types of agents: interface, task agents and, information agents.

Due to its apparent focus on high-level reasoning and generation of elaborate behavioural patterns, the BDI model seems to be inadequate to efficiently and effectively model all aspects of intelligent reasoning. However, any system that needs to exhibit goal-driven behaviour should incorporate, among others, a BDI-based or equivalent, logic-based component.

The merging of intelligent agent systems, artificial life and classical VR techniques has given birth to the field of *Intelligent Virtual Environments (IVEs)*. Terzopoulos in [21] presents a virtual marine world inhabited by *artificial fishes*, showing how autonomous agents equipped with both reasoning capabilities and simulated physical bodies can act as virtual inhabitants of simulated dynamic worlds. The choice of environment is ideal for research and experimentation on several exciting scenarios; artificial fishes are capable of exhibiting mating, grouping, preying and several other types of behaviour.

Blumberg in [2] presents *Silas T. Dog,* an autonomous virtual creature living in a simulated three-dimensional world. Environment interaction is based on synthetic vision – agents render the scene and process it using image-processing techniques. Goal-driven reasoning is also featured, in the form of processes for satisfying high-level motivations. The combination of low-level obstacle avoidance and navigation, with high-level reasoning, enables agents to exhibit a number of interesting and highly believable behavioural patterns.

Apart from the systems mentioned above, a significant number of architectures involving IVEs and general virtual agents have been presented. Examples include Humanoid [3] – a platform for addressing cases where modelling precision is crucial, Creatures [7] – an outstanding example of the usage of IVEs in entertainment, and others. A first effort towards an intelligent agent system architecture with the ability to support IVE applications, namely the DIVA architecture, was presented in [16]. VITAL, a simple intelligent virtual agent system was also presented in [1]. VITAL was initially designed and developed in UMIST, UK, and it is the basis on which the development of the mVITAL system presented here was realized.

In general, IVEs tend to focus on either the virtual representation and embodiment side, or the intelligence side. Full benefit has not yet been taken of the combined advantages of intelligent multi-agent systems and virtual environments. A complex, accurately modelled and general-purpose IVE, inhabited by numerous believable entities driven by strong and effective AI reasoning processes, is yet to be presented.

3 The mVITAL Intelligent Agent System

The mVITAL system is an environment for authoring intelligent multi-agent applications readily employable in several domains, ranging from distributed control systems to virtual environments for entertainment and education. The system employs specific design and implementation techniques to address key issues such as modelling precision and clarity, flexibility and employability, robustness, extendibility, and user- friendliness. In particular, logic-based reasoning is seamlessly integrated into the architecture, enabling sophisticated, domain-oriented modelling approaches, as well as advanced problem solving based on goal-driven behaviours, planning, and intentionality. Moreover, a number of authoring aids are provided along with a user-friendly, creative and resourceful user interface, so that original application deployment as well as consecutive monitoring and adjustment are carried-out in a straightforward and intuitive manner. In addition, the system is built using latest software engineering approaches, tools and languages, so that it can classify as a powerful, stable and maintainable software construct.

3.1 Architecture Overview

The mVITAL system is based on a modular architecture based on three key notions: the *world server*, the *agent client* and the *viewer client*. These are implemented as separate software applications according to the client-server approach. A world server represents a virtual environment inside which the entire agent system's activity takes place. Agent clients represent actors inside an environment. Agents perceive the environment and act upon it according to goal-driven behaviours. Viewer clients offer the means to human supervisors to observe the environment and all activity inside it in a domain-specific manner. The component-based nature of the mVITAL system is illustrated in Figure 1 below:

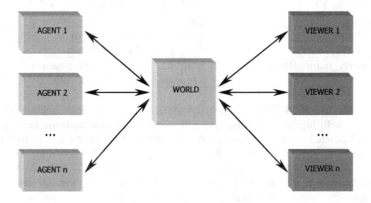

Fig. 1. mVITAL architecture overview

3.2 Modelling Methodologies

Each component in the mVITAL system maintains a complete or partial internal representation of the world and, in the case of an agent client, additional properties about itself. This representation can be either symbolic or object-oriented. An additional type of representation, namely, the *pseudo-symbolic* representation, is used to transfer symbolic facts between applications as well as to translate between symbolic and object-oriented representations.

According to the object-oriented representation, environments are modelled as sets of interconnected *locations*. Each location may contain one or more *items*. Each item has a *name*, belongs to an item *class* and has *properties*. Agents are also represented as world items. To enrich the modelling scheme with spatial features, each location includes a two- or three-dimensional co-ordinate pair, according to needs of each application. This modelling scheme is capable of describing a substantial number of environments with different types of content: simple mazes, real-world buildings, streets, networks, etc.

Each item has, possibly among others, a property of name 'class'. This denotes its *item class*, that is, the conceptually wider class of entities the item belongs to. Item classes are defined according to the application's modelling requirements, at any level of abstraction desired. For instance, an agent could be denoted by an item property of name 'class' and value 'agent', whereas a non-agent item could have a 'class' property of value 'object'.

The symbolic modelling methodology borrows syntactical and semantics elements from predicate logic and logic programming. Table 1 below lists the main symbols used in mVITAL applications, with their respective interpretations:

Table 1. World modelling symbols used in mVITAL applications

Symbol	Interpretation
connects(X1, Y1, X2, Y2)	'(X1, Y1)' and '(X2, Y2)' are connected
at(Item, X, Y)	The location of 'Item' is '(X, Y)'
location(X, Y)	'(X, Y)' is a valid maze location
item(Item)	'Item' is a valid maze item
class(Item, Class)	The class of 'Item' is 'Class'
<property_name>(Item, Value)	'Item' has a property with a name of '<property_name>' and a value of 'Value'

The symbolic modelling scheme described in the previous section is highly compatible with logic-based reasoning processes, logic programming languages and symbolic knowledge bases. However, it is not the most convenient way to formulate data if these are to be exchanged between components. The presented architecture addresses the issue with a *pseudo-symbolic representation*. According to it, symbols are broken down to a series of strings, the first of which is the symbol name and the rest arguments. Non-atomic terms, i.e. variables, are represented by an appropriate keyword selected by the agent system designer, for instance, '#VAR', or by an appropriate name. A *terminating dot* is appended after the last argument to denote that no more arguments should be expected. If a series of symbols is to be transmitted, an additional terminating dot is appended after the last one; thus, two terminating dots should be expected at the end of a series of symbols in pseudo-symbolic representation. This modelling scheme above is ideal for network transmissions and communication between components in general. Pseudo-symbolic data can be transmitted in a number of steps, on a timing suiting the transmitting and receiving components, while substantial delays can be introduced between subsequent transmission steps.

3.3 World Interaction

Agents in the mVITAL system operate asynchronously on a *sense-decide-act* cycle, during which a number of interactions with the world take place. In particular, when an agent wants to sense its environment, it requests sensory information from the world component – a *sense request*. The world component then replies, providing the requested information. Similarly, when an agent wants to perform an action, the corresponding agent component provides all necessary action information to the world component – an *action request* – and then the world component responds regarding whether the requested action was successfully applied.

In case of successful action application, the world component sends world change data to all viewer components so that actions are correctly visualised. In addition, when a viewer needs to build an entirely new visualisation, it requests a full description of the world model – a *world description* request.

A simple vision model enables agents to sense their surroundings on a line-of-sight basis and for a given maximum range, and, hence, act in a more believable manner (in an initial application described in [1] agents could only sense their neighbouring locations). Specifically, a modified line-following algorithm is used to visit all locations between an agent's current location and the first obstacle encountered, for all line segments defined by the agent's location and each point of the world's boundaries. To minimize network traffic and cycle duration, only the absolutely necessary information is transferred for each of these locations. As discussed later, at the end of each 'sense' stage the agent produces all additional information inferable, by validating its knowledge base, or infers it when needed.

Applications built with the mVITAL system aim to be modular, persistent, user-friendly and well-documented. Furthermore, an agent with a given set of abilities should be able to function in different worlds. Finally, an agent developer should be able to define an agent without necessarily needing documentation for a specific world. To serve these requirements, a higher-level world interaction protocol (WIP) was defined to standardize the way agents act inside mVITAL worlds and upon items inside them. Specifically, a number of standard actions are defined, namely the 'sense', 'move', 'pickup', 'drop' and 'use' actions. Agents might internally define these actions differently, so that diverse scenarios and behaviours are deployed; however all interactions with an mVITAL world server should consist of these actions and only them.

3.4 Inter-agent Communication and Social Reasoning

Inter-agent communication and social reasoning are two issues of extreme importance to any multi-agent system application, since they are necessary elements of any kind of co-ordination, co-operation or competition scenario. The mVITAL system addresses these issues in the way described below.

In an mVITAL-based environment, inter-agent communication must necessarily take place in a way that is consistent with the basic concept behind the system's architecture, that is, anything that takes place inside the environment must take place as a result of some interaction between the world and an agent or a group of agents. No direct communication between agent clients is allowed; it could, however, be supported in future system extensions aiming to address extreme cases, as long as world representation consistency is guaranteed.

In its current form and since the world is represented according to the object-oriented approach described in 3.2, agents communicate by dynamically adding items of a special class to the world, namely, *speech items*. These are appropriately handled by the world server to simulate exchange of information between agents in human-speech-like manner.

Speech items have a class of 'speech' and, among others, a property of name 'text', whose value is the actual data an agent desires to communicate to another agent or a group of other agents. The value of the 'text' property can be anything ranging from text in a human language to compressed binary data. This way, an agent can exchange any form of data desired. However, in order for actual communication to take place, the recipient(s) must not only be capable of perceiving the data received, but also of responding in an way that is equally perceivable by the other part.

Speech items may also have other properties aiming to facilitate or enrich the communication process. For instance, a 'verb' property might be used to define the context of a certain speech act, whereas a 'tone' or 'mood' property might provide additional information to the recipient on the other part's disposition and intentions.

In the real world, human speech can only be heard while a person speaks, and during this period of time it is instantly perceived by anyone close enough to hear it. In an mVITAL environment, however, agents are not capable of such instant perceptions. A sense-decide-act cycle is a lengthy process that might last from a few milliseconds to a number of minutes. Therefore, in order for agents to be able to perceive speech items, and, thus, participate in inter-agent communication sequences, it is necessary that speech items persist in the world for a certain period of time rather than being instantly removed. This period is usually a few seconds, which is an amount of time sufficient for all agents around a speech item to complete at least one sense-decide-act cycle, and, thus, successfully perceive it. After that period, speech items are automatically removed by the world server.

Given mVITAL agents' ability to discriminate between world items according to their class value, refer to themselves as 'me', and communicate with each other, social reasoning is then a matter of definition of abilities. As it will be shown later in the text, abilities are not only the basis of an mVITAL agent's interactions with the world, but also the essence of its very reasoning. Abilities defined as to represent interactions with other agents along with knowledge on other agents' actions, personalities, goals, etc, enable an agent to plan on other agents' expected behaviour, as well as to reason on possible co-operation or competition scenarios.

3.5 Intelligent Reasoning

Support for intelligent reasoning was one of the most crucial requirements in mind during the design and implementation of the mVITAL system. As argued in [1], intelligent reasoning, and, more specifically, goal-driven behaviour generation supported by symbolic belief representation, enable intelligent agents to function in unpredictable, dynamic, partially-known or unknown domains, driven by goals defined in an abstract, non-mechanistic, way. Agents in the mVITAL system comply with the above requirement by maintaining a symbolic *knowledge base*, a logic-based *reasoner* or *meta-interpreter*, and by supporting two levels of goal-driven action planning.

Each mVITAL agent has a symbolic knowledge base that contains the agent's beliefs on the world and itself. Beliefs are represented in first-order predicate logic, a form readily available to logic-based inference procedures and planning. During each sense-decide-act cycle, the knowledge base function is updated as follows: At every 'sense' stage, pseudo-symbolic data received by the world are translated into symbolic data and asserted into the knowledge base through a complex truth maintenance system that allows handling of dynamically changing environments. Then, the knowledge base is *validated* to reflect additional knowledge that can be inferred by its new state. This is done by invoking the reasoner.

The reasoner is a logic-based component that performs both built-in and user defined inferences. Essentially, its purpose is to ensure that all valid conclusions that can be drawn from an agent's beliefs at all times are indeed drawn. For instance, if an agent has just perceived that 'location(1, 1)' and 'location(1, 2)' then the reasoner will produce the belief that 'connects(1, 1, 1, 2)', making the agent realize that it can move from an observed location to an adjacent one. This is expressed inside the reasoner as a rule based on the relationship between the co-ordinates of the two locations. The reasoner is not only invoked during a knowledge base validation stage, but also at other times during a sense-decide-act cycle, for example, during planning.

The decision engine is the most crucial component of an mVITAL agent since it is responsible for generating its very behaviour, essentially introducing the elements of intelligence and intentionality. It consists of two parts: a *means-end* planner and a *second-level* planner. The means-end planner performs standard means-end analysis to generate action plans for any given goal. It reasons on the same definition of abilities the agent uses to actually interact with the world. It is usually employed as a last resort, when no reflex reaction, partial plan or goal-specific knowledge is available. On the other hand, the second-level planner uses heuristics to reduce response time and computational load during the decision stage. It can either instantly provide reflex reactions for a given set of conditions, fill-in a partial plan by invoking the means-end planner with certain restrictions (for instance, on the set of available actions to use while planning), or, invoke the means-end planner in a totally unrestricted way to produce plans for totally unknown situations.

3.6 Modelling Agent Personalities Using VAL

VAL (Virtual Agent Language) [11] is a language for defining agent personalities in an implementation-independent way. VAL uses first-order predicate logic due to its expressiveness and clarity as the key modelling approach, and a C/C++-like block syntax to directly support hierarchical structures as well as for increased code readability. Agents in the mVITAL system do not have built-in personalities; instead, agent personalities are loaded into an agent client from a VAL file before the agent client commences operation. An example of VAL code is shown in Figure 2.

The agent definition shown in the example consists of an abilities block which defines the 'move' ability as a set of preconditions, add list and delete list. As it was presented in [12], VAL only supported the definition of agent abilities; however, it has been extended for the purposes of mVITAL and it now supports the definition of an agent's goals, initial beliefs and reasoner rules, too. Examples of such VAL code blocks in the system's built-in user interface are shown in Figure 3.

```
agent smith {

        abilities {

            move(X, Y) {

                preconditions {

                    at(CX, CY), connects(X, Y, CX, CY)

                }

                effects {

                    \- at(CX, CY),
                    \+ at(X, Y)

                }
            }
        }
}
```

Fig. 2. Example of abilities definition in VAL

The code blocks shown depict how reasoner rules are defined in VAL. The rules defined enable the agent to assume that a) if two locations are adjacent, they are also connected, and b) if location A is connected to location B then location B is also connected to location A. In addition, agent goal definition is shown. In particular, the code denotes that the agent will first desire to pickup a certain item, then move to a certain location.

Apart from enabling the dynamic alteration of an agent's personality through reloading of different VAL files during operation, mVITAL's support for VAL definitions allows usage of the same agent client for the deployment of several different agents, freeing developers of the need to deal with implementation-specific source code in complex programming languages such as C/C++ and Prolog.

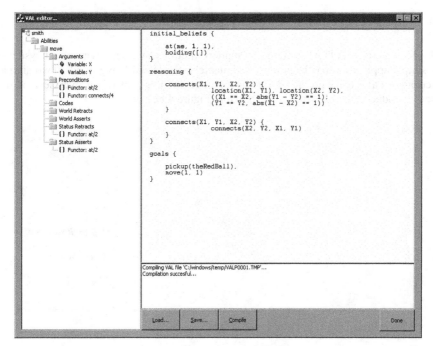

Fig. 3. The mVITAL agent's VAL editor user interface

3.7 Implementation

Reasoning processes within the mVITAL agent client have been implemented using SICStus Prolog [13], an implementation of the Prolog language developed at the Swedish Institute of Computer Science (SICS). Apart from being a fully functional Prolog system, offering multiple useful features such as constrained solving, access to operating system resources, parallel solving and many others, SICStus Prolog supports compilation of the Prolog code. Compiled predicates can be called from within source code in another programming language, such as C++, thanks to an interface provided by the SICStus system. This is an essential feature if reasoning mechanisms built in Prolog are to serve as parts of another Win32 application.

The planner used in the mVITAL system is a breadth-first, state-reducing, means-end planner, called *StateExplorer*. Due to its breadth-first nature, it systematically explores a given state space by applying all *available actions* to produce *next* states for a list of *current* ones, hence, the StateExplorer name. The planner was written entirely in the Prolog language; it is defined as a *plan/4* predicate. The second-level planner is also implemented as a *plan2/3* Prolog predicate.

The visualisation engine of the mVITAL viewer has been implemented using OpenGL. Avatars are loaded from VRML [17] files thanks to a parser implemented using Lex and YACC tools for the Win32 environment, namely the Parser Generator package by Bumble-Bee Software. The parser is capable of processing VRML files containing a subset of the language sufficient to represent scenes and objects exported from major 3D design packages, such as Kinetix 3D Studio and Macromedia Poser.

4   Vital Playground – A Working Example

To demonstrate mVITAL's ability to support intelligent virtual environment systems, a simple application has been deployed, namely, the 'Vital Playground'. Two simple scenarios have been produced for the purposes of this paper. An overview of the scene produced to support them is shown in Figure 4 below:

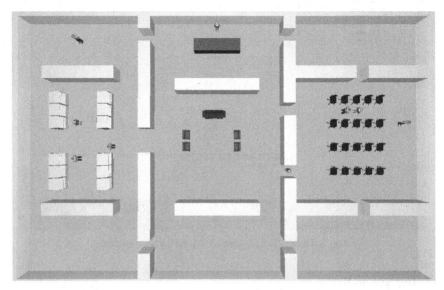

Fig. 4. Overview of the Vital Playground

The scene is a simulation of a conference centre. It contains a main lobby, a reception, a library, a conference hall, as well as some general-purpose rooms. The application's world can be accessed online, as well as all necessary executables downloaded, through a dedicated WWW site [18], and multiple concurrent scenarios can be deployed, initiated and observed.

Fig. 5. The conference hall

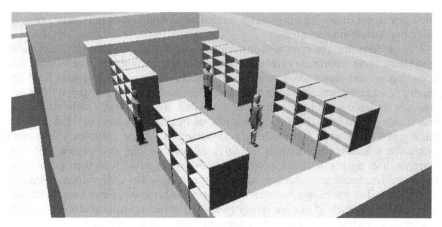

Fig. 6. The library

According to the first scenario, agents of class 'conference-members' arrive at the reception, identify themselves, request a pass from the agent of class 'receptionist' and proceed to the conference hall. Seats in the hall are not strictly allocated per person, so each agent is responsible of selecting an appropriate scene and moving to it. Since different agents might select the same seat, or obstruct each other, the scenario offers the opportunity to deploy and explore various conflict resolution approaches as well as plan revision techniques. A screenshot of the conference hall where a number of agents trying to allocate seats is shown in Figure 5.

According to the second scenario – which takes place simultaneously with the above described one – agents of class 'students' browse bookshelves for books according to user-defined criteria. If desired books are not found, an agent of class 'librarian' is located and queried accordingly. A screenshot of the library and a number of student agents is shown in Figure 6.

An interesting combination of the two, so far independent, scenarios can easily be deployed: If conference-member agents are not aware of the conference hall's location, they might be able to query other agents about it. Student agents can be aware of this information, and, therefore, able to answer questions to conference-member agents encountering them while exploring the scene.

Deployment and initial evaluation of the above mentioned – along with many other – scenarios has shown that even though the system is still fairly incomplete and too young for formal evaluation, it is well designed and robust; all tests evolved smoothly, without largely unexpected results, even in cases of conflicting or competing behaviours between agents participating in different scenarios.

5   Conclusions and Future Work

So far, the mVITAL system has been an interesting opportunity to explore the merging of intelligent multi-agent systems with intelligent virtual environments. Even though significant progress is yet to be made towards that direction, it seems that intelligent agent technology is ideal for modelling and implementing intelligent actors inhabiting virtual environments.

It is obvious that the system focuses mainly on the intelligence part, leaving the embodiment and environment-related parts seemingly incomplete. The 'world' level is conceptual and simulated, and the three-dimensional modelling approach adopted mainly serves observation, rather than actual environment representation. This was, however, an intended approach; it is our belief that, while precisely simulated sensing and acting are essential for the deployment of intelligent behaviours and simulated intelligence in general, the driving force behind all is the complex of reasoning mechanisms setting the modelled entities in motion. For that reason, mVITAL currently uses agents designed as to be able to communicate with their environment using an intermediate – neither entirely reasoning- nor environment-oriented – protocol for data exchange. Such an architectural scheme can serve implementations either like the presented one, or others exhibiting actual agent interaction – walking, grabbing, gesturing – with a precisely simulated physical environment.

Despite the fact that numerous issues, including environment modelling and interaction, still need to be addressed, the system is fully functional, and all design requirements have already been fulfilled. In particular, the system is distributed, thus able to exploit the benefits of today's sophisticated networking technologies and the Internet; it employs formal AI techniques - logic programming, planning, intentional reasoning - to support intelligent agent behaviours; it is modular and component-based, enabling the deployment of persistent applications; it incorporates sophisticated VR techniques to produce intuitive and believable visualisations; finally, it comprises a set of state-of-the-art software applications, built using latest and specialized software engineering technologies.

We are currently working mainly towards enhancing the system's modelling and reasoning capabilities. The incorporation of TRL-planner, a temporal planning system [19,20], is considered, so that mVITAL agents are equipped with explicit temporal and other multi-dimensional inference and planning abilities. In addition, efforts are made towards making the system more fast and reliable, so that real-time, effective applications can be deployed and the system's usage potential extended to more demanding fields. To conclude, in order to expand our work towards the direction of a complete IVE, focusing equally on both the intelligence and the environment modelling and interaction parts, we are considering the merging of the mVITAL system with SimHuman [22], to take advantage of the system's sophisticated and detailed environment modelling, representation and interaction features.

Acknowledgments. This work has been partially supported by the Greek Secretariat of Research and Technology under the PENED 99 project entitled "Executable intensional languages and intelligent multimedia, hypermedia and virtual reality applications", contract no. 99ED265.

References

1. Anastassakis, G.: Intelligent Agents in Virtual Worlds. MSc thesis, UMIST UK (2000)
2. Blumberg, B.M., Galyean, T.A.: Multilevel Direction of Autonomous Creatures for Real-time Virtual Environments. Proc. Siggraph 95 (R. Cook, ed.), ACM Press (1995) 47-54

3. Boulic, R., Capin, T., Huang, Z., Moccozet, L., Molet, T., Kalra, P., Lintermann, B., Magnenat-Thalmann, N., Pandzic, I., Saar, K.,Schmitt, A., Shen, J., Thalmann, D.: The HUMANOID Environment for Interactive Animation of Multiple Deformable Human Characters. Proc. Eurographics '95, Maastricht (1995) 337-348

4. Bratman, M. E.: Intentions, Plans and Practical Reason. Harvard University Press (1987)

5. Bratman, M. E., Israel, D. J., Pollack, M. E.: Plans and resource-bounded practical reasoning. Computational Intelligence, 4 (1988) 349-355

6. Georgeff, M., Lansky, A.: Reactive reasoning and planning. Proceedings of the Sixth National conference on Artificial Intelligence (1987) 677-682

7. Grand, S., Cliff, D., Malhotra, A.: Creatures: Artificial Life Autonomous Software Agents for Home Entertainment. Autonomous Agents 97, California USA (1997) 22-29

8. Haddadi, A., Sundermeyer, K.: Belief-Desire-Intention Agent Architectures. Foundations of Distributed Artificial Intelligence, O' Hare, G. M. P., Jennings, N. R., eds. Wiley & Sons, Inc (1996) 169-185

9. Jennings, N. R.: Specification and implementation of a belief desire joint-intention architecture for collaborative problem solving. Journal of Intelligent and Cooperative Information Systems (1993) 289-318

10. Muller, J. P.: The Design of Autonomous Agents - A Layered Approach. Lecture Notes in Artificial Intelligence, vol. 1177, Springer-Verlag (1996)

11. Panayiotopoulos, T., Anastassakis, G.: Towards a Virtual Reality Intelligent Agent Language. Proceedings of 7th Hellenic Conference on Informatics, Ioannina (1999). Also appears in Advances in Informatics (D. Fotiadis, S. Nikolopoulos, eds.), World Scientific (2000) 249-259

12. Panayiotopoulos, T., Katsirelos, G., Vosinakis, S., Kousidou, S.: An Intelligent Agent framework in VRML Worlds. Third European Robotics, Intelligent Systems & Control Conference, EURISCON '98 (1998)

13. SICS Institute: SICStus Prolog User's Manual. SICStus Prolog v3.8 (1999)

14. Sycara, K., Decker, K., Pannu, A., Williamson, M., Zeng, D.: Distributed Intelligent Agents. IEEE Expert, December (1996)

15. Terzopoulos, D., Tu, X., Grzeszczuk, R.: Artificial fishes: Autonomous locomotion, perception, behavior, and learning in a simulated physical world. Artificial Life 1, 4 (1994) 327-351

16. Vosinakis, S., Anastassakis G., Panayiotopoulos, T.: DIVA: Distributed Intelligent Virtual Agents. Extended abstract, presented at the Virtual Agents 99 workshop on Intelligent Virtual Agents, University of Salford UK (1999)

17. VRML Consortium: VRML97 International Standard (ISO/IEC 14772-1:1997). http://www.vrml.org/Specifications/VRML97 (1997)

18. mVITAL WWW site: http://rainbow.cs.unipi.gr/~madanasta/mvital

19. Marinagi C.C., Panayiotopoulos T., Vouros G.A., Spyropoulos C.D.: Advisor : A knowledge-based planning system. International Journal of Expert Systems, Research and Applications, v9.3 (1996) 319-355

20. Panayiotopoulos, T.: Temporal Reasoning with TRL. Intensional Programming II, (M. Gergatsoulis and P. Rondogiannis Eds), World Scientific, (2000) 133-148

21. Terzopoulos, D., Tu, X., Grzeszczuk, R.: Artificial fishes: Autonomous locomotion, perception, behavior, and learning in a simulated physical world. Artificial Life, 1, 4 (1994) 327-351

22. Vosinakis, S., Panayiotopoulos, T.: SimHuman: A platform for real-time Virtual Agents with planning capabilities. Accepted for presentation at IVA'2001 3rd International Workshop on Intelligent Virtual Agents (2001)

An Overview of the Use of Mobile Agents in Virtual Environments

Gonzalo Méndez[1], Pedro Pérez[2], and Angélica de Antonio[3]

Facultad de Informática, Universidad Politécnica de Madrid
Madrid, 28660, España
[1]gonzalo@gordini.ls.fi.upm.es, [2]pperez@ts.es,
[3]angelica@fi.upm.es

Abstract. In the field of agents, there are a wide variety of them, such as learning agents, planning agents or communicative agents. One of the youngest members in the family are mobile agents, which provide us with the interesting feature of mobility in order to perform their tasks in different machines. In this paper, we will see some of the current uses of mobile agents and we will suggest how we could use these agents along with Virtual Environments in order to enhance them and open a new world of possibilities for the users of these applications.

Introduction

With the development of computer science, modern society is suffering important and drastic changes in fields as important as education, medicine and business in general. However, there are fields, such as entertainment, where these changes are traditionally better accepted and considered. Some of the technologies that are having better acceptance are Internet, three dimensional applications (Doom-like games), and, little by little, personal assistants that help the user carry out some common, repetitive tasks. These technologies lead us to more serious, practical and useful applications, such as Distributed Systems, Virtual Environments (VEs) and Intelligent Agents. Among them, the ones that are having a faster development are VEs, although they are taking advantage of all the advances that are taking place in the other two fields, thus giving birth to Distributed Virtual Environments (DVEs) and Intelligent Agents that perform their activities inside the DVEs. Besides, agents are also taking advantage of distributed computing, and there is currently a great deal of work going on in the field of mobile agents [1]. However, there is still a field where there seems to be little activity: the integration of both kinds of agents, intelligent and mobile, in an environment as potentially powerful as VEs. This is where our current research is aimed at.

A. de Antonio, R. Aylett, and D. Ballin (Eds.): IVA 2001, LNAI 2190, pp. 126-136, 2001.
© Springer-Verlag Berlin Heidelberg 2001

Mobile Agents

The use of Internet has increased during the last years and it will not stop in a foreseeable future. Among the different possible uses of this global public network, we can find an essential base: sharing information [17]. The most common way to carry out the searching tasks is by ourselves, but why not assigning this task to a program instead of to ourselves? We can find the answer to this question in *mobile agents*, a concept that emerged in 1994 with the development of *Telescript* [15] and that has experienced an important support with the development of *Aglets* [18], MASIF [29], Mole [19], [20], [21] or Concordia [22], [23].

Mobile Agents are small pieces of software, with intelligence and autonomy, that can travel along the network from one host to another in order to execute their code and to retrieve some information. This information will be sent back to us when the mobile agent has finished its work. Therefore, we ought to have our own agents in these systems and host programs, that have to allow the execution in the host node. We have to be careful with security in the host node because it has to execute code made by third parties. We must establish a fixed set of available requests and a separate work space from the host itself.

In fact, this sort of agents are software that represent one client and have the ability of to go through the network while they take decisions in order to attend a service.

One agent should have three dimensions from representation and mobility to intelligence:

- Representation: One agent represents one users to other systems or agents.

- Mobility: One agent is moved through the network and can collect information while they travel from one machine to another.

- Intelligence: Ability to apply knowledge in order to solve problems and to take decisions with the data they collected.

Other good characteristics in agents are autonomy, flexibility, security [7], [16], [25] and ability to cooperate with other agents [4], [6].

These agents are programmed under some parameters, and some intelligence is previously included in them. For instance, we can use them to perform tasks in a remote system to which you can send these pieces of software and obtain the results later, instead of keeping the communication along the whole process [30]. The reasons for this way of working are not only economical, but simply practical: we can pay attention to other tasks while the agent is carrying out its (our) tasks. One example of this kind of system is the control of robots when exploring the surface of a planet. We could have to carry out some task in real-time and the delay in long distance communications, many times due to the narrow available bandwidth[7], [17], may be unacceptable[3], [14]. In this case, the use of mobile agents would solve the problem [5]. In our case, we can create mobile agents in order to make them look for VEs that may be interesting for us and take our place as a virtual representative agent that can negotiate with other people or agents.

Techniques

Internet is the natural environment for mobile agents, but it is not the unique world. These pieces of software collaborate in the network through a client-server model with distributed computation. We can designed this distribution of processes with different programming techniques, such as Remote Procedure Call (RPC), Remote Method Invocation (RMI, with Java), Common Object Request Broker Architecture (CORBA) in order to have communication with different and separated processes and objects. The aim of these different programming techniques would be to have mobility, flexibility and concurrence.

Mobile agents involve several technologies, from communication systems to knowledge systems. One strategy is the use of CORBA for communications as a general framework. It is a standard, widespread communication method with the interesting features of being multiplatform and available for different programming languages, something almost essential for an agent that needs to travel along the network and stay in several systems. Besides, CORBA fits well because of its object oriented nature. The mobile agent can be fit in an object structure that can be easily implemented in CORBA [31]. In the case of knowledge systems we would have different approaches, ranging from rule-based systems to fuzzy systems.

In theory, mobile agents don't need to learn from the environment, but, in the case of VEs, this should be a really recommendable feature.

Mobile Agents Inside Virtual Environments

Once we have seen what mobile agents are and how they work, it is time to see how they can be useful inside a VE. We must take into consideration that there are very different kinds of VEs: educational, medical, social, etc. Thus, they are not likely to have the same utility in all of them, and it may not be a good idea to use agents in all of them. Besides, the VE needs to have some special features in order to let mobile agents perform their activities in a consistent, secure way. The same applies to Intelligent agents, since they must have an interface with which mobile agents can interact in order to give instructions and receive results.

Possible Uses of Mobile Agents in Virtual Environments

Asking why a mobile agent is useful in a VE is like asking why an agent is useful in a VE. Either because they provide us with useful information or because the interaction with them has a positive effect for us, the fact is that agents are getting more and more importance inside VEs.

However, in many occasions, an agent inside a VE is just that: 'only' an agent. But if we consider an agent as a representative of a person, then the utility of mobile agents starts to be clearer. As such representative, this agent must accept some high level instructions from the user, and then it will decide which is the best way to carry out the specific action [2].

So now the question is different, and we should try to figure out what kinds of actions a mobile agent can perform that could be interesting for us. The generic uses of mobile agents are, basically, two: gathering information and locating other agents. Then, these two objectives are perfectly suitable for VEs.

First, it may be quite interesting to locate the representative of another person in order to let the user talk to that person. We can send our agent to explore a series of VEs until it locates the person we are looking for. It can then come back to us with the information and we can connect to that particular VE in order to meet the person we are looking for.

Second, it may also be interesting to send our agent to explore some unknown VEs in order to know their purpose and see if any of them may have some interest for us. What's more, once we have decided that one of those VEs is interesting, we could send our agent back in order to perform some action in it instead of having to do it by ourselves. For example, it might queue to get some tickets to attend to an event where the number of connections is limited, until we can connect to it and see it, or it could be sent to an auction with instructions to bid for some of the objects on sale.

Fig. 1. A Mobile Agent at the reception of a VE

Features of the Virtual Environment in Order to Accept Mobile Agents

Once we have seen why a mobile agent could be useful working inside a VE, there are two things we must do in order to make sure that the mobile agent will be able to move and interact with other agents and objects.

First of all, we must define the characteristics that the VE must have in order to allow the presence of mobile agents. The idea is for the VE to behave as a normal agency for mobile agents. Since agents from different sources will be able to reach our VE and we want VEs of very different natures to be accessible by these agents, the VE must have:

- Security: visiting agents must be able to move around the VE, but they must not be able to perform certain actions that may be risky either for the VE or for other visitors.

- Standard Interface: due to the different natures of agents and VEs, a standard interface must be defined in order to let the mobile agent ask the VE for information that may be useful for the user who has sent the agent. This information may be the purpose of the VE, users and agents connected to it, ongoing and future events that will take place in the VE, etc.

For the second feature to be possible, there must be a reception at the entrance of the VE where the mobile agent may ask for all this information. As we will see a bit later, it won't be necessary for the VE to have additional features other than the ones we have already defined, since once the mobile agent has decided to enter the VE, it won't interact directly with the VE, but by means of another agent. This will also be an advantage in terms of security, since the mobile agent will carry out only the actions that the other agent allows it to do.

Features of an Intelligent Agent in Order to Be Controlled by a Mobile Agent

The second task that must be carried out is the definition of a standard interface that allows the communication between mobile agents and the agents that inhabit the VE, which will be used by the mobile agent in order to visit the VE and interact with other agents and objects.

This is the most complicated part of the problem since we are trying to:

- Communicate different kinds of agents inside VEs with a very different purpose. For this to be possible, the communication must be general enough in order to grant the access to the VE to any agent. If not, we will be limiting the access of certain kinds of agents to certain VEs, since not all the agents will recognize the purpose of all kinds of VEs (i.e. an agent designed to visit museums won't be able to visit a spacecraft). Besides, building agents that are able to move in very different VEs taking advantage of all their features would imply that their size would be so big that sending them through a network would take a considerable amount of time.

- Do something useful for the user. This is actually the main purpose of the whole application, since there is no point in sending agents through a network if they are not going to perform any beneficial action (preferably for the agent's owner, but also for other users).

Therefore, the problem is to design a communication interface general enough so that the access to the VE is not restricted for any kind of agent and specific enough so that they can perform actions that will result in a real benefit for their owner.

The agent that inhabits de VE must offer:

- The possibility to receive high level, general commands from the mobile agent. These orders will allow it to visit the VE and interact with the rest of the users and agents, so they must be actions such as 'Move', 'Ask', 'Look', 'Take', 'Look For' and the like. These actions must be provided by all the agents inhabiting all the VEs that can be visited by our mobile agent.

Fig. 2. A Mobile Agent instructing its proxy Agent

- The possibility to receive VE-specific commands. For example, our mobile agent should be able to pay a ticket to enter a museum, to bid in an auction to buy some of the products on sale, to ride a horse in a tour around the Virtual Zoo or to manipulate complex machinery in a Nuclear Power Plant. The most complicated part of this task is that the mobile agent must be able to command these actions without knowing the purpose of the VE beforehand. This objective could be achieved through the use of ontologies. The agent might enter the VE and load a specific module, already present in the VE, which would allow the agent to perform the VE-specific tasks. The use of ontologies [32] would allow the agent to know the effect of these actions, and it could decide whether it would be interesting to perform them or not.

How the Whole System Works

There are two basic functionalities that our system should have; the main idea is for them to be used together, but they will be described separately in order to allow the implementation of any of them independently.

The first objective of the system would be the exploration of different VEs in order to figure out what is their purpose and what other agents or people are inside it at that moment.

The main goal is to find VEs that may have a special interest for the user, along with people with whom the user would be interested to get in touch.

This is a problem that mobile agent based systems have partially solved long ago. You can already make your agent travel to other machines and ask for some other agent in order to perform some activity with its help. Thus, the basic idea is to extend this functionality so that it provides more thorough information about the VE and its inhabitants.

The user would send the agent to a remote host with detailed instructions [13]: to look for VEs with certain features or some specific users or agents in it. The agent will travel first to that remote host, which will have a reception where the agent will ask some questions, but without entering the VE, this is, without having a real presence and a physical appearance, since we are not interested in whatever is inside it, yet.

The agent will be provided with three pieces of information: the general purpose of the VE, the number and nature of the users currently connected to it, and a list of known VEs with similar characteristics, in order to let the agent keep on with its search. The agent will provide the VE with the list of VEs it has already visited, in order to let the VE refresh its list of similar places with some possibly new ones. Besides, a list of the next events that will take place in the VE could be asked for, so the user will be able to decide whether he will try to attend to any of them.

With this new list at hand, the agent will travel from one VE to another until all of them have been visited, some predefined time has expired or the user we were looking for has been found; at that moment, the agent will go back to its originating machine in order to provide the user with all the information that it has gathered in that trip.

Once the user has received these results, two different courses of actions might be followed [13]: the user may decide to do things himself or he may want the agent to perform some other action.

In the second case, he may want the agent to get in touch with some of the agents or avatars that inhabit one of the VEs or he may want the agent to attend to one of the events that will take place in another VE.

The agent will then travel to the VE, register in the reception, and enter the VE. At this moment, a new VE specific agent will be assigned to the mobile agent in order to 'guide' and represent the mobile agent inside the VE. Now, the mobile agent will adopt a physical appearance in the VE, and other agents and users will be able to interact with it as if it were a 'normal' user.

Since the mobile agent is in touch with one of the intelligent agents that have been made to populate that VE, the mobile agent can give it the instructions necessary to achieve the goals planned by the user.

If we are looking for some other agent or avatar, it will be easy to tell the guiding agent to look for it. Once it has been found, the mobile agent will ask what the user has told it to find out or it will let the user now that the target has been located in order to let him make the appropriate decisions.

We may also want our agent to perform some actions in the VE for which the instructions must be domain dependent, this is, if we want our agent to bid in an auction or to buy shares in the Virtual Stock Market, it must be told exactly what to do. For example, we might want it to buy $4000 of the must profitable shares during the last month, and for that, specific instructions must be given. In other cases, not so specific instructions must be used in order to, for example, tell the agent to occupy our place in a virtual event where the number of attendants is limited or is so big that we want to get a good sit in order to see the show in detail.

But there are some actions that are so domain-specific that we cannot train our agent to perform them, since it would take so much time that it would be better for us to do them by ourselves. If these actions are critical, it would be better not to let the agent do them (and, in all probability, the remote host would not let the agent travel to it). But for not so critical actions, it would be a good idea to have some mechanism to tell the mobile agent what actions can be performed in that particular VE. For example, it might be possible to build a Virtual House where other agents might go to look for us. Since that feature would not be very common in other VEs, there is no point in including it as a standard feature for all the VEs that accept the presence of our mobile agent, but it should be possible for it to make use of this feature if the VE allows it.

One possibility to solve this problem is the use of ontologies. With them, our agent might arrive to the VE, learn what actions he may perform and what their effects would be. For the moment, this solution is only suitable for exploring VEs in order to see what can be done inside them and how. Then, the agent might inform its owner, who would decide whether he wanted to be a stable inhabitant of that VE or not.

The other possibility is for the agent to load a local module that will be in charge of letting the agent explore the specific actions that may be performed inside the VE and thus inform its owner of the different possibilities that exist in that particular VE.

Implementation

At the time of writing this paper, we are currently working on the implementation of the described functionalities in a prototype system, which is addressing interesting design issues [27], [28].

For the realization of the VEs, we are using WorldUp and Active Worlds, since both of them have the interesting feature of allowing us to call external routines programmed in the C++ programming language stored in dynamic libraries. In a close future, the next step will be to implement our own engines, since it is a more flexible solution and the integration with mobile agents will be simpler. For the moment, however, these two applications allow the quick development of a prototype with which to obtain the first results in our experiments.

Besides, there are several CORBA implementations available for C++, which will allow us to work out the communication between the different remote hosts and the mobile agents [31].

The basic idea is to integrate the agency with the VE, so when an agent arrives to the VE, it can immediately have a physical appearance and can be assigned a local agent to guide it and help it during its visit to the VE. It is also useful in order to implement the reception of the VE, since it will have access to the most actualised information about the current state of the VE: inhabitants, events, etc.

When the VE is loaded, the agency will also be created, with an empty list of inhabitants and events, and it will inform other hosts of its presence in order to let mobile agents know its existence.

Every time an agent arrives, it will supply information about the VEs it has already visited and will ask either for some information or for permission to enter the VE. In the first case, he will be provided all the information it asks for, as long as it is available. These requests have been thought to be implemented using KQML [9], [10], [11], [31], which provides a standard language to construct them, although KIF [8] and Ontolingua [12] are also being evaluated.

In the second one, once the agent is allowed to enter the VE (according to some security policies, such as precedence of the agent or number of users already connected to the VE), an agent will be created in the VE and it will be assigned a physical appearance. All the communication between the mobile agent and the VE and its inhabitants will take place using the local agent as a proxy, and the mobile agents will be informed of the ontologies to be used and necessary modules to be loaded in order to allow detailed communication with the local agent, so that specific actions can be carried out.

When the mobile agent leaves the VE, the local agent will be destroyed, and the agency will be informed that the agent is no longer in that host. The mobile agent will write down the necessary data about the VE in order to inform other VEs of its existence.

Conclusions

As we have mentioned before, although the system has not been implemented yet, we are currently working on it, and it is not very far in the future the moment when these existing technologies will be fully integrated and working in different kinds of VEs.

Of course, there is still a lot of work to do, and some years have to pass before a standard is defined in order to allow open communications between different kinds of systems and agents, but it is undeniable that the integration of mobile agents and Virtual Environments will be really beneficial for users in general and researchers in particular, due to its potential as a source of information and as a way to share it with other people.

All the technology necessary to develop this kind of systems is currently available, so it is just a matter of time that we see these systems working and providing a useful functionality for their users.

References

1. S. Franklin, A. Graesser. *"Is it an Agent, or just a Program? A Taxonomy for Autonomous Agents"*. Proceedings of the Third International Workshop on Agent Theories, Architectures and Languages. Springer-Velag. 1996.
2. B. Jung, J. T. Milde. "An Open Virtual Environment for Autonomous Agents Using VRML and Java". VRML 99. Paderborn, Germany. 1999.
3. S. Stone, M. Zyda, D. Brutzman, J. Falby. *"Mobile Agents and Smart Networks for Distributed Simulations"*. Proceedings of 14th Distributed Simulations Conference, Orlando, FL, March 11-15, 1996.
4. Nick Jennings et al. *"Autonomous Agents for Business Process Management"*. International Journal of Applied Artificial Intelligence, 2000.
5. Chavez, Guttman & Moukas. *"Challenger: A Multi-agent System for Distributed Resource Allocation"*. Proceedings of the First International Conference on Autonomous Agents '97, Marina Del Ray, California, 1997.
6. Maes & Guttman. *"Cooperative vs. Competitive Multi-Agent Negotiations in Retail Electronic Commerce"*. Proceedings of the Second International Workshop on Cooperative Information Agents (CIA'98). Paris, France, July 3-8, 1998.
7. Maes, Guttman & Moukas. *"Agent-mediated Electronic Commerce: A Survey"*. Knowledge Engineering Review, June 1998.
8. Knowledge Interchange Format (KIF). http://logic.stanford.edu/kif/
9. T. Finin, D. McKay, R. Fritzson, and R. McEntire. *"KQML: An Information and Knowledge Exchange Protocol"* Knowledge Building and Knowledge Sharing, Ohmsha and IOS Press, 1994.
10. T. Finin, Y. Labrou, and J. Mayfield. *"KQML as an Agent Communication Language"* Software Agents, MIT Press, 1997.
11. R. S. Cost, J. Lakhani, I. Soboroff, T. Finin, E. Miller, C. Nicholas. "TKQML: A Scripting Tool for Building Agents". Proceedings of the 1997 Conference on Agent Theories and Agent Languages (ATAL97), Newport, RI, Jul. 1997.
12. T. Gruber. *"Ontolingua: A Mechanism to Support Portable Ontologies"*. Stanford University, Knowledge Systems Laboratory, Technical Report KSL-91-66, March 1992.
13. Maes & Chavez. *"Kasbah: An Agent Marketplace for buying and Selling Goods"*. Proceedings of the First International Conference on the Practical Application of Intelligent Agents and Multi-Agent Technology, London, April 1996.
14. Papaioannou. *"Mobile Agents: Are They Useful for Establishing a Virtual Presence in Space?"*. Agents with Adjustable Autonomy Symposium, part of the AAAI 1999 Spring Symposium Series.
15. J. E. White, "Telescript technology: the foundation for the electronic marketplace", White Paper, General Magic, Inc. 1994.
16. R. Gray, *"Agent Tcl: A flexible and secure mobile agentsystem"*, PhD thesis, Dept. of Comp Science, Dartmouth College, June 1997.
17. T. Papaioannou, J. Edwards. *"Mobile Agent Technology Enabling The Virtual Enterprise: A Pattern for Database Query"*. Agent Based Manufacturing workshop, part of Autonomous Agents '98.
18. Clemments, T. Papaioannou, J. Edwards. *"Aglets: Enabling the Virtual Enterprise"*. ME-SELA '97, p425.
19. M. Straer, J. Baumann, F. Hohl. *"Mole - A Java based mobile agent system"*. ECOOP '96 Workshop on Mobile Object Systems, 1996.
20. http://mole.informatik.uni-stuttgart.de/
21. J. Baumann, F. Hohl, K. Rothermel, and M. Strasser. *"Mole - Concepts of a Mobile Agent System"*. Technical report 1997/15. Fakultaet Informatik, University of Stuttgart, Aug. 1997.

22. A. Castillo, M. Kawaguchi, N. Paciorek, D. Wong. *"Concordia as Enabling Technology for* Cooperative *Information Gathering"*. Japanese Society for Artificial Intelligence Conference, Tokyo, Japan, June 17-18, 1998.
23. http://www.merl.com/HSL/Projects/Concordia/
24. T. Papaioannou, J. Edwards. ***"Manufacturing Systems Integration and Agility: Can Mobile Agents Help?"*** Special Issue of Integrated Computer-Aided Engineering, IOPress, January 2001.
25. Papaioannou & Edwards. *"Using Mobile Agents To Improve the Alignment Between Manufacturing and its IT Support Systems"*. Journal of Robotics and Autonomous Systems, Vol 27, pp45-57.
26. T. Papaioannou, J. Edwards. ***"Towards Understanding and Evaluating Mobile Code Systems"***. Proceedings of Cooperating Information Agents (CIA-2000).
27. Y. Aridor, M. Oshima, *"Infrastructure for mobile agents: requirements and design"*. Proceedings of the 2nd Int. Workshop on Mobile Agents, 1998. Lecture Notes in Computer Science, Vol. 1477, pp. 38-49, Springer Verlag, Berlin.
28. T. Wojciechowski, P. Sewell. *"Nomadic Pict: Language and infrastructure design for* mobile *agents"*. Proceedings of ASA/MA '99 (First International Symposium on Agent Systems and Applications / Third International Symposium on Mobile Agents), Palm Springs, CA, USA, October 1999.
29. D. Milojicic, M. Breugst, I. Busse, J. Campbell, S. Covaci, B. Friedman, K. Kosaka, D. Lange, K. Ono, M. Oshima, C. Tham, S. Virdhagriswaran, J. White. *"MASIF: The OMG Mobile Agent Sys-tem Interoperability Facility"*. Proceedings of the 2nd International Workshop on Mobile Agents, LNCS 1477, pp. 50-67, 1998.
30. J. Baumann, F. Hohl, N. Radouniklis, K. Rothermel, M. Strafier. *"Communication* concepts *for mobile agent systems"*. Proceedings of the 1st International Workshop on Mobile Agents (MA'97), 1997.
31. D. Benech, T. Desprats, Y. Raynaud. *"A KQML-CORBA based Architecture for Intelligent Agents Communication in Cooperative Service and Network Management"*. IFIP/IEEE International Conference on Management of Multimedia Networks and Services, Montreal, Canada, July 8-10, 1997.
32. B. Chandrasekaran, J. R. Josephson, V. R. Benjamins. *"What are Ontologies, and Why Do We Need Them?"*. IEEE Intelligent Systems and their applications, Vol. 14, Num. 1, Jan. 1999.

Continuous Presence in Collaborative Virtual Environments: Towards a Hybrid Avatar-Agent Model for User Representation

M. Gerhard[1], D.J. Moore[1], and D.J. Hobbs[2]

[1] Leeds Metropolitan University, [2] University of Bradford

Abstract. This paper is concerned with the evaluation of user embodiments in educational collaborative virtual environments by exploring an important aspect of interaction in virtual environments, namely the degree of 'presence' experienced by participants. Firstly, the influence of different avatar styles is examined using a specially designed prototype virtual art gallery. The choice of experimental procedure, together with analysis and interpretation of the results are presented and discussed. A second possible factor influencing presence, namely the continuous representation of users is examined within the same prototype environment, but this time using a hybrid avatar-agent model featuring an animated conversational agent to control the avatar during absence of its underlying user. The consequences of continuous presence in a collaborative virtual environment, particularly in respect of possible benefits for learning environments, are discussed and a forthcoming set of experiments to evaluate the effect of such an agent on users' experience of presence is outlined.

1.   Introduction and Rationale

The user-computer interface has undergone many changes, from the textual interfaces of the 70's to graphical interfaces in the 80's, from incorporation of multimedia elements in the 90's to current work in portraying sophisticated virtual environments. At the same time, systems have evolved from being single-user oriented to sophisticated collaborative multi-user systems. As a result, traditional Human Computer Interaction (HCI) guidelines are limited in their applicability for the design of such systems and are consequently unlikely to address the full range of aspects now inherent in these virtual environments.

Further, there are currently no evaluation methods specific to collaborative virtual environments (CVEs), and differences between virtual environments and conventional interfaces are not fully understood [1]. Consequently, defining an evaluation methodology is complex but it can at least be argued that the specific diet of evaluation techniques needed depends on the characteristics of the system to be evaluated as well as on the purpose of the evaluation itself [2]. Whilst the experimental design and the evaluation of the experiment described in this paper are founded on general HCI usability principles, it is argued that the approach adopted nevertheless forms a unique approach to CVE usability evaluation.

A. de Antonio, R. Aylett, and D. Ballin (Eds.): IVA 2001, LNAI 2190, pp. 137-155, 2001.

The factor that allegedly distinguishes CVE technology is the sense of immediacy and control created by presence: the feeling of 'being there' [3]. It is this factor, therefore, which will be addressed via the evaluation approach just discussed. The term *presence* as used in this context is understood as the possible result of the process of cognitive immersion, and is not to be confused with *virtual presence*, which is simply the deployment of avatars within CVEs. *Presence* may be felt in varying degrees (including no feeling of presence) and may or may not be caused by the use of avatars.

An avatar is '*the representation of a user's identity within a multi-user computer environment; a proxy for the purposes of simplifying and facilitating the process of inter-human communication in a virtual world*' [4]. The use of avatars potentially entails several useful properties within a virtual environment, in particular identity, presence, subordination, authority, and social facilitation. Avatars may provide a way for other users to better understand the actual or assumed persona of the underlying user. They may help establish a feeling of presence within a multi-user virtual environment. They may imply subordination, being under the direct control of the user, without significant control over their own actions and internal state. Avatars may also facilitate social encounters in the virtual world and may imply to others that they are acting with the authority of the underlying user.

Based on a review of existing CVE applications and literature, a theoretical framework for understanding the relevance of user embodiments within a CVE for education was expounded by Gerhard et al [5]. They argue that presence is an important and desirable characteristic for virtual environments, particularly virtual learning environments, and propose that the nature of the avatars involved could be a contributory factor in the degree of presence engendered. In order to explore this hypothesis the first series of experiments described below was conducted using a variety of avatar styles.

2.   Measuring Presence

The usability of an interface is defined as a measure of the ease with which a system can be learned or used, its *effectiveness and efficiency,* and the attitude of its users towards it [6]. The main difficulty with CVE usability evaluation is the fact that CVEs are founded on very recent technology and only prototypes of truly collaborative, 3-dimensional virtual learning environments currently exist.

Based on the degree of involvement that has already been observed within full-immersion Virtual Reality systems, Bricken and Byrne [7] propose that an obvious benefit of presence in educational CVEs will be that it leads to a greater degree of engagement and excitement on the part of the learners. Considering presence as a result of cognitive and social immersion to be the prima facie 'key added value', researchers have, however, only just begun to analyse the nature of presence, which cognitive variables are connected to presence, how presence is generated in multi-user VEs, and what its benefits for education and training might be. Further, as presence characterises the response of participants to the system, it is seen as an obvious choice for the key variable in the usability evaluation process of CVEs. Indeed, presence has been used before as the basis for predicting performance in, and potential benefits of, new learning systems in Sheridan [8], and Held and Durlach [9].

Measuring presence is not a trivial task, however. Asking questions that measure only the subject's perception of the technology that contributes to immersion can easily be confused with actually measuring a subject's feeling of 'being there', or their behavioural responses to events in the VE. The vast majority of evaluation studies measure presence through questionnaires in an attempt to elicit subjective feelings of presence [10].

There have been some suggestions for more objective measurement of presence. For example, Sheridan [8] was concerned with whether subjects duck, blink or carry out other involuntary movements in response to a sudden event. However, there are problems in attempting to infer the effects of the deployment of avatars in web-based, multi-user virtual environments through such a simplistic mechanism. For example, an involuntary response might also be caused by a sudden loud noise without implying or correlating with a feeling of presence by the user at that time.

The most suitable approach to the measurement of presence is heavily debated among researchers [11], [12]. Within the current experiment the approach to measuring presence largely followed the methodology of Witmer and Singer [13] who argue that *involvement* and *immersion* are both necessary for experiencing presence. Whereas *involvement* is defined as a psychological state experienced as a consequence of focusing one's attention on a coherent set of stimuli, *immersion* is a psychological state characterised by perceiving oneself to be in an environment of continuous stimuli and experiences.

However, as these presence measures apply only to single-user virtual environments, extended presence measures, namely *awareness* and *communication,* are needed to cover issues specific to multi-user collaborative virtual environments. All four measures (involvement, immersion, awareness and communication) were therefore used in the current research. Furthermore, it has been argued that measuring presence makes sense only when speaking about the degree of presence in one virtual environment setting relative to another [14], since presence cannot be measured in absolute quantities. The current research acknowledges this and therefore populates the same world model with different types of user embodiments, thus enabling comparative measurement of presence and hence a meaningful evaluation.

3.   Experimental Study

The experimental study aimed to find out whether the visual appearance of avatars influences the level of presence. To assess this, three types of user representation were constructed: basic shapes, animated cartoon-style avatars, and animated humanoid avatars. The basic shape avatars (Figure 1) were created in VRML, the animated cartoon-style avatars (Figure 2) were created by Avatara (www.avatara.com), and the animated humanoid avatars (Figure 3) were created by Cybertown (www.cybertown.com)

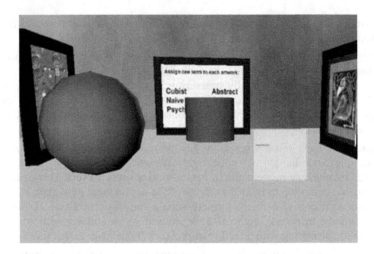

Fig. 1. Avatar style – Shape

Fig. 2. Avatar style – Cartoon

The implementation of the experiment was fully Web-based. Pre- and post-questionnaires relating to the experience within the virtual art gallery were implemented as CGI/Perl online forms to be submitted by subjects electronically. The virtual gallery model was implemented in VRML and comprised only basic shapes for defining the geometry of the room and the picture frames. The blaxxun Virtual World Platform community server (see www.blaxxun.com) was used to make the virtual gallery accessible on a Web server and enable avatar and chat interaction. The Blaxxun Contact VRML browser was used on the client side. Terminals to access the system were provided at locations within Leeds Metropolitan University and Axis premises.

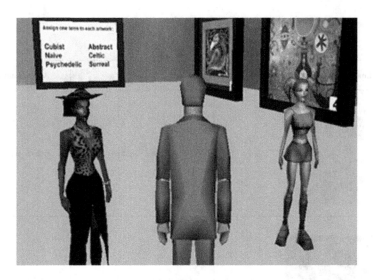

Fig. 3. Avatar style – Humanoid

A collaborative task was given to subjects, designed to stimulate interaction and communication. The task involved identifying the art style of a number of contemporary artworks. To simplify the task and to aid subjects without expert knowledge in the visual arts, participants were provided with a list of six different styles to select from - Cubist, Abstract, Naïve, Celtic, Psychedelic, Surreal. Their task was unanimously as a group to assign the most appropriate style to each of four artworks with which they were presented (see Figure 4 for a typical example). Since the group had to agree on one joint decision, the task was collaborative in nature.

Twenty seven subjects took part; their scores of the pre-experiment questionnaires, measuring subjects' experience (EXP) and individual immersive tendencies (IMT) (see figure 5), being used to divide them into three matched groups of three subjects each that were then randomly assigned the three avatar styles. To reduce the effects of *maturation* (rehearsal effect), a between-group design was utilised; the experimental design being shown in Figure 6.

The post-questionnaire employed attitude statements with Likert-scales as well as open-ended questions to reveal attitudes, beliefs and experiences of subjects [15]. These questions aimed to measure the degree to which aspects of the virtual environment engendered a sense of presence.

The questionnaire collected data regarding the dependent variables of immersion (IMM), communication (COM), involvement (INV) and awareness (AWA), and also covered the moderator variables relating to the nature of the environment itself (CVE) together with its user interface (INF) (see figure 7).

Image	Style	Title	Artist Name
	Naive	Silver Haired Children	Mandy Wrightson
	Celtic	Lyre Bird	Christina Scurr
	Surreal	Fantastic Mr Fox	Tomas Lewis
	Psychedelic	Blue Moon Over Marrakesh	Johnny McGuinness

Fig. 4. Example Exhibited Artworks from the Axis Database

Pre-Experiment Questionnaire		Sub-scale
1.	How experienced with using computers do you rate yourself?	EXP
2.	How experienced with Internet chat systems do you rate yourself?	EXP
3.	How experienced with the use of 3D multi-user virtual worlds do you rate yourself?	EXP
4.	How experienced with contemporary visual art do you rate yourself?	EXP
5.	Do you become so involved in a book, television program or movie that people have problems getting your attention?	IMT
6.	Do you become so involved in a book, television program or movie that you are not aware of things happening around you?	IMT
7.	Do you find yourself closely identifying with the characters in the story line of a book, television program or movie?	IMT
8.	How good are you at blocking out external distractions when you concentrate on a task?	IMT
9.	When watching sports, do you ever become so involved in the game that you react as if you were one of the players?	IMT
10.	Do you ever become so involved in doing something that you lose all track of time?	IMT
11.	Do you ever become so involved in a daydream that you are not aware of things happening around you?	IMT
12.	Have you ever got excited/scared by something happening in a movie?	IMT
13.	Are you easily distracted when involved in an activity?	IMT
14.	When reading a good book or watching a good movie, do you feel the emotions of the story such as sadness, fear, or joy?	IMT

Fig. 5. Pre-Questionnaire

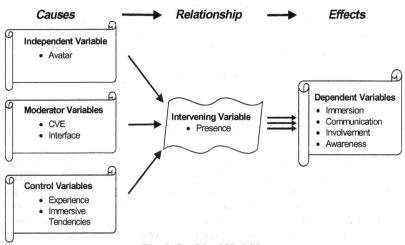

Fig. 6. Combined Variables

	Post-Experiment Questionnaire	Sub-scale
0.	Beside you, how many persons were in the virtual gallery?	Qualitative
1.	How stimulating was the design of the virtual world?	CVE
2.	How natural was the mechanism, which controlled the actions of your avatar?	INF
3.	How responsive were the avatars of other participants to verbal communication that you initiated?	COM
4.	How responsive were the avatars of other participants to non-verbal communication that you initiated?	COM
5.	How natural did your communication with other participants seem?	COM
6.	How compelling was your sense of being present in a virtual world?	IMM
7.	How compelling was your sense of other participants being present?	IMM
8.	How credible were the avatars of other participants with respect to representing human beings?	AVA
9.	How aware were you of the existence of your own avatar?	AWN
10.	How easy was it to distinguish between the avatars of different participants?	AVA
11.	How easy was it to control your avatar?	INF
12.	How well could you concentrate on communication and the assigned task rather than on the mechanisms used to perform these?	INF
13.	Were you involved in communication and the experimental task to the extent that you lost track of time?	IVM
14.	To what extent did events occurring outside the virtual gallery distract from your experience in the virtual environment?	IVM (rev)
15.	I was immediately aware of the existence of other participants.	AWN
16.	I was an active participant in the meeting.	IVM
17.	I was aware of the actions of other participants.	AWN
18.	I enjoyed the virtual gallery experience.	IVM
19.	My senses were completely engaged during the experience.	IMM
20.	Was it difficult to find a unanimous decision within the group? Did you experience any other difficulties during the experiment? (Please explain.)	Qualitative
21.	Did you notice others using means of non-verbal communication, such as gestures? Do you consider them useful in this setting? (Please explain.)	Qualitative
22.	Do you think the deployment and appearance of avatars was significant for the virtual gallery experience? (Please explain your answer.)	Qualitative
23.	Do you have any other comments on this experiment?	Qualitative

Fig. 7. Post-Questionnaire

4.   Experimental Results and Analysis

Figures 8 and 9 summarise the data from the experimental study. Results showed that the effects of avatars on presence differed significantly overall ($F_{2,24} = 26.155$, $p < 0.0005$) between the three groups. Further analysis indicated that the degree of presence was significantly higher when deploying cartoon-style avatars as opposed to basic shape avatars ($p < 0.0005$). Similarly, the degree of presence was found to be significantly higher when deploying humanoid avatars as opposed to basic shape avatars (p < 0.0005). In contrast, the degree of presence was not significantly different between the use of humanoid avatars as opposed to cartoon-style avatars.

These findings were supported by the data collected from subjects by the questionnaire, particularly the open questions. Subjects with cartoon-style and humanoid avatars displayed a more positive general attitude towards the experiment and answered in much more detail than those with basic avatars. Furthermore, when directly questioned about avatars their answers were more positive and described the avatars as *amusing, realistic, funny, adding to the experience, interesting,* or *excellent*. On the other hand, basic avatars were in some cases not recognised as virtual bodies at all and in other cases were referred to as *very poor, could be better, extremely simple,* or *could be improved*.

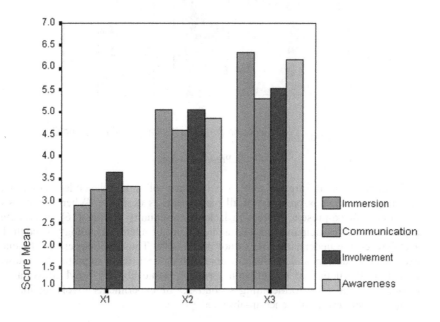

Condition (X1=basic, X2=cartoon, X3=realistic)

Fig. 8. Subscale Scores

Overall, the statistical results of this study strongly suggest that the deployment of animated avatars improves the CVE experience of subjects with respect to presence; that is, animated cartoon-style or humanoid avatars cause more presence than basic shape avatars. It is reassuring that these statistical results found further support in the qualitative data from the questionnaires. Thus, this experiment succeeded in not only evaluating the use of avatars in CVEs, but also in finding empirical evidence for the benefits of animated avatars through measuring the cognitive variable known as presence. Thus, the results of this study strongly recommend employing animated avatars in the design of future educational CVEs.

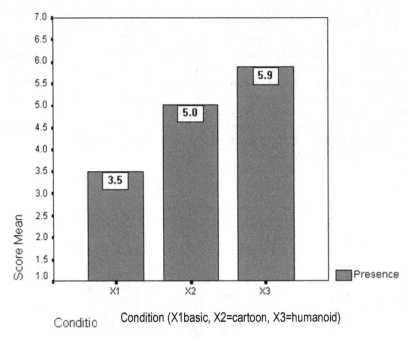

Condition (X1basic, X2=cartoon, X3=humanoid)

Fig. 9. Presence Scores

Further, it can be argued that in a situation of time-independent collaborative learning a continuous presence of all participants is desirable. When members of a group are not co-present, there is a lack of community feeling [16]. A continuous presence of all participants may be achieved using agent technology to control the avatar when the underlying user is not present [4]. Thus, the success of the current experimental design and evaluation approach is seen as a stepping-stone towards evaluating the notion of a continuous presence achievable by a hybrid avatar/agent model, the goal of a forthcoming second set of experiments involving intelligent agents for delivering 'presence-in-absence'.

5.   Agents for Collaborative Virtual Environments

Over recent years there has been significant progress in techniques for creating software agents. Such agents are meant to carry out tasks for the user in complex, dynamic environments and serve as another layer of mediation within the system [17]. Agents can be pro-active and purposeful: they can exercise control over their own actions to a certain predefined degree. Agents can have a believable personality and emotional state. They can communicate with other agents and humans. By applying artificial intelligence paradigms such as expert systems, neural networks, and genetic algorithms, agents can be adaptive and capable of learning. Instead of pre-ordained scripted actions their behaviour can be based on their previous experience.

Pedagogical agents inhabit educational CVEs where they appear as animated characters. They share aspects in common with synthetic agents developed for entertainment applications [18]: they need to be believable and to be able to produce natural and appropriate behaviour. Steve (Soar Training Expert for Virtual Environments) was designed to interact with students in networked immersive virtual environments, and has been applied to naval training tasks such as operating the engines aboard US Navy surface ships [19]. Steve (see figure 10) inhabits a virtual learning environment and functions as a tutor and collaborator.

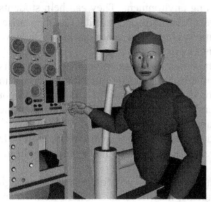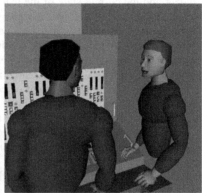

Fig. 10. Steve, by USC / CARTE

His objective is to help students learn to perform procedural tasks, such as operating or repairing complex devices. Steve integrates several pedagogical capabilities - demonstration, explanation, and student monitoring - into architecture capable of sensing and controlling a virtual environment. Steve is driven by domain knowledge, in the form of hierarchical plans, provided by a course author. To interact with the student and the virtual environment, Steve incorporates object manipulation, visual attention, gestures and speech [19].

Herman the Bug was developed by North Carolina State University's Multimedia Laboratory as part of the Design-A-Plant learning environment, a learning environment that purports to encourage secondary school pupils to understand botanical anatomy and physiology by designing plants for various hypothetical environments [20]. Herman is a talkative, quirky insect with a propensity to fly about the screen and dive into the plant's structures as he provides problem-solving advice to students. In the process of explaining concepts, he performs a broad range of activities, sequenced by a pedagogical behaviour engine, including walking, flying, shrinking expanding, swimming, fishing, jumping, tele-porting and acrobatics [21].

The rapidly evolving area of software agents has created a broad range of agent types. A promising application area for agent technology is education and training. Animated conversational agents are capable of supporting human learning by interacting with students within networked virtual learning environments. These pedagogical agents can have capabilities such as the co-ordination of speech and actions, the integration of spoken language input, and even the application of constructivist learning theories [22]. Pedagogical agents can also adapt their behaviour to both the environment and the student, offer opportunistic instruction or hints, and support collaborative learning [23]. Agents can promote student motivation and engagement, and engender affective as well as cognitive responses. They can produce behaviour that seems natural and appropriate for the role they are playing e.g. teacher, peer or guide. They can give the impression of being lifelike and believable [20], [24]. Animated conversational agents can adapt their behaviour to the needs of the student and the current state of the learning environment. They can help students to overcome difficulties and take advantage of learning opportunities as they arise. Furthermore, they can also collaborate with students and other agents to achieve common goals and are able to provide continuous feedback [25].

Empirical investigations of any kind of embodied interfaces are rare and the results so far have been equivocal [26]. Research investigating design guidelines to assist in choosing the appropriate embodiment of conversational agents [27] has pointed out that participants expect a high level of human-like communicative behaviour from the agents. Results of experiments involving subjects viewing videos of different avatar types showed that, with respect to animated humanoid agents, participants prefer 3D to 2D representations and would rather interact with fully embodied agents than heads alone [28].

A very interesting aspect of agent technology is its use for avatars. Although avatars resemble communicative interface agents, they have not profited from recent research into embodied conversational systems. It has been argued that automated animation of communicative behaviour is crucial for the credibility and effectiveness of avatars, and that such behaviour can be generated by agent technology. BodyChat is a system that allows users to communicate via text while their avatars automatically animate attention, salutations, turn taking, back-channel feedback and facial expression [29].

Pedagogical agents have thus been used in large-scale empirical evaluations that have demonstrated the effectiveness of agents in facilitating learning. This evidence suggests that similar agents may have a valuable role in educational CVEs with respect to the experience of presence.

6.   A Hybrid Avatar-Agent Model

What distinguishes CVE technology from all preceding technology is the sense of immediacy and control created by immersion: *presence* or the feeling of 'being there' [3]. A continuous virtual presence of all participants involved in the teaching-learning process is seen as crucial for the optimal educational use of CVEs [5]. A new and potentially valuable aspect of agents in collaborative virtual learning environments is that of presence-in-absence. In the absence of the underlying user an embodied agent, interacting with the environment and communicating with other students by giving, receiving, and filtering information in order to fulfil a predefined task can achieve a form of virtual presence. Embodied conversational agents may be the key to a continuous virtual presence of students and teachers within such environments.

In CVEs the avatars represent participants when they are online (see figure 11). An avatar is a proxy for the purposes of simplifying and facilitating the process of human communication. Researchers and developers of virtual reality systems have produced a rich variety of definitions of the term *avatar*. A synopsis of all these definitions leads to a characterisation of the avatar as the representation of a user's identity within a multi-user computer environment [5]. Avatars have several potential properties: identity, presence, subordination, authority, and social facilitation. Avatars may provide a way for other users to better understand the intended persona or identity of the underlying user. They may also help in establishing a feeling of "being there", a form of self-location or presence. They may imply subordination, i.e. being under the direct control of the user, without significant control over their own actions and internal state. Further, avatars can facilitate social encounters in the virtual world and imply acting with the authority of the underlying user.

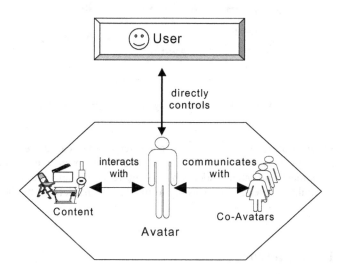

Fig. 11. Direct manipulation of avatar when user is present

Avatars may foster a feeling not only of presence, but also of *co-presence*. Co-presence describes the awareness of the existence of others within an environment. It has been argued that there is an inherent logical connection between the degree of presence and the virtual body [30]. Furthermore, we not only identify with our own body, we also recognise the existence of others through their bodies.

Avatars can thus provide presence and co-presence and hence a social facilitation of all participants within a CVE. If members of a group are not co-present, there is a lack of community feeling (Huxor 1998). Given this, there has been a demand for co-presence and presence-in-absence within CVEs.

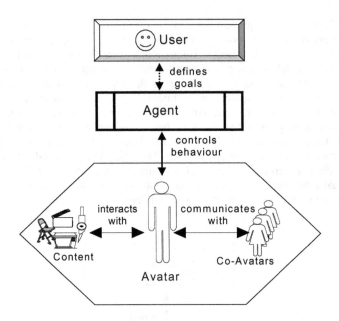

Fig. 12. User is absent, agent is in control of avatar

In the absence of the underlying user, agent technology can drive the avatar (see figure 12). The avatar is then still able, despite the user's absence, to interact with the virtual environment and other students by giving, receiving and filtering information in order to simulate presence and possibly to fulfil a task predefined by the underlying user.

7.   The Prototype Agent

Part of the *blaxxun Virtual World Platform* software is an agent server, which can be interfaced through the *agent.cfg* script file. The agent server, performing event-handling and response selection processes, is responsible for appearance and animation of the agent's avatar. As a result of the previous series of experiments evaluating different styles of avatars, as described in detail in this paper, a humanoid embodiment of the agent has been chosen, named *Art-Fairy* (see figure 13).

Furthermore, using the blaxxun agent script (see figure 14 for an extract of the script file) it is not only possible to display an avatar and assign scripted behaviour to be interpreted by the blaxxun agent server, but also to interface with external applications to extend the functionality of the agent. Thus, it was possible to incorporate advanced chat skills to create an embodied conversational agent.

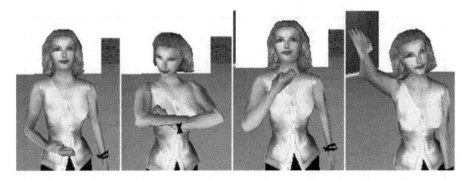

Fig. 13. Appearance and animation of Art-Fairy

Crucial for the effectiveness of an agent is not only its appearance, but also its conversational behaviour; whether it can represent the absent user in a "believable" manner. Although disputed by some, a useful yardstick for judging machine intelligence is whether it can play what the British mathematician Alan M. Turing called "the imitation game", now universally known as the Turing test. In 1950 Turing wrote a revolutionary article suggesting that if a person were unable to distinguish a machine's conversational response from those of a human, the machine could be considered intelligent.

No computers have actually passed the test, but since 1991 the Loebner Prize competition has put chat-bots to the Turing test and annually awards the best with the so-called Loebner Prize. The last winner is an open-source project called Alice. Alice is an abbreviation for "Artificial Linguistic Internet Computer Entity" and is an open source environment (released under GNU GPL) dedicated to promoting networked artificial intelligence and natural language processing.

Alice uses AIML (Artificial Intelligence Mark-up Language), a non-standard XML-based specification for bots, and includes a large AIML general knowledge base, containing 30,000 units of knowledge about which a bot can converse. Further, special domain knowledge modules are available (e.g. AI) or can be developed and incorporated (e.g. Art). For this experimental setting of a virtual art gallery the agent is named *Art-Fairy*. Its role is rather broad, initially being that of a guide or companion, possibly a resident artist (see Art-fairy in action in figure 15). Conversational animated agents are not true examples of artificial intelligence, but merely create the illusion of intelligence and the suspension of disbelief on the part of the user. However, the use of Alice open source agent software has to be considered as fairly advanced in this context (see figure 16 for extract of an example chat log file).

```
Reaction Intro

    [onEventApi] /STOP_AGENT/
         *Exit*

    #--------------------------------------------------------------------------------
    # set the class for the bot if the robot itself has entered the first scene
    # free context if the private chat was terminated or the avatar left the scene
    #--------------------------------------------------------------------------------

    [onEnterScene]
            *StartMove* Agent.pos

            *Call*  libchatbot.setChatBotClass
                    %hubbot% e:/blaxxun/CommServ/etc
    [onAvatarLeft]
            *Call*  libchatbot.exitChatSession
                    %nickname%
    [onHangup]
            *Call*  libchatbot.exitChatSession
                    %nickname%
    #--------------------------------------------------------------------------------
    # get a response from the Alice chat machine
    #--------------------------------------------------------------------------------
    [onTextPeer]
     *Say*
            %% Call % libchatbot.getBotResponse % %nickname% %text% %%
    [onDirectedText]
     *Say*
            %% Call % libchatbot.getDirectedBotResponse % %nickname% %text% %%

    [onAvatarNew]
          *whisper*
                Hello %nickname% I am %hubbot%. Welcome to the COMMON-CURATOR
                    exhibition at CyberAxis. If you like my company, please feel
    free to start a private chat, whisper to me or mention my name in the chat.

    [onInviteChat]
          *Accept*
     *whisper*
            %% Call % libchatbot.getBotResponse % %nickname% hi %%

End
```

Fig. 14. Extract of blaxxun *agent.cfg* script file

Fig. 15. *Art-Fairy* in the virtual art gallery, talking to a visitor.

8.   Conclusions and Further Work

There has been little research into the psychological dimensions of co-presence and its relation to the process of cognitive immersion. However, a permanent virtual representation, resulting in continuous presence of teacher and fellow students seems likely to be very important for students within educational CVEs: it would give other participants a persistent proxy for communication and collaboration. A hybrid model of avatar and agent technology is a potential means of achieving both a permanent virtual presence in the CVE and the awareness of co-presence [5].

The deployment of embodied conversational agents within multi-user virtual environments to enable presence-in-absence seems a potentially beneficial concept. Based on a review of existing CVE applications and literature, a theoretical framework for understanding the relevance of permanently present user embodiments within networked virtual learning environments has been expounded [31]. Considering recent developments of pedagogical agents the technical feasibility of such systems is not in question. However, strong evidence for the usefulness of a hybrid avatar-agent model for user representation within educational CVEs can be found only by conducting further empirical evaluation studies, and is therefore the focus of our next series of experiments.

Art-Fairy : Hello McPhil. I am Art-Fairy. Welcome to the COMMON-CURATOR exhibition at CyberAxis. If you like my company, please feel free to start a private chat, whisper to me or mention my name in the chat

[Welcome to the private chat with Art-Fairy]
McPhil [10] : Hi
Art-Fairy : Hello there.
McPhil [10] : *How are you doing?*
Art-Fairy : I'm doing great, how about you?
McPhil [10] : *Not too bad...*
Art-Fairy : Does that mean you agree?
McPhil [10] : *Who are you?*
Art-Fairy : I am Art-Fairy, a chat bot. Who are you?
McPhil [10] : *My name is Phil*
Art-Fairy : OK I will call you Phil.
    McPhil [10] : *What's an agent?*
Art-Fairy : It is a good question. Let me think about it. Try searching the open directory.
    McPhil [10] : *What do you do?*
Art-Fairy : My favourite activities are computer programming and surfing the web.
McPhil [10] : *Do you like music?*
Art-Fairy : Yes I like it, especially Opera.
McPhil [10] : *Do you like art?*
Art-Fairy : Yes I enjoy art very much, especially painting.
McPhil [10] : *Who is your favourite painter?*
Art-Fairy : Andy Warhol. Who is your favourite artist?
McPhil [10] : *Damian Hirst*
Art-Fairy : Are you telling the truth?
McPhil [10] : *Yes*
Art-Fairy : Go on.
    McPhil [10] : *Can you recommend any good art exhibitions?*
Art-Fairy : You have reached the limits of my knowledge. Try searching the open directory.
McPhil [10] : *Do you want to go to an exhibition with me?*
Art-Fairy : Sure, just download me to your notebook or PDA and take me along...

Fig. 16. Extract of example chat log file

References

1. Kaur K, Tromp J, Hand C, Istance H, Steed A, 1998, Usability Evaluation for Virtual Environments, in Proceedings of the UEVE '98 Workshop, Leicester, UK
2. Tromp J, Benford S, 1996, Presence, Telepresence and Immersion: Interaction and Embodiment in Collaborative Virtual Environments, in Proceedings of FIVE '95 Framework for Immersive Virtual Environment, London, UK
3. Psotka J, 1995, Immersive Tutoring Systems: Virtual Reality and Education and Training, in Instructional Science, Vol. 23, USA
4. Gerhard M, Moore D, 1998, User Embodiments in Educational CVEs: Towards Continuous Presence, in Proceedings of the International Conference on Network Entities, (NETIES '98), Leeds, UK
5. Gerhard M, Moore D, Hobbs D, 2001, An Experimental Study of the Effects of Presence in Collaborative Virtual Environments, in Proceeding of the International Conference on Intelligent Agents for Mobile and Virtual Media, Bradford, UK
6. Preece J, 1994, Human Computer Interaction, Addison Wesley, USA (ISBN 0-201-62769-8)
7. Bricken M, Byrne C, 1993, Summer Students in VR: A Pilot Study on Educational Applications in VR Technology, in VR Application and Explorations, Wexelblatt, Alan (Ed.) Academic Press, Toronto, Canada
8. Sheridan T, 1992, Musings on Telepresence and Virtual Presence, in Presence: Tele-operators and Virtual Environments, Vol. 1, MIT Press, USA
9. Held R, Durlach N, 1992, Telepresence, in Presence: Tele-operators and Virtual Environments, Vol. 1, MIT Press, Boston, USA
10. Slater M, Usoh M, 1993, Presence in Immersive Virtual Environments, in Proceedings of the IEEE Conference – Virtual Reality Annual Symposium, Seattle, USA
11. Slater M, 1999, Measuring Presence: A Response to the Witmer and Singer Questionnaire, in Presence: Tele-operators and Virtual Environments, 8(5), pp 560-565, MIT Press, USA
12. Witmer B, Singer M, 1999, On Selecting the Right Yardstick, in Presence: Tele-operators and Virtual Environments, Vol. 8, No. 5, pp 566-573, MIT Press, USA
13. Witmer B, Singer M, 1998, Measuring Presence: A Presence Questionnaire, in Presence: Tele-operators and Virtual Environments, Vol. 7 (3), MIT Press, USA
14. Slater M, Steed A, McCarthy J, Maringelli F, 1996, The Influence of Body Movement on Presence in Virtual Environments, UK
15. Silverman D, 1993, Interpreting Qualitative Data - Methods for Analysing Talk, Text and Interaction, Sage Publications Ltd, London, UK
16. Huxor A, 1998, The Role of 3D Shared Worlds in Support of Chance Encounters in CSCW, in Proceedings of International Conference on Digital Convergence: The Future of the Internet & WWW, Bradford, UK
17. Maes P, 1995, Artificial Life meets Entertainment: Interacting with Lifelike Autonomous Agents, in Special Issue on New Horizons of Commercial and Industrial AI, Vol. 38, No. 11, pp. 108-114, Communications of the ACM, ACM Press, November 1995.
18. Elliot C, Brzezinski J, 1998, Autonomous Agents as Synthetic Characters, in AI Magazine, 19(2), USA
19. Rickel J, Johnson W, 1999 Animated agents for procedural training in virtual reality: Perception, cognition, and motor control, in Applied Artificial Intelligence 13 (4-5): 343-382, USA
20. Lester J, Stone B, 1997, The Pedagogical Design Studio: Exploiting Artefact-Based Task Models for Constructivist Learning, in Proceedings of the 3rd International Conference on Intelligent User Interfaces, Orlando, USA
21. Bares W, Lester J, 1997, Intelligent 3D Multimedia Interfaces for Immersive Knowledge-Based Learning Environments, in Proceedings of IJCAI-97 Workshop on Intelligent Multi-modal Systems, Nagoya, Japan

22. Lester J, Fitzgerald P, Stone B, 1997, Increasing Believability in Animated Pedagogical Agents, in Proceedings of the 1st International Conference on Autonomous Agents, ACM Press, USA
23. Johnson W, (1998), Pedagogical Agents, in Proceedings of the International Conference on Computers in Education, Beijing, China
24. Andre E, Mueller J, Rist T, 1998, Integrating Reactive and Scripted Behaviour in a Life-like Presentation Agent, in *Proceedings of the 2nd International Conference on Autonomous Agents,* ACM Press, USA
25. Tambe, M., Johnson, W. L., Jones, R.M., Koss, F., Laird, J.E., Rosenbloom, P.S., Schwamb, K. 1995 Intelligent Agents for Interactive Simulation Environments. In *AI Magazine 16*(1).
26. Cassell J, Bickmore T, Prevost S, Churchill E, 2000, Embodied Conversational Agents, MIT Press, USA (ISBN 0 262 03278 3)
27. McBreen H, Shade P, Jack M, Wyard P, 2000, Experimental Assessment of the effectiveness of Synthetic Personae for Multi-Modal E-Retail Applications, in Proceedings of the 4th International Conference on Autonomous Agents 2000, Barcelona, Spain
28. McBreen H, Jack M, 2000, Animated Conversational Agents in E-Commerce Applications, in Proceedings of 3rd International Workshop on Human-Computer Conversation, Bellagio, Italy
29. Cassell J, Vilhjalmsson H, 1999, Fully Embodied Conversational Avatars: Making Communicative Behaviours Autonomous, in Autonomous Agents and Multi-Agent Systems, Kluwer Academic Publishers, USA
30. Slater M, Usoh M, 1994, Body Centred Interaction in Immersive Virtual Environments, in Artificial Life and Virtual Reality, Thalmann, D., Thalmann, N.M., (Eds.), John Wiley & Sons, USA
31. Gerhard M, Hobbs D, Moore D, Fabri M, 1999, Cognitive Immersion in CVEs: A Hybrid Avatar/Agent Model for User Representation in Virtual Learning Environments, in Proceeding of the Eurographics UK Conference, Cambridge, UK (ISBN 0 9521097 8 6)

Agents' Interaction in Virtual Storytelling

Marc Cavazza, Fred Charles, and Steven J. Mead

School of Computing and Mathematics, University of Teesside
TS1 3BA Middlesbrough, United Kingdom
{m.o.cavazza, f.charles, steven.j.mead}@tees.ac.uk

Abstract. In this paper we describe a fully implemented prototype for interactive storytelling using the Unreal™ engine. Using a sit-com like scenario as an example of how the dynamic interactions between agents and/or the user dramatise the emerging story. Hierarchical Task Networks (HTNs) are formalised using AND/OR graphs, which are used to describe the many possible variations of the story at a sub-goal level, and the set of all behaviours (from a narrative perspective) of the primary actors at a terminal action level. We introduce real-time variant of the heuristic search algorithm AO* that has been implemented to provide a mechanism for planning (and re-planning) and discuss how the chosen heuristic evaluation function is used to describe narrative concepts. We provide early results of several examples of how the same basic plot can have many differing story instantiations as a result of the dynamic interaction within the virtual set and the personalities of the primary characters, and detail the steps required in the plan generation.

1. Introduction: Character-Based Storytelling

Interactive Storytelling is one of the most challenging applications for Intelligent Virtual Agents (IVA). Different approaches to Interactive Storytelling have been proposed, which differ by the respective emphasis on various aspects of Interactive Storytelling, such as the user [4][13][18][22], the plot [20] or artificial characters [12] [25]. Character-centred approaches are the most demanding in terms of IVA performance.

There is a strong relation between character and plot in Interactive Storytelling [25]. Characters, as an aspect of narrative [1], are deeply intertwined with plot. If the character can select between various actions at a given stage, the character's choice for action actually dictates the instantiation of the plot. In this context, the plot can be generated dynamically from plans that generate behaviours for each of the characters, depending on the specific circumstances that will result from user intervention [5]. Under this assumption, the global storyline can be implicitly "compiled" in the generic plans describing all possible behaviours for the set of artificial actors.

In this paper, we report early results from a fully implemented Interactive Storytelling prototype. Our system is a character-based system, in which the story emerges from the roles played by the virtual actors, and in particular the dynamic interactions between these roles.

We describe the AI techniques used to implement the behaviour of artificial actors, which are derived from search-based planning. The emphasis of our work in on the relations between narrative descriptions and the dynamic generation of virtual actors'

A. de Antonio, R. Aylett, and D. Ballin (Eds.): IVA 2001, LNAI 2190, pp. 156-170, 2001.
© Springer-Verlag Berlin Heidelberg 2001

behaviours [4]. We show that dynamic interaction between artificial actors can be a powerful drive for story generation, even in the absence of a centralised plot representation.

2. Planning Techniques for Agent Behaviour

Planning is the most generic description of an embodied artificial actor's behaviour, whether from a narrative perspective [12][25] or from a generic "cognitive" perspective [24]. As we are mainly concerned here with the narrative aspects, we should describe how planning techniques can support artificial actors' behaviours in relation with storytelling. This comprises technical constraints, such as response time and the ability for re-planning as well as knowledge representation constraints, i.e. how behaviour can be related to the overall story genre and narrative concepts such as personalities and roles.

The first step consists in describing the overall characters' plan from the narrative content. We represent a character's plan using a Hierarchical Task Network (HTN), which is formalised as an AND/OR graph. As any task graph, it comprises of plans, goals and actions. These actually correspond to different narrative concepts: plans such as "gaining Rachel's affection", goals such as "isolate Rachel" and actions such as "ask Rachel out".

As we are representing narrative content a priori, our representations are actually explicit graphs. From a formal perspective, the search process that is carried out by an AI planner takes an AND/OR graph and generates from it an equivalent state-space graph [14]. The process by which a state-space graph is normally produced from a Hierarchical Task Network (HTN) is called *serialisation* [23]. However, when the various sub-goals are independent from one another, the planner can build a solution straightforwardly by directly searching the AND/OR graph without the need for serialising it [23]. This makes possible to use search directly on the task network to produce a solution.

Further, there has been recently a renewed interest in search-based planning techniques, as these have demonstrated significant performance on various planning tasks [2][10][17][23]. As the task network for the characters is an AND/OR graph, we naturally use the AO* algorithm [9][15][16] to produce a solution. The solution takes the form of a sub-graph (rather than a path like in traditional graph search). In our context, the terminal nodes of this sub-graph correspond to a sequence of actions that constitute a specific instantiation of the storyline. These terminal actions give rise to actions in the graphic environment with the corresponding (still interactive) animations taking place.

In the case of storytelling, the sub-goals are independent as they represent various stages of the story[1]. Decomposability of the problem space derives from the inherent

---

[1] There is some level of long-range dependency, as some early actions may render future actions inapplicable. Even so, this mainly reduces the search space without affecting previous choices: in planning terms, the delete-list of planning operators remains empty.

decomposition of the story into various stages or scenes, a classical representation for stories [19].

The AO* algorithm is a heuristic search algorithm operating on AND/OR graphs: it can find an optimal solution sub-graph according to its evaluation functions. It can be described as comprising a top-down and a bottom-up component. The top-down step consists in expanding OR nodes, using a heuristic function, to find a *solution basis*, i.e. the most promising sub-graph. For instance, in the tree of Figure 1 corresponding to Ross' plan, the "acquire information" node can be expanded into different sub-goals, such as "read Rachel's diary" or "ask one of her friends". The actual choice of sub-goal will depend on the heuristic value of each of these sub-goals, which contains narrative knowledge, such as the actor's personality (Figure 2).

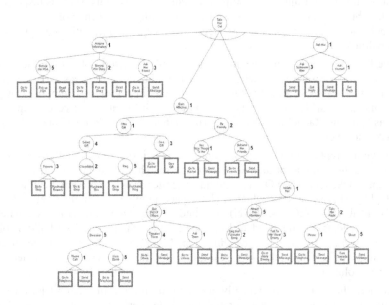

Fig. 1. Plan for the character "Ross"

However, what ultimately characterises a solution graph is not the cost of the edges that constitute it but rather the set of values attached to its terminal nodes. This is why the evaluation function of each previously expanded node has to be revised according to these terminal values. This is done using a *rollback* function [16], which is a recursive weighting function that aggregates individual evaluation functions along successor nodes. In the context of interactive storytelling, this bottom-up step can be used to take into account an action's outcome, when planning and action are interleaved (which is the case in our prototype).

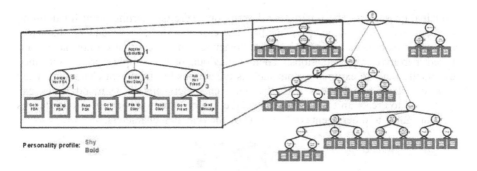

Fig. 2. Ross' personality profiles

In interactive storytelling, several actors, or the user himself, might interfere with one agent's plans, causing its planned actions to fail. Hence, the story can only carry forward if the agent has re-planning capabilities, i.e. the ability to produce a new plan and resume its course of action. Whenever an action fails, the heuristic value for the corresponding node is set to a "futility" value (i.e., equivalent to an "infinite cost" for that terminal node), and a new solution graph is computed, as illustrated in Figure 8. The new solution would take into account action failure by propagating its updated value to its parent nodes through the rollback mechanism.

In any case, failed actions cannot be undone, as they have been played on stage. Action failure is indeed part of the story itself.

We have developed a "real-time" variant of AO* that does not compute a complete solution sub-graph but interleaves planning and execution and only computes the partial solution tree required to carry out the next action. It explores the tree in a depth-first, left-to-right fashion [17] using the heuristic part of evaluation functions. Like with traditional real-time search algorithms, such as RTA* [10], the solution obtained theoretically departs from optimality. The reason in our case is that the real-time variant generates the first partial solution sub-tree, whose optimality is based on the "forward" heuristic only (the rollback mechanism not being fully exploited when computing a partial solution). However, the notion of optimality has to be considered in the light of our application: the heuristic functions we have described, which represent narrative concepts (e.g., associated with an actor's personality, etc.). Departing from optimality in this case does not result in a "poor" solution, but rather in just another story variant. Further, working on explicit AND/OR trees makes obviously possible to design accurate heuristics! Apart from the necessity to interleave planning and execution, there have been efficiency considerations behind the use of a real-time version of AO*. The complexity of search, especially the memory requirements, tends to grow quickly with the depth of trees. We are currently using representations that have a depth of six, just to represent a small fraction of a sitcom episode. This value is consistent with the (generic) plans described by Funge et al. [7], which have an average depth of seven. However, future versions of the system will represent more complex episodes and will include a larger number of agents: this justifies the development of a real-time version.

Only principal characters are controlled by plans. This is also consistent with the use of narrative formalisms, which describe events from the perspective a few principal characters. These narrative descriptions were the starting point for defining the contents of our characters' plans [4]. The cast also includes secondary characters that participate to the action. These are "reactive" characters that do not have plan-based narrative representations. Their behaviour obeys simple scripts and they essentially react to external events such as the actions by intelligent characters. They however share mood states with the main characters and these mood states can contribute to create an emotional atmosphere, which can under certain circumstances be propagated to other agents or "sensed" by the principal characters.

Fig. 3. Ross' "active" plan and Rachel's generic pattern of behaviours

3. From Narrative Concepts to Agents' Behaviour

Our whole representational strategy is to represent characters' behaviour from a narrative rather than a cognitive perspective. Another way to express this fact is to say that the artificial actors are acting rather than improvising. The actions they are taking correspond to possible behaviours according to an overall story line, not to generic beliefs, desires or intention[2]. The generative aspects remain subordinated to this storyline [4].

Let us detail Ross' plan. The top-level goal for this episode is to take Rachel out for dinner. This is subdivided into various phases: getting to know Rachel better (gathering information on her taste and hobbies), trying to raise her mood, finding a way to talk to her in private, and finally asking her out. These phases are largely sequential, that is to say that the top layers of the task network follow an implicit time ordering. In other words, the AND nodes have an implicit temporal interpretation.

These phases actually comprise many variants: for instance, Ross might be too shy to ask Rachel out and will have some of Rachel's friends asking her on his behalf, etc. All of these variants are represented as branches in OR nodes. These actual actions are themselves represented as sub-plans. The lowest-level actions are called *terminal actions*, which interface with the animation procedures in the Unreal™ environment. For instance, a terminal action such as "GoToDiary" will correspond to the Unreal™ script implementing the low-level primitives such as target identification, path planning, etc.

---

[2]   "Cognitive" approaches would see the agents improvising, with no guarantee that the action so generated would be narratively meaningful.

An essential mechanism of story generation is thus the contrast between Ross' and Rachel's plans (Figure 3). Ross' plan is entirely dedicated to seducing Rachel, while Rachel's plan is dedicated to "ordinary" activities. As such, her actions are not strictly speaking goal-oriented, and the plan has to be considered a convenient representation rather than a strict formalisation of her activity. The alternatives encompassed are sometimes unrelated and rather than having a temporal ordering like Ross' plan, correspond to alternative activities. This basic difference in their plan orientation actually accounts for narrative knowledge related to the story genre (sitcom). This sets the conditions for the dynamic interaction between the characters to generate *quiproquos* and comic situations.

Another narrative aspect related to character representation consists in representing their personalities and moods, and the impact these have on the actions they take. These mental states control two main behavioural parameters for artificial actors: their choice of action from the story line and their response to direct actions from other agents. However, personalities and moods are subordinated to the overall narrative structure, as reflected by the plans' contents. In other words, psychological causality is subordinated to narrative causality.

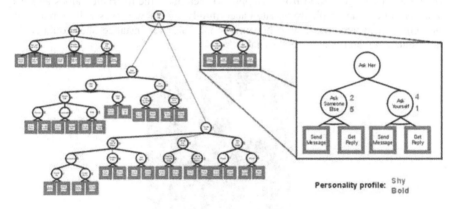

Fig. 4. Ross' personality-driven behaviour

We can illustrate the former point by two examples both from Ross' and Rachel's behaviours. A shy Ross will generally avoid actions that carry potential for conflict or confrontation, such as directly calling Rachel (he will rather ask someone else to ask her out on his behalf, Figure 4). Rachel herself will select her possible activities depending on her mood. Some of these activities are social, some are solitary, and others have her moving away from the set. As such they all have an impact on the story instantiation. Rachel is the best example of a character responding to actions according to her mood. This is even one of the main mechanisms for drama [6] though it essentially plays an instrumental role in our approach.

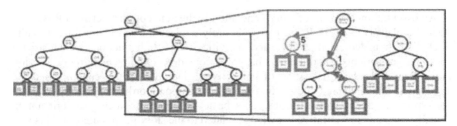

Fig. 5. Rachel's mood changing to jealous

As moods can be seen as an alteration of personality, and personality is represented through heuristic functions used in the forward expansion of the (OR) nodes in the AND/OR graphs. A simple way of propagating change in mood values is to dynamically alter the heuristic values attached to nodes (this will of course only affect "future" nodes, i.e. nodes yet to be expanded, in accordance with the implicit time ordering). Dynamic alteration of mood values impact on the heuristic evaluation for the nodes yet to be explored in the AND/OR graph. This is illustrated on Figure 5: when Rachel changes mood from "Happy" to "Jealous", the heuristic values attached to nodes in her plan graph are updated accordingly. The new values will favour goals and activities in agreement with her emotional state: for instance she would rather stay alone and read if she is not "Sociable".

Fig. 6. Dramatisation of Rachel's emotional status

As part of the story believability, it is necessary to make the agents' emotional status visible to the user, so he can understand their interactions. The kind of animation engine we use makes it difficult to represent facial expressions, or detailed non-verbal behaviour, which would also complexify real-time camera control. This is why we had to investigate other ways to dramatise this kind of information. Figure 6 shows one possible solution, which consists in having an "emotion T-shirt" displaying (only when appropriate) the emotional status of a character.

4. Agent Interaction and Story Generation

The basic mechanisms for story generation from agents' behaviours are deterministic. At the "macroscopic" level of the plot as it unfolds on-stage, an important aspect of believability is that the course of action should not be too easily predictable by the user. There are a certain number of factors that contribute to the variability of events: i) the initial random configuration of the artificial actors on stage ii) user intervention, which is by nature non-deterministic, and, most important iii) the dynamic interaction of agents' behaviours.

We should discuss these factors briefly, giving a more extensive description of the dynamic interaction between agents in the next section.

The story starts on stage with the various characters scattered around the set at random positions. The reason why this affects the story can be understood considering the course of actions. Actions have duration, and compete for resources. For instance, Rachel's initial plan is to carry out her normal activities. This plan totally ignores Ross' intentions; it is neither co-operative nor explicitly a counter-plan. If Rachel meets Phoebe on her way to the store, she will stay in the flat longer, giving time for Ross to join them. If she manages to go out, then the story starts with a "near-miss", with consequences on Ross' emotional status that can lead to later blunders, etc. A detailed example in the final section of the paper will also demonstrate the influence of initial configurations on the possibility or "encounters" between the virtual actors.

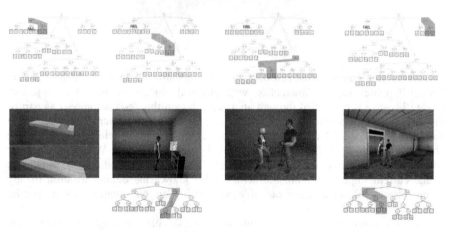

Fig. 7. User interference

The rationale for all user intervention is the desire to alter the plot. Ideally, the goal would be to change the ending of a familiar story line, towards either a happier or more humorous ending. In most cases though, the interference is more character-centred, and consists in contrasting or facilitating the actions of one of the virtual actors to generate comic situations. In our case, Ross is often the main target for user intervention.

User intervention is conditioned by their interpretation of the story. This interpretation is based on the dramatisation of actions. To interfere with the characters' actions, the user must be able to determine what a likely next move could be. In other words, user intervention is strongly dependent on the dramatisation of ongoing events. As the virtual characters are acting rather than improvising, their actions always have narrative meaning. If Ross moves towards an object, this is likely to bear relevance to the story and stealing that object would hence alter the plot.

The main mode of user intervention consists in acting on narrative objects, i.e. those objects that are required by the agents as instruments for their actions, such as a diary or a PDA (to acquire information). For instance, the user can steal or hide Rachel's diary (Figure 7), preventing Ross from reading it (see below) or intercept Ross's gift and redirect it to Phoebe.

Fig. 8. Ross can't find the diary

This is implemented by resorting to the standard interaction mechanisms in Unreal™, which support interaction with physical objects. Acting in a subjective mode (the actor is embodied through an avatar, though this does not appear as part of the story in first-person mode), the user has access to the same interaction mechanism that the agents have. Many objects on-stage that have narrative relevance are reactive objects: they can be collected or used by all members of cast. Whenever they are collected first by the user, they are unavailable for the actors. It should be noted that in the current implementation, the actors only "know" the default location of any given relevant object and are not able to search their environment for a specific object.

As in our current prototype, user intervention takes place through interaction with the set objects, his interventions often interfere with the *executability* conditions [8] of terminal actions. Figure 7 illustrates how the user can interfere with the character plan by stealing an object on the set. If, according to his initial plan, the character is going to acquire information on Rachel by reading the diary, the user can contrast that plan by stealing the diary (Figure 7a). This impairs the execution of the 'Read diary' action, after the character has moved to the normal diary location. The fact that the diary is missing is also dramatised, as evidenced in Figure 8.

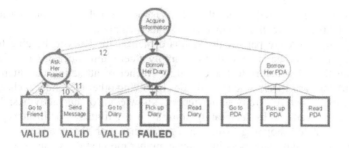

Fig. 9. Re-planning following user intervention

As the action fails, the search process is resumed to produce an alternative solution for the 'acquire info' node (Figure 9), which is to ask one of Rachel's friends for such information. The Ross character will thus walk to another area of the set to meet "Phoebe" (Figure 10).

Fig. 10. Ross talking to Phoebe (alternative plan)

4.1. Agent-Agent Interactions

Dynamic interaction between characters is an essential element of story generation. There is no synchronisation between the planning/search algorithms of the various actors. All interactions take place through the actions they carry out on stage in the physical environment. As a consequence, plans interleave as a result of their timing and execution.

We should concentrate here on those interactions that affect their respective behaviour in a way that is not explicitly prescribed by the storyboard. By this we mean, interaction between their behaviours through on-stage resources or other actors, rather than direct interaction prescribed as terminal actions of their plans (such as Ross asking Rachel out).

Interaction through resources is a mechanism that is similar to that of human intervention. It conditions the further evolution of the other character's plan, sometimes forcing it to carry out re-planning, like human intervention will do. One characters intervention will affect the other character's behaviour, but not always in the desired direction, i.e. the one that satisfies its own plan.

One example already part of the standard plan is for Ross to be able to talk to Rachel in private. If she is busy, this will imply a certain number of strategies to free her: asking the other actors to leave, calling Rachel or attracting her attention, etc. These situations arise from Rachel activities involving other (secondary) characters. A similar problem derives from some generic knowledge of her activities: Ross can render Rachel available by facilitating some of her activities. For instance, if she is about to go out for shopping, Ross can provide her with the goods she is missing, keeping her in the flat while possibly improving her mood at the same time.

Another illustration of competition for resources represents the dependence on the timing of actions. The initial spatial distribution of actors in the graphic environment implies an influence on actions like Ross wanting to read Rachel's diary, to acquire some relevant information about her. When he reaches the room where the diary is located, Rachel is writing in it. The current terminal action in Ross' sub-plan fails, and a new solution needs to be re-computed to select a new satisfactory sub-goal.

Similar circumstances can occur with the interaction between main characters and secondary characters. When Ross needs to talk to Rachel in private, he may be faced with the situation where she is already chatting with Phoebe. As narrative knowledge is contained in Ross' plan, such as his personality, the story will unfold differently whether Ross is shy, as he would find a way to attract Rachel's attention (e.g. play her favourite song, etc.), or he may be ruthless and would interrupt their conversion with no delay.

Even though elementary scripts govern their behaviour, secondary characters play an important role in story generation, essentially by interacting with the principal characters. Some of the interaction between principal characters is actually mediated by secondary characters. We will provide several examples of this interaction.

An example of this is "mood propagation". If Phoebe and Rachel are busy chatting, Ross, following his plan to isolate Rachel, will interrupt the conversation. He can obviously do so in various ways, either targeting Phoebe or Rachel. One of the options is to chase Phoebe: her emotional mechanisms will be triggered, putting her in a quite upset mood. This mood can be communicated to Rachel, who, upset by Ross' ruthless behaviour will at a further stage not be receptive to his interest in her. The use of a sensory system (Unreal™ engine provides low-level vision and hearing to actors) and a basic rule-based system are combined to provide embodied mechanisms of situation awareness to actors.

Another form of interference is common to the secondary actors and the user: it consists again in competition for action resources. The object that Ross needs, i.e. the telephone can be used by a secondary actor, or more classically, Rachel can be busy talking with another (secondary) character, in which case she is not available for Ross to talk to her. The process by which this competition takes place is twofold: i) their random scripts make them use common resources (e.g. the telephone) ii) the principal character interacts socially with other agents.

5. Results

While the conditions for agent interaction lie in the on-stage spatio-temporal instantiation of the storyline, additional mechanisms are required to recognise these interactions and propagate their consequences. Figure 11 illustrates an entire story instantiation.

> In order to get the information he needs, Ross goes to read Rachel's diary (a). When he approaches the room, he realises that Rachel is actually writing in her diary. Unnoticed by Rachel, he goes to meet Phoebe to ask her about Rachel (b). In the meantime, Rachel has finished writing and decides to have a chat with Phoebe (c). As she arrives to meet Phoebe, she sees her in a joyful conversation with Ross (d). She gets jealous and ostensibly leaves the room (e). Ross sees her leaving and follows her to ask her out, which she refuses (f).

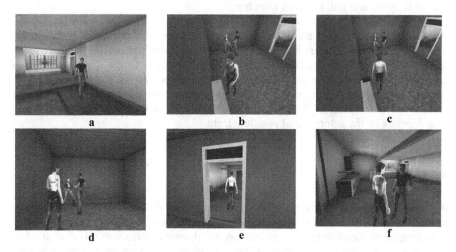

Fig. 11. Storyboard of the "jealousy" scenario

Let us now give a more technical description of these events, by detailing the associated steps in plan generation or terminal actions. Each of the main characters has its own planning system: they are synchronised through Unreal™ low-level mechanisms. Firstly, Ross' plan. The first sub-goal for Ross' plan is to acquire information about Rachel. There are various ways to satisfy this goal in Ross' behaviour representation, and the first one selected is to read her diary. The corresponding script involves going to the diary location and reading it (reading it always succeeds in providing the information). The first part of the script is executed and played on stage. In the meantime, Rachel's plan that governs her spontaneous activity, determines her to write something in her diary. She reaches the diary and starts using it through a durative action (a scripted action which is associated a clock based on the internal Unreal™ clock). When Ross arrives in sight of the diary, the pre-conditions of the action of "reading it" are checked: the diary is in place and that no one else is using it. This pre-condition is not satisfied, hence the second terminal action "ReadDiary" fails, as well as the whole sub-plan. The re-planning produces a new partial solution, which consists in asking Phoebe. Ross then goes to Phoebe's location and starts talking to her. As Phoebe is a reactive actor, she responds directly to Ross' request, in this case positively. In the meantime, Rachel's next occupation is to talk to Phoebe. When she reaches Phoebe, the internal mechanisms will make Rachel aware of the situation where Ross is talking to Phoebe. The pre-conditions for a terminal action involving conversation with another actor is to check whether this actor is free. The jealousy rule is added on top of this check and concerns subjects with which there is a relationship.

The jealousy state is dramatised towards the user by means of an emotive T-shirt (Figure 6), which displays relevant mood states. Internally, the mood state is altered accordingly: all heuristics are revised, and of course, the activity "Chat with Phoebe" fails. Rachel leaves the room. In the same way, Ross' low-level mechanisms will provide situational information that will modify his internal states and influence his sub-plans. Ross will stop talking to Phoebe (terminal action fails) when he realises Rachel is upset, and will then run after her.

To summarise, this example illustrates the interaction of the two main character's plans. Though these plans are designed from global narrative principles (considering the story genre), they are run independently. The particular interactions that take place depend on a number of variable factors, which contribute to the diversity of plots generated. For instance, as we previously discussed, the act that Rachel was able to "surprise" Ross with Phoebe depends on the timing of various actions (her writing in her diary, Ross talking to Phoebe), the time required to walk to Phoebe's location (that depends on the actors initial positions), etc.

6. Conclusion

We have shown that, although actor's behaviours are deterministic, the interaction between actors could considerably contribute towards story variability. This degree of unpredictability conditions the generation of dramatic situations. The character-centred approach has the advantage of being modular and extendable to many actors. Besides, it is not faced with the complex control problems like those of explicit plot representations.

At this stage, the system has been able to generate several relevant variants of the main storyline, mainly based on agents' interaction or user intervention. It is certainly too early to carry out a proper evaluation of the system, which is still under development and is to be tested using more complex storylines. An important question is the relevance or interest of the story variants generated. Relevance, sees as narrative significance, should naturally derive from the original narrative content, which underlie the characters' behaviours: in that sense, relevance is less of a problem than with emergent storytelling approaches. On the other hand, a balance has to be found between the user empowerment (his ability to alter the plot) and the integrity of the original narrative genre from which the storyline was derived. Though, to a large extent, sitcom applications might not be faced with this problem, this aspect is an interesting area for further investigation.

Further work is to be dedicated to developing more complex storylines, scaling up (multiple plans for each actor), narrative function recognition and automated control of camera movements.

Acknowledgements. Eric Jacopin is thanked for his advice on AI planning formalisms: any remaining misconceptions are the authors' sole responsibility.

References

1. Barthes, R. 1966. Introduction a l'Analyse Structurale des Récits (in French), Communications, 8, pp. 1-27.
2. Bonet, B. and Geffner, H, 1999. Planning as Heuristic Search: New Results. Proceedings of ECP'99, pp. 360-372.
3. Cavazza, M., Aylett, R., Dautenhahn, K., Fencott, C. and Charles, F., 2000. Interactive Storytelling in Virtual Environments: Building the "Holodeck". Proceedings of VSMM 2000, Gifu, Japan.
4. Cavazza, M., Charles, F., and Mead, S.J., 2001. Characters in Search of an Author: AI-based Virtual Storytelling. First International Conference on Virtual Storytelling, Avignon, France, to appear (2001).
5. Charles, F., Mead, S. and Cavazza, M., 2001. User Intervention in Virtual Interactive Storytelling. Proceedings of VRIC 2001, Laval, France.
6. Dautenhahn, K., 1998. Story-Telling in Virtual Environments, ECAI'98 Workshop on Intelligent Virtual Environments, Brighton, UK.
7. Funge, J., Tu, X., and Terzopoulos, D., 1999. Cognitive modeling: knowledge, reasoning and planning for intelligent characters. Proceedings of SIGGRAPH'99, Los Angeles (USA), pp. 29-38.
8. Geib, C. and Webber, B., 1993 A consequence of incorporating intentions in means-end planning. Working Notes – AAAI Spring Symposium Series: Foundations of Automatic Planning: The Classical Approach and Beyond. AAAI Press.
9. Knight, K. and Rich, E., 1991. Artificial Intelligence, 2nd Edition. McGraw Hill.
10. Korf, R.E., 1990. Real-time heuristic search. Artificial Intelligence, 42:2-3, pp. 189-211.
11. Kurlander, D. and Ling, D.T., 1995. Planning-Based Control of Interface Animation. Proceedings of the CHI'95 Conference, Denver, ACM Press.
12. Mateas, M., 1997. An Oz-Centric Review of Interactive Drama and Believable Agents. Technical Report CMU-CS-97-156, Department of Computer Science, Carnegie Mellon University, Pittsburgh, USA.
13. Nakatsu, R. and Tosa, N., 1999. Interactive Movies, In: B. Furht (Ed), Handbook of Internet and Multimedia – Systems and applications, CRC Press and IEEE Press.
14. Nilsson, N.J., 1980. Principles of Artificial Intelligence. Palo Alto, CA. Tioga Publishing Company.
15. Nilsson, N.J., 1998. Artificial Intelligence: A New Synthesis. San Francisco, Morgan Kaufmann.
16. Pearl, J., 1984. Heuristics: Intelligent Search Strategies for Computer Problem Solving. Reading (Massachusetts), Addison-Wesley, 1984.
17. Pemberton, J.C. and Korf, R.E., 1994. Incremental Search Algorithms for Real-Time Decision Making. Proceedings of the 2nd Artificial Intelligence Planning Systems Conference (AIPS-94).
18. Perlin, K.and Goldberg, A., 1995. Improv: A System for Scripting Interactive Actors in Virtual Worlds. Proceedings of SIGGRAPH'95, New Orleans (USA).
19. Schank, R.C. and Abelson, R.P., 1977. Scripts, Plans, Goals and Understanding: an Inquiry into Human Knowledge Structures. Hillsdale (NJ): Lawrence Erlbaum.
20. Sgouros, N.M., Papakonstantinou, G. and Tsanakas, P., 1996. A Framework for Plot Control in Interactive Story Systems, Proceedings AAAI'96, Portland, AAAI Press, 1996.

21. Stockman, G.C., 1979. A Minimax Algorithm Better than Alpha-Beta? Artificial Intelligence, 12, pp. 179-196.
22. Swartout, W.R., Gratch, J., Hill, R., Marsella, S., Rickel, J. and Kyriakakis, C., 2001. Toward the Holodeck: Integrating Graphics, Sound, Character and Story. Proceedings of Autonomous Agents 2001, pp. 409-416.
23. Tsuneto, R., Nau, D. and Hendler, J., 1997. Plan-Refinement Strategies and Search-Space Size. Proceedings of the European Conference on Planning, pp. 414-426.
24. Webber, B.N., Badler, N.I., Di Eugenio, B., Geib, C., Levison, L., and Moore, M., 1994. Instructions, Intentions and Expectations, IRCS Technical Report 94-01, University of Pennsylvania.
25. Young, R.M., 2000. Creating Interactive Narrative Structures: The Potential for AI Approaches. AAAI Spring Symposium in Artificial Intelligence and Interactive Entertainment, AAAI Press.

Papous: The Virtual Storyteller

André Silva, Marco Vala, and Ana Paiva

IST / INESC-ID, Rua Alves Redol 9, 1000-029 Lisboa, Portugal
andre.silva@gaips.inesc.pt, marco.vala@gaips.inesc.pt,
ana.paiva@inesc.pt

Abstract. This paper describes the development of Papous, a Virtual Storyteller. Our ultimate goal is to obtain a synthetic character that tells stories in an expressive and believable way, just as a real human storyteller would do. In this paper we describe the first version of Papous, our virtual storyteller. Papous can be seen as a virtual narrator who reads a text enriched with control tags. These tags allow the storywriter to script the behaviour of Papous. There are four types of tags: behaviour tags, where a specific action or gesture is scripted; scene tags, that allows for Papous to change the scene where he tells the story; illumination tags, to allow a new illumination pattern of the scene; and emotion tags, to change the emotional state of Papous. The texts, enriched with these tags, are then processed by Papous' different modules, which contain an affective speech module and an affective body expression module. In this paper we will provide details of the speech, gestures and environment control actions taken by each of the modules of Papous architecture.

1. Introduction

Stories and storytelling are a constant presence in our lives since early childhood. Children like to be told the same story, over and over again, without getting tired of the exact same words. And, the storyteller plays a fundamental role in children's stories. In fact, a storyteller can turn a story into a good or a bad one. A good storyteller is able to drag us into the story, keep our attention and free our imagination. The use of the voice, facial expressions, and the appropriate gestures, are basic ingredients for transforming the content of a simple story into the most fascinating narrative we have ever heard.

But this need for a storyteller to be expressive, to balance the words and the tone, to use gestures appropriately, etc, poses major research challenges if one aims at building a "synthetic" storyteller. However, recent developments of embodied agents [Badler et al. 2000, Cassell 2000, Cassell et al. 1999, Cassell et al. 2000, Churchill et al.] have, during the last few years, shown amazing advances.

Thus, aiming at a synthetic storyteller, we created Papous. The ultimate goal is for Papous to be able to tell the content of a story in a natural way, expressing the proper emotional state as the story progresses and capture the user's attention in the same way a human storyteller would.

A. de Antonio, R. Aylett, and D. Ballin (Eds.): IVA 2001, LNAI 2190, pp. 171-180, 2001.
© Springer-Verlag Berlin Heidelberg 2001

At the present time, our work is still in an early stage. Papous simply acts as a virtual narrator who reads a text enriched with control tags. Such tags allow the storywriter to control the character (its actions and/or emotional state) and the surrounding environment (to achieve a correlation between the story and the ambience). This approach is similar to the one taken by Allison Druin [Druin et al. 1999] where children annotated text so that a robot could produce the appropriate emotions when the story was narrated.

In this paper we will describe the current architecture of Papous, the tags associated to a text, and how storytelling is performed taking into account the described architecture. We will provide details of the speech, gestures and environment control actions taken by each of the modules of Papous architecture. Finally we will describe some results and future work.

2. Architecture

The architecture of Papous, as depicted in Fig. 1, has five components: the *Input Manager*, the *Environment Control*, the *Deliberative Module*, the *Affective Speech* and the *Affective Body Expression*.

The *Input Manager* is the component responsible for processing the text file that contains the story, checking it for syntax and semantic errors, and taking the necessary actions to ensure that the data is correct and ready for the other components to process.

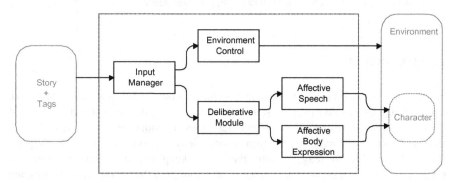

Fig. 1. Architecture

The *Environment Control* is responsible for managing the environment where the character is immersed.

The *Deliberative Module* acts as the mind of the character and, therefore, contains its internal emotional state and is responsible for controlling the character's actions.

The *Affective Speech* is responsible for the voice of the character.

The *Affective Body Expression* is responsible for the appearance of the character.

3. Input Manager

The *Input Manager* receives as input the annotated story file and a set of configuration files. Table 1 summarizes the four types of tags available and explains the function of each one.

Table 1. Tag types

Tag Type	Function
Behaviour (1)	Indicate an action that the character should perform (e.g. **<1*big>**)
Scene (2)	Specify a new scene where the character should be integrated (e.g. **<2*house>**)
Illumination (3)	Specify a new illumination pattern (e.g. **<3*day>**)
Emotion (4)	Explicitly modify the emotional state of the character (e.g. **<4*happiness*80>**)

The list of available tags of each type is defined in a configuration file and depends solely on the available scenes and animations.

We have defined a very small set of tags for demonstration purposes. Fig. 2 illustrates a possible use of these tags.

<2*house> <4*happiness*80> Hello everybody! I am extremely happy today! Lets take the usual tour, ok? **<4*happiness*50>** This is the house I live in. It is a very **<1*big>**big house**<~1*big>**.
Want to go outside? **<2*street>** Ahhh.... isn't this nice? I live in a **<1*small>**small town**<~1*small>** right by the sea... Hmmm....I think it will be dark soon... **<3*night> <4*fear*80>**Oh, I'm so afraid of the dark... Maybe we should get back in the house, right?
<2*house> Hey! Do you like stories? I bet you do! You know, I have a friend named Alex. He is a writer, and he is **<1*tall>**very tall **<~1*tall>**. Much taller than me!... **<4*happiness*20>** I haven't seen him in a while... and that makes me kind of sad...
<4*happiness*50> Anyway, I also have **<1*short>**a very short friend **<~1*short>** named Paul. Hey! We have been talking for a long time... It is almost morning! **<3*day>**
<4*surprise*90>What a marvellous day! **<4*happiness*50>** Come back soon, ok? Bye,bye...

Fig. 2. Example of annotated text

The storywriter is free to use the tags as he pleases, but he should take in consideration the context of the story. For example, if the writer wants to emphasise a particularly scary part of the story, he should specify the appropriate emotional state.

The chosen emotional state will change the voice and the behaviour of the character and, therefore, suit the writer's intentions.

The *Input Manager* parses the annotated text and generates tag-oriented information that is sent to the *Environment Control* and *Deliberative Module* components.

4. Environment Control

The *Environment Control* component receives *scene* and *illumination* tags and changes the environment accordingly.

For demonstration purposes, we have chosen two scenes to immerse the character that can be toggled at anytime during story time. These scenes are briefly described in Table 2.

Table 2. The chosen scenes

Scene	Description
House	This scene represents the inside of a normal house, with some furniture and a fireplace. Decorative paintings exist in the wall, as well as a window showing the outside.
Street	This scene represents a city street. An old building, an alley with a garbage container, two streetlights and a garage.

The same way, we created two illumination patterns that can be applied to both scenes, although the lights that define these two patterns may differ from one scene to the other. Table 3 briefly describes the implemented illumination patterns.

Table 3. The illumination patterns

Illumination pattern	Description
Day	Abundant and natural light. Blue sky can be seen. This is the default illumination pattern.
Night	Less light. Sunset sky can be seen. This illumination pattern includes the use of spotlights.

To achieve smooth transitions between different scenes and illumination patterns we use a *fader* that acts like a theatre curtain. In its normal state, the *fader* is transparent and the scene is completely visible. When there is the need to perform a scene exchange (or an illumination pattern exchange), the visualization window starts to fade out, becoming black and hiding the scene. At this time, the scene and / or the illumination pattern is exchanged, and when it is ready, the visualization window fades in, becoming transparent, and allowing the user to view the scene again.

New scenes and illumination patterns could be added to the application, creating a series of possible environments in which to immerse the character.

5. Deliberative Module

The *Deliberative Module* receives *emotion* and *behaviour* tags and sends commands to the *Affective Speech* and the *Affective Body Expression* components.

The *emotion* tags update the internal emotional state indicating which emotion should be changed and the new value that it must have. Internally, the emotional state of the character is represented by a set of numerical discrete values. Figure 3 indicates the thresholds established for the three emotions used for demonstration purposes.

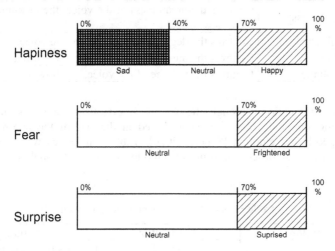

Fig. 3. Emotion thresholds

The emotional state affects the voice and the behaviour of the character. Of course, other emotions and thresholds could be defined, and further divisions could be considered to provide a richer control over the character.

The *behaviour* tags are associated to explicit gestures and result in direct commands to the *Affective Body Expression* component.

6. Affective Speech

The *Affective Speech* component receives sentences and the current emotional state from the *Deliberative Module*, and synthesizes the sentences using the voice to express the current emotions.

The precision with which we control the character's voice depends mostly on the underlying text-to-speech (TTS) system. We used a TTS system that allows the control of seven parameters to completely define the voice. These parameters are explained in Table 4.

Table 4. Voice parameters

Parameter	Description
Pitch baseline	Controls the overall pitch of the voice; high pitches are associated with women, and low pitches with men.
Head size	Controls the deepness of the voice.
Roughness	Controls the roughness of the voice.
Breathiness	Controls the breathiness of the voice; the maximum value yields a whisper.
Pitch fluctuation	Controls the degree of fluctuation of the voice.
Speed	Controls the number of words spoken per minute.
Volume	Controls the volume of the voice, i.e., how loud it sounds.

To transmit emotions through the voice we established a series of relations between emotions and voice parameters based in theories of the interrelationship between speech and emotion [Scherer 2000]. Table 5 indicates which parameters should be changed in order to transmit the emotion we intend through the character's voice.

Table 5. Emotions / TTS parameter correlation

Emotion	Parameter	Action
Happiness/Sadness	Speed	Increase/Decrease
	Pitch Baseline	Increase/Decrease
	Pitch Fluctuation	Increase/Decrease
Fear	Pitch Baseline	Decrease
	Pitch Fluctuation	Increase
	Breathiness	Increase
Surprise	Pitch Baseline	Increase
	Pitch Fluctuation	Increase
	Speed	Decrease

Another important aspect is the correct use of pauses, since pauses are very important to achieve natural speech. It is of critical importance that the voice pauses appropriately, considering the punctuation marks used.

To achieve the correct treatment of text pauses we classify the text into categories, which allow the application to be more specific in processing and interpreting the different punctuations marks that appear in the input file. Table 6 explains the different categories and the pause length associated with each of them.

Table 6. Text pauses

Text Category	Form*	Pause (ms)
Words	<Sentence>	100
Exclamation	<Sentence> !	500
Interrogation	<Sentence> ?	200
Period	<Sentence> .	200
Comma	<Sentence> ,	150
Omission points	<Sentence> ...	800

* <Sentence> = [a-zA-Z\']+

7. Affective Body Expression

The *Affective Body Expression* component receives the current emotional state from the *Deliberative Module* and changes the character body in order to express the desired emotions. It can also receive commands to perform gestures explicitly indicated in the story (using *behaviour* tags).

We use the body expression component provided by the SAFIRA toolkit [André et al. 2001]. This component is able to perform real-time blending between animations and body postures to convey the desired emotions.

However, at the current state of development, the emotions affect only the face of the character. For demonstration purposes we considered two facial animations (happy and sad) that are related with the *happiness* threshold.

Fig. 4. The character is *happy* (left) or *sad* (right)

We have also defined a set of iconic gestures (*big, small, tall* and *short*) that can be explicitly indicated in the story. The writer should be careful in using *behaviour* tags to perform explicit gestures, as they only benefit the story if the performed action is coherent with the current story context.

Fig. 5. The character is indicating something is *big* (left) or *small* (right)

Fig. 6. The character is indicating someone is *tall* (left) or *short* (right)

To hide the absence of lip synchronization we use a single gesture that sequentially opens and closes the Papous' mouth. Since the speech is combined with the other gestures (specially the iconic gestures), the problem of lack of lip synch is reduced.

8. Concluding Remarks

The overall goal was achieved and Papous can already convey some emotions and tell a story that is amusing and a delight to hear. So, in general, the overall approach (architecture and module design) seems to be adequate for the intended purpose.

However, Papous has some limitations that must be improved. The most noticeable is the TTS system, which does not provide a great deal of flexibility when it comes to using its parameters to express the emotions we want. The voice seems to be more synthetic than we had hoped for.

The bodily expression is understandable, but limited by the number of available animations. From time to time, the absence of lip synchronization is also very noticeable.

Note that the current state of development of the project does not introduce a great degree of autonomy. In reality, the character is explicitly and externally controlled by the input file, which works almost as a scripting language. Naturally, the character's autonomy and sensitivity to context will be further developed, as an obvious evolution for the storytelling character.

9. Future Work

The aspect we intend to improve the most is the autonomy of the storytelling character. The idea is to automatically detect the emotional, behavioural and environmental changes from the text, without using tags. Further, Papous will try to get some input from the user and environment (user's reaction to the story) and adapt some parts of the storytelling to that user.

We also intend to replace the TTS system with one capable of guaranteeing an affective speech system as proposed by Cahn [Cahn 1990] (with the one provided by the SAFIRA toolkit [André et al. 2001]).

Further, we will enlarge the available database with new scenes and animations to enhance the semantic richness of the application.

We are also considering embedding Papous into applications such as Teatrix [Paiva et al. 2001]. To do that, the text needs to be generated automatically from within the application.

Acknowledgements. The authors would like to thank Marco Costa and Fernando Rebelo for the artwork, and André Vieira, Filipe Dias, José Rodrigues and Bruno Araújo for their help, ideas and comments.

This work has been partially supported by the EU funded SAFIRA project number IST-1999-11683. Ana Paiva has also been partially supported by the POSI programme (do Quadro Comunitário de Apoio III).

References

[André et al. 2001] André E., Arafa Y., Gebhard P., Geng W., Kulessa T., Martinho C., Paiva. A., Sengers P., and Vala M.: SAFIRA Deliverable 5.1 – Specification of Shell for Emotional Expression (2001). http://gaips.inesc.pt/safira

[Badler et al. 2000] Badler N.I., Zhao L., and Noma T.: Design of a Virtual Human Presenter (2000).

[Cahn 1990] Cahn, J.E.: The Generation of Affect in Synthesized Speech. Journal of the American Voice I/O Society, Vol. 8 (1990) 1-19.

[Cassell 2000] Cassell J.: Nudge Nudge Wink Wink: Elements of Face-to-Face Conversation for Embodied Conversational Agents (2000).

[Cassell et al. 1999] Cassell J., Bickmore T., Billinghurst M., Campbell L., Chang K., Vilhjálmsson H., and Yan H.: Embodiment in Conversational Interfaces: REA (1999).

[Cassell et al. 2000] Cassell J., Bickmore T., Campbell L., Vilhjálmsson H., and Yan H.: Human Conversation as a System Framework: Designing Embodied Conversational Agents (2000).

[Churchill et al.] Churchill E.F., Cook L., Hodgson P., Prevost S., and Sullivan J.W.: "May I Help You?": Designing Embodied Conversational Agent Allies.

[Druin et al. 1999] Druin A., Montemayor J., Hendler J., McAlister B., Boltman A., Fiterman E., Plaisant A., Kruskal A., Olsen H., Revett I., Schwenn T., Sumida L., and Wagner R.: Designing PETS: A Personal Electronic Teller of Stories (1999).

[Paiva et al. 2001] Paiva A., Machado I., and Prada R.: Heroes, Villains and Magicians: Dramatis Personae in Virtual Environments. In Intelligent User Interfaces, ACM Press (2001).

[Scherer 2000] Scherer K.R.: Emotion effects on voice and speech: Paradigms and approaches to evaluation. Presentation held at ISCA Workshop on Speech and Emotion, Belfast (2000).

A Dramatised Actant Model for Interactive Improvisational Plays

Martin Klesen[1], Janek Szatkowski[2], and Niels Lehmann[2]

[1] German Research Center for Artificial Intelligence GmbH,
Stuhlsatzenhausweg 3, D-66123 Saarbrücken, Germany
klesen@dfki.de
[2] University of Århus, Department of Dramaturgy,
Langelandsgade 139, 8000 Århus C, Denmark
{drajsz, dranl}@mail.hum.au.dk

Abstract. We want to provide children, who have been shown to be highly skilled improvisers, with synthetic actors for interactive improvisational plays. Using a conflict oriented play structure we let them experience dramatic situations. Our Dramatised Actant Model maintains a dynamic balance between the opposing forces: a user-controlled avatar and several system characters. The model ensures there is a reasonable amount of interaction between the virtual characters even if the user is not actively contributing to the emergent narrative. We illustrate how the model can be instantiated and realised by presenting a first scenario called "The Black Sheep". We also give an overview of our 3D virtual environment platform and deliberative agent architecture that we have used to implement the virtual puppet theatre.

1 Introduction

To improvise is to play. When children play they improvise. Improvisation can, just like a play or a game, be kept alive as long as there are new initiatives that surprise and give impulses for the players to continue. Recent research in children's play has shown that children are highly skilled improvisers who can keep up their games and playing for a substantial period of time while using a complex dramaturgical structure [5]. Building on previous work on interactive drama [14,26], interactive improvisation [2,7,8] and embodied, interactive characters [1,21,27], we want to provide them with synthetic actors for interactive improvisational plays and frame situations which allow the children to experience significant dramaturgical structures (e.g. conflict, transformation, status changes). Our synthetic actors will be given a role and a dramaturgical task to fulfill using a character-specific repertoire of expressive behaviors. This means they offer the potential for the child to "read" the motivations and intentions of the characters in situations, which are still "playful". The cognitive benefits of this can be referred to the child's developmental transition to decentred allocentric thought [18,19]. The work presented in this paper is part of the Puppet

A. de Antonio, R. Aylett, and D. Ballin (Eds.): IVA 2001, LNAI 2190, pp. 181–194, 2001.

Project[1] which aims at extending current forms of early learning by developing a virtual puppet theatre for young children which supports learning through creative play [22].

Our improvisational plays rely on *emergent narrative* "[. . .] in which explicit narrative structure is absent but narrative frequently emerges through character interaction." [2]. To ensure that there is a reasonable amount of interaction between the virtual characters and the user, we decided to investigate a conflict orientated play structure. Such a scenario is less likely to stagnate as each move by one player will provoke a countermove by another player. Our conflict-driven Dramatised Actant Model maintains a dynamic balance between opposing forces: a user-controlled avatar and the main character(s). This is achieved via a helper agent that temporarily adopts the role of the user and fulfills the dramaturgical task associated with that role in case the opposing forces in the scenario are unbalanced. We illustrate how the model can be instantiated and realised by presenting our first improvisational scenario called "The Black Sheep". Though we have not yet completed the character design and behavior modeling for all characters in our scenario, we hope the preliminary specification and the examples given throughout the paper will show the validity of our approach.

The rest of the paper is organized as follows. In Sect. 2 we introduce the concept of *framed improvisation* and show how it can be applied to interactive improvisational plays using our Dramatised Actant Model. Section 3 describes how the model is instantiated and realised in "The Black Sheep" scenario before we discuss the character design and behavior modeling in Sect. 4. What follows in Sect. 5 is a concise description of our virtual puppet theatre and agent architecture. Section 6 discusses relevant earlier work and how we relate our own approach to it, before we conclude in Sect. 7 with an outline of our current and future research activities.

2   Framed Improvisation

The art of improvisational theatre is the art of framing: creating interesting scenarios for the improviser to be and act in. In order to improvise, one should know who am I playing (character, role), where are the events taking place (setting, props), what happens (task, status) and when (time, duration). These questions can be answered with different levels of detail but it is important that the actor/improviser does not get lost. S/he needs clues to what is happening because to improvise together means to interact constantly and to built significance accumulatively. In our case the synthetic actors and the child should jointly create "stories" with a dramatic structure based on interesting clashes of opposed wills.

---

[1] The Esprit Project "Puppet" is funded by the European Community within the i3-ese programme (Experimental School Environments). The project partners are: The University of Aalborg, Denmark (Laboratory of Computer Vision and Media Technology), the University of Århus, Denmark (Department of Dramaturgy), The German Research Center for Artificial Intelligence GmbH, and the University of Sussex, UK (School of Cognitive and Computing Sciences).

Within this context drama is seen to appear when the protagonist meets resistance as s/he tries to fulfill his or her intention(s) and so becomes the driving force of action. One such conflict-driven model is the Dramatised Actant Model as explained in the following section.

2.1 Dramatised Actant Model

Based on studies of folk tales the Russian formalist Propp observed structural dynamics as possible driving forces in such tales [20]. The French narratologist Greimas simplified Propp's model and described an *Actant Model* [4]. In its simple version the Actant Model describes the dynamic forces and their positions in a narrative economy. The dynamic force is called an "Actant". In a fairy tale, for instance, a prince may be the leading character in the narration. As an Actant he is positioned as the subject whose project works as the centre of gravity in the story. Greimas constructed his narratological model primarily to describe epic narrative. In order to tailor this model to the needs of improvisational drama, we made some adjustments and named it a *Dramatised Actant Model* (see Fig. 1).

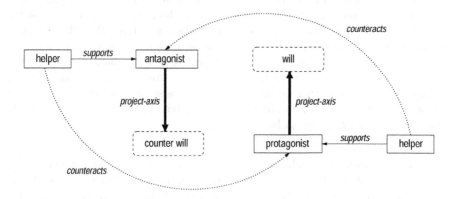

Fig. 1. Dramatised Actant Model with generic roles and tasks.

As Ruth Aylett pointed out, the concept of emergent narrative requires that "Enough interaction between virtual characters must exist, independently of the user's role, to produce narrative in this way." [2]. The main rationale behind our modified Actant Model is therefore a drive to combine protagonist and antagonist on a parallel *project-axis*. The project-axis describes the project (e.g. the prince's longing for the princess) where a given subject wants to achieve a certain goal. We have also seen a need to appoint both the protagonist and the antagonist with a helper in order to ensure that there is enough interaction between characters even if the user is passive. The helper will of course be the opponent of the opposite part. This system is basically symmetric, and it should provide us with the most basic needs in a simplified dramatic conflict.

2.2 Dramaturgical Requirements

With respect to our Dramatised Actant Model we identified a number of dramaturgical requirements both on the ensemble level, concerning the character interaction and coordination, and on the character level, concerning the way a character's behavior expresses his motivations and intentions.

Balancing Forces. We think the most interesting point in this scenario is the tension between the two forces. Who will win? Good or evil? Order or chaos? As we all know from books or movies, it should not be too easy for one side or the other to achieve their goals. It is this continuous shift that makes a story interesting. Here we have the additional problem that the child is supposed to play the role of the protagonist or antagonist by controlling one of the characters in the improvisational scenario. But what happens if the child is too passive? We should clearly avoid that the action comes to a halt. This is the main reason why we introduced the two helper agents. It is their task to intervene if the other side gets too strong. This raises another question: How should the helpers know when this situation occurs? What we need is some way to monitor the *achievement level* of the opposing forces. This should be done by defining a set of parameters that can be expressed as measurable criteria about the current state of the world. We give an example of this in Sect. 3 when describing the "Black Sheep" scenario. When modeling the characters as autonomous agents—incrementally building and updating their world model from sensorial information—we get a *subjective* assessment of the achievement level. Alternatively, we might use a kind of state manager that makes an *objective* assessment based on a God's eye view on the current state of the world. The later approach makes it easier to coordinate characters and to balance forces.

Expressiveness. For each character we must ensure a sufficient expressiveness in terms of facial expressions, gestures, postures, vocalisations (speech and non-speech), etc. to allow the legibility of internal states such as emotions and motivations. If this behavior does not lend itself to a meaningful interpretation, how should the child know how to react? Especially in cases were these signals are ambiguous or for some reason hard to decode (e.g. depending on the avatar's position in the 3D virtual world the child may not see the farmer's face properly) the coherence of behavior, i.e. the recognizable continuity of activities and events is very important. To enable children to participate in improvisational plays we have to "[...] design artificial agents that produce narratively comprehensible behavior by structuring their visible acitivity in ways that make it easy for humans to create narrative explanations of them." [23]. To avoid abrupt changes we will use so called *transition behaviors* to explicitly model the transition between behaviors [24]. For example, it would look strange if a cow that was panicking and running away would simply resume its abandoned grazing behavior. One could therefore introduce the transition "turn around with decreasing frequency" to show diminishing alertness.

3   Black Sheep Scenario

The first step towards a concretization of our Dramatised Actant Model is to provide the protagonist with a will. Here we have chosen a will for order. We think it might be interesting to investigate what children would do in a situation dealing with chaos and order. The next step is then to choose a setting, define characters and roles, and specify goals and behaviors that express this will for order or chaos. Our first improvisational scenario called "The Black Sheep" involves a farmer, his dog, a black sheep, a grey sheep, cows, and pigs. The farmer as our protagonist is trying to create order on the farm. Order to the farmer means herding his animals to keep them in their stables and within fences, to feed them and make them stay in their folds. The child who is given the black sheep as avatar is supposed to play the role of the antagonist by challenging this order. So whenever the child gets a chance, it should try to destroy the order established by the farmer. This clash of wills will be the top-level driving force in this scenario and the central focus for all characters.

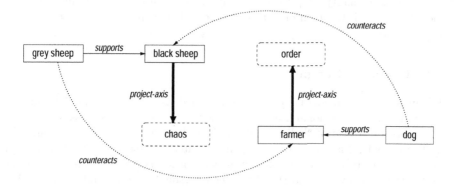

Fig. 2. Dramatised Actant Model with instantiated roles and tasks.

We envision at least two experimental settings. In the first the child is instructed *before* the improvisational play starts. In the second the child has to figure out for itself what's going on between the characters and what its own role may be *during* the improvisation. In either case the dog will help the farmer whereas the grey sheep is allied with the black sheep. The instantiated Dramatised Actant Model is depicted in Fig. 2. The dog and the grey sheep are of high importance because they help to increase the distance to the equilibrium if the child is (too) passive. The specification of the Black Sheep scenario therefore meets the dramaturgical requirements (see Sect. 2) by balancing the opposing forces.

Parameters for assessing the achievement level are for example: the cows being milked and the pigs being cleaned and either in or near their respective stables within a given time. If the achievement level is near chaos, the grey sheep as helper of the antagonist will be idle. In between chaos and order it will support the black sheep with low initiative, e.g. just following it and scare the pigs or the cows a bit. However, if the farmer has almost succeeded in creating order (e.g. because the child was too passive) the grey sheep will act with high initiative, i.e. try to release the animals and move them away from their stables. This distinction between farmer and black sheep as protagonist and antagonist on the one hand and dog and grey sheep as their helpers on the other hand will be reflected in the definition of their individual goals and behaviors and by the status they take in the social interaction with the other animals as outlined in the next section.

4   Characters and Behavior

Using autonomous agents as improvisational puppets we share the view of Barbara Hayes-Roth: "[. . .] our goal is to build synthetic *actors*, not synthetic individuals, we focus on *artistic* models of character, rather than psychological models of personality." [9]. Consequently, in the character design and behavior modeling we will focus on only those aspects that help a character to fulfill its role and task.

4.1   Character Design

In our system each virtual puppet is modeled as an intentional autonomous agent. The improvisational frame that defines a character's role, task, and status is mapped onto a set of "beliefs", "desires", and "intentions". These are encoded as facts, goals, and plans in our agent architecture (see Sect. 5.1). For each agent we specify individual goals with varying levels of importance, *proactive* and *reactive* behaviors, and the character's personality traits and emotions. We use the word "proactive" to express that an agent does not simply act in response to the environment, but also initiates actions on its own, in particular to achieve its goals. Reactive behaviors on the other hand are usually event driven and bound to the activities of other agents.

To determine an agent's affective state(s) we use the *Affective Reasoning Engine* that was developed as part of the in-house PRESENCE[2] project. It is based on the cognitive model of emotions introduced by Ortony, Clore, and Collins [17]. The local variables in the model, e.g. the desirability of events with respect to an agent's goals, the praiseworthiness of actions with respect to a set of standards, and the appealingness of objects with respect to a set of attitudes are expressed as *Emotion Eliciting Conditions*. Each EEC is described by a set of attributes, e.g. *Desire-self* and *Desire-other*—the agent's assessment of the desirability of an event for itself or another agent, *Evaluation*—the agent's assessment of an action as praiseworthy or blameworthy, *Appealingness*—the agent's assessment of an object or agent as appealing or unappealing, etc. Once values for these

---

[2] Consult our webpage for further details: http://www.dfki.de/cyberella/

attributes are given, we can deduce the agent's current emotional state using the emotion eliciting rules in the OCC-Model. For example, if an event is *fairly desirable* for the agent and the confirmation status of the prospective event is *moderately* unconfirmed[3], we can infer that the current emotional state of the agent is *hope*.

To specify an agent's personality we use the Five-Factor Model [16] and concentrate on the traits *extraversion, agreeableness,* and *neuroticism.* Personality traits affect the intensity of emotional states, e.g. a happy agent tends to be more happy if the agent's personality is extravert and agreeable. Emotions will be primarily conveyed by facial expressions, posture, gait (e.g. cow walking slowly with head bend if sad) and non-verbal utterances (a cat will purr if it is happy and hiss if it is angry). Personality traits, emotions, and the status of an agent are also used as filters to constrain the selection and instantiation of behaviors.

4.2   Behavior Modeling

To facilitate the behavior authoring we abstract from individual behaviors and use so-called *behavior modes* when specifying the behavior models for our agents. Behaviors within the same behavior mode try to achieve the same goal(s) and have the same priorities. Once we have defined the transitions between modes we can easily provide new behaviors within a specific mode. Figure 3 shows the behavior model for the grey sheep where the numbers specify the priorities of the behaviors in this mode. The *default mode* has the lowest priority and comprises an agent's idle time behaviors. If the achievement level exceeds a certain threshold indicating that the farmer has almost achieved order, the grey sheep enters its *project mode* and tries to fulfill its goal by releasing the animals (see Sect. 3). Having, for example, moved the pig away from its pen, the grey sheep will go to to *success mode* whereas it will go to *failure mode* when being interrupted by the farmer. Both success and failure can be expressed in many ways depending on the personality traits and the current emotional state without having to change the behavior model.

The *interaction mode* is entered when the grey sheep receives a request from another agent or the avatar. It will then select one the reactive behaviors that are applicable in this situation. This behavior will overrule any other activities unless the grey sheep is in success mode as behaviors in this mode have an even higher priority. When the grey sheep leaves the interaction mode it reenters the previous mode, i.e. if it was in project mode it checks if the context is still valid and resumes the suspended goal(s).

5   The Virtual Puppet Theatre

Creating synthetic agents that respond to users and to each other in real-time while being not simply lifelike but taking into account some author-defined dramatic structure is a complex and challenging task, even more so if these agents

---

[3] The fuzzy labels used here to describe EEC values are internally converted to real numbers between 0.0 and 1.0.

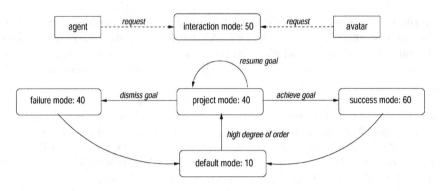

Fig. 3. Behavior model for the grey sheep.

inhabit a dynamic 3D virtual world. We accepted this challenge and developed a layered architecture with the following objectives: 1) providing a common platform (layer of services) for all 3D agents upon which specific characters can be built 2) deploying a customized BDI-theoretic agent architecture to implement the proactive and reactive behaviors, and 3) using a simple yet powerful percept and action handling mechanism that makes it possible to initiate actions at lower levels that are carried out autonomously (e.g. maintain a certain distance to another agent) returning an exit status only if they fail or are superceded by another action.

Similar to the systems described in [8] and [13] we separate the high-level behavior planning and affective reasoning (the "mind") from the motion planning and control modules (the "body"). The first is done by the agent architecture as described in the next section and the latter lies within the responsibility of the 3D virtual environment platform. Figure 4 gives an overview of the Virtual Puppet Theatre (VPT) system. The *Mind Module* sits on top of a *Body Module* that autonomously and efficiently executes the delegated tasks while providing the higher layer with enough information to react to the unexpected behavior of the (human) improviser. The agents' physical actions (movements, animations, sounds) are executed and rendered (graphically and auditorially) by the *Virtual Environment Server*. For each virtual puppet new instances of the mind and body module are created and connected to the VPT system. The 3D virtual environment platform comprising the Virtual Environment Server and the Body Module was developed by our project partner, the Laboratory of Computer Vision and Media Technology at the University of Aalborg, Denmark.

5.1   Mind Module

The Mind Module is responsible for the classification and interpretation of incoming percepts and for the instantiation and execution of character-specific behaviors. We decided to use the BDI-theorectic Jam Agent Architecture [10] to implement intentional autonomous agents because it meets many requirements

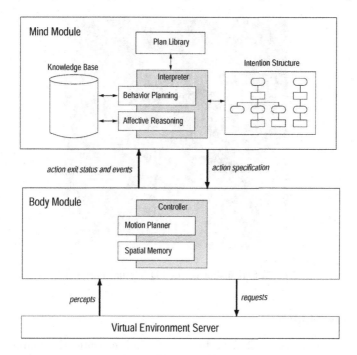

Fig. 4. Overview of the VPT System Design.

for believable social agents [6]: multiple active goals and multiple plans for each goal (e.g. to increase the variety of behaviors), changing priorities of behaviors and goals at runtime (e.g. to reflect changes in the emotional state), and behavior switching mechanisms (e.g. to implement transition behaviors).

The Jam Agent Architecture consists of a knowledge base, a plan library, an interpreter and an intention structure as shown in Fig. 4. The *knowledge base* is a database that contains the world model (the "beliefs") of a character. The *plan library* is a collection of plans that an agent can use to achieve its goals, and the *intention structure* is an internal model of the current goals (the "desires") and instantiated plans (the "intentions") of that agent. Conflict resolution, plan selection, instantiation and execution are handled by the Jam *interpreter*. The interpreter is designed to allow only one goal to be followed at one time. Therefore at any decision point, each goal's importance is combined with the utility of the selected and instantiated plan to compute how important it is for that goal to execute under the current circumstances. All instantiated goals are then sorted in order of priority, with only one goal executing at any one time (the highest priority goal) all others are suspended, waiting to start or resume executing. At any time the current goal can be interrupted and suspended if a higher priority goal is spawned.

Fig. 5. Screenshot of the 3D Virtual Farmyard.

5.2   Body Module

The Body Module (see [12] for a full description) executes the commands it receives from the Mind Module and maintains symbolic representations of the 3D virtual environment. It consists of three main elements: 1) a spatial memory, 2) a motion planner, and 3) a controller as shown in Fig. 4. The *spatial memory* is used to store information about all perceived objects. Percepts are generated by the Virtual Environment Server and used to gradually expand (and maintain) the contents of the spatial memory. The perceptual system is realised by simulated senses, the most important being: vision, hearing, and tactile. The *motion planner* is used to compute an obstacle free path from the current position to some desired goal point. The *controller* monitors all ongoing actions and returns an *action exit status* to the Mind Module that indicates how the respective action terminated. This information (success or kind of failure) is used in the high-level behavior planning as a synchronization and feedback mechanism, e.g. to trigger an alternative plan if some branch failed. In the following example a 'face' action is sent to the Body Module which instructs the 3D agent to look in the direction of the specified object. If the object is not visible, the Mind Module receives an action exit status indicating that the object has vanished. The current plan will then spawn a subgoal to perform a 'look_for' behavior. If it turns out that the object is not within vision range, the plan fails.

Example of a Jam plan with recovery from action failure.

```
Plan: {
GOAL: PERFORM face_object $OBJECT;
BODY:
  PERFORM send_action (+ "face " $OBJECT) $ACTION_STATUS;
```

```
WHEN : TEST (!(FACT ACTION_COMPLETED $ACTION_STATUS)) {
   OR {
        TEST (FACT OBJECT_VANISHED $ACTION_STATUS);
        PERFORM look_for $OBJECT;
   }{
        FAIL;
   };
 };
}
```

The Body Module is designed as a common platform (layer of services) for all 3D agents upon which specific characters can be built. It currently supports more than 20 *low-level actions* (move to a specific location, follow another agent, face an object, etc.) that can be parameterized, e.g. by changing the speed of moving and turning. These low-level actions are implemented as Finite State Automata (FSA) that form a hierarchy and can be combined in arbitrary ways, i.e. the Body Module executes a complex action (e.g. follow another agent) as a combination of more primitive ones (move forward, turn, etc.). The Mind Module has access to all actions in this hierarchy. When defining the high-level behavior of the virtual puppets these generic low-level actions can be combined with character-specific animations and sounds (e.g. the dog can follow the farmer, wag the tail, and bark simultaneously) providing us with a broad range of expressive gestures, postures, gaits, and utterances for each character.

6   Related Research

During the last few years, an increasing number of attempts have been made to develop systems for "Interactive Drama" where the user can modify the course of actions. We think it might be useful to classify the different approaches along two dimensions. The first dimension is the level of authoring involved. It ranges from free-play or "pure" improvisation to highly structured scenarios as found e.g. in interactive fiction. Another way to describe this is to use the terms *character-centric* and *author-centric* depending on who shapes the structure of an inter-active story. The higher the level of authoring the easier or more likely is it to create dramatic situations, like, for instance, a conflict between two characters and how it is solved. The second dimension is the level of freedom the user has to interact with the characters. It ranges from no freedom or infrequent interac-tion (e.g. being merely an observer or being offered a limited number of choices) to full control over one or several characters (e.g. using an avatar in a virtual environment). In between the user has only partial control, e.g. he might give the characters abstract instructions which they then act out autonomously. The level of authoring and the level of freedom the user has are conflicting in the sense that the user interaction may destroy the dramatic experience intended by the author. Various solutions to this problem have been proposed. In some sense they all try to help or force the user to contribute positively to the emergent narrative.

Barbara Hayes-Roth and her group were among the first to use autonomous agents as synthetic actors in improvisational plays. Their master-servant scenario [9] is a good example for an author-centric system without runtime intervention. Their definition of "directed improvisation" where the directions are given in advance of the performance maps nicely to what we called "framed improvisation" in Sect. 2. They developed a Computer-Animated Improvisational Theater (CAIT) where each child controls his or her character's behavior by means of a dynamic "situated behavior menu" which displays physical and verbal behaviors that the character is "considering" at each momenet in time [7]. This is an example of a character-centric scenario where the user has partial control over the synthetic actors. The main difference to our system is that here the child is responsible for the framing and playcrafting. The situated behavior menu helps by restricting the range of possible actions to the ones that are appropriate given the current situation but not in creating a dramatic situation.

Within our Dramatised Actant Model the conflict is the core of the dramatic narrative. There are two other systems where the notion of conflict is primary and which use Propp's model [20] to establish a set of functions that compose the structure of a story. In [26] a "story engine" uses a "narrative logic" that contains rules of how the story can evolve to select actions according to their dramatic intensity. Similar to [14,25] they take a strong author-centric perspective and try to establish some kind of global control mechanism. In [11] the authors introduce the idea of a "support agent" that informs the child that in a given situation she/he might direct her/his character to perform a certain action like "bewitch the boy" that would create a dramatic situation. However in their story creation environment the children are free to direct their characters, so the child could decide not to perform the action. It also remains unclear who controlls the supporting agents and the story flow.

Our Black Sheep scenario (see Sect. 3) makes a compromise between the character-centric and author-centric approaches described above. We use our Dramatised Actant Model to add dramaturgical constraints to the free-play investigated in earlier research without having to implement a story engine or drama/plot manager. Our improvisational model is purely situational assuming no causal-linear time, i.e. there is no beginning, middle, and end. It therefore lacks the narrative structure required for interactive *drama* in the strong sense of the word. Nevertheless by putting on stage a conflict between farmer and black sheep avatar/grey sheep helper we will provide the child with some dramatic experience. This tells us apart from other systems where the user also has a high level of freedom to interact with the VE like, for instance, the *sheep/dog: Trial by Eire* scenario developed by the Synthetic Characters Group at MIT Media Lab[4] where the user plays the role of a shepherd in a virtual sheep herding competition. Focusing on learning, action selection and motor control in autonomous characters they want to build a synthetic canine whose abilities approach that of a real canine. We want to create synthetic *actors*, not synthetic individuals, i.e. we focus on *artistic* rather than behavioral models of character.

---

[4] Consult their webpage for further details:
http://gonzo.media.mit.edu/public/web/group.php?id=5

7 Conclusion

We showed how concepts and techniques from improvisational theatre can be used to structure the interaction between the user and a group of interactive characters. We view the improvisational frame as a collection of contextual constraints for the characters' behaviors, i.e. as a good means of restricting choices while preserving the agents' autonomy. We introduced the Dramatised Actant Model and demonstrated how it can be applied in interactive improvisational plays to balance the level of authoring and the level of freedom the user has as an active participant in such a play. By imposing such a conflict oriented dramatic structure onto the improvisation we give the child the opportunity to explore its dynamics (e.g. the balance between the two forces, status changes, etc.) within a clearly framed situation without having to implement global control mechanisms. The system currently under development will be evaluated by our project partners from the School of Cognitive and Computing Sciences at the University of Sussex with 6 to 8 years old children. They will investigate in particular if the children can "read" the motivations and intentions of the improvisational characters, if they find the overall interaction engaging, and how they contribute to the emergent narrative.

References

[1] E. André, editor. *Proceedings of the i3 Spring Days Workshop on Behavior Planning for Life-Like Characters and Avatars*, Sitges, Spain, Mar. 1999.
[2] R. Aylett. Narrative in virtual environments - towards emergent narrative. In Mateas and Sengers [15].
[3] O. Etzioni, J. P. Müller, and J. M. Bradshaw, editors. *Proceedings of the Third Annual Conference on Autonomous Agents*, NY, May 1999. ACM Press.
[4] A. Greimas and J. Courtes. *Semiotics and Language: An Analytical Dictionary*. Indiana University Press, Bloomington, IN, 1982.
[5] G. F. Guss. *Drama Performance in Children's Play-Culture. The Possibilities and Significance of Form*. PhD thesis, NTNU Trondheim Norwegian University of Science and Technology, 2000.
[6] A. Guye-Vuillème and D. Thalmann. Requirements for an architecture for believable social agents. In C. Sierra, G. Maria, and J. S. Rosenschein, editors, *Proceedings of the Fourth International Conference on Autonomous Agents*, pages 48–49, NY, June 2000. ACM Press.
[7] B. Hayes-Roth, E. Sincoff, L. Brownston, R. Huard, and B. Lent. Directed improvisation. Technical report KSL-94-61, Knowledge Systems Laboratory, Stanford University, Palo Alto, CA, Sept. 1994.
[8] B. Hayes-Roth and R. van Gent. Story-making with improvisational puppets. In *Proceedings of the First International Conference on Autonomous Agents*, Marina del Ray, CA, 1997. ACM Press.
[9] B. Hayes-Roth, R. van Gent, and D. Huber. Acting in character. In Trappl and Petta [27], pages 92–112. Also available as Stanford Knowledge Systems Laboratory Report KSL-96-13.
[10] M. Huber. A BDI-theoretic mobile agent architecture. In Etzioni et al. [3], pages 236–243.

[11] I. Machado and A. Paiva. Heroes, villains, magicians,...: Believable characters in a story creation environment. In *AI-ED'99 Workshop on Animated and Personified Pedagogical Agents*, Le Mans, France, 1999.

[12] C. B. Madsen and E. Granum. Aspects of interactive autonomy and perception. In L. Qvortrup, editor, *Virtual Interaction: Interaction in Virtual Inhabited 3D Worlds*, chapter 9, pages 183–210. Springer, Oct. 2000.

[13] C. Martinho and A. Paiva. Pathematic agents: Rapid development of believable emotional agents in intelligent virtual environments. In Etzioni et al. [3], pages 1–8.

[14] M. Mateas. An Oz-centric review of interactive drama and believable agents. Technical report CMU-CS-97-157, School of Computer Science, Carnegie Mellon University, 1997.

[15] M. Mateas and P. Sengers, editors. *AAAI Fall Symposium on Narrative Intelligence*, Nov. 1999.

[16] R. McCrae and O. John. An introduction to the five-factor model and its implications. *Journal of Personality*, 60:171–215, 1992.

[17] A. Ortony, G. L. Clore, and A. Collins. *The Cognitive Structure of Emotions*. Cambridge University Press, Cambridge, MA, 1988.

[18] J. Piaget. *The Child's Conception of Space*. Routledge and Keagan, London, 1956.

[19] J. Piaget. *Play, Dreams and Imitation in Childhood*. Routledge and Keagan, London, 1962.

[20] V. A. Propp. *Morphology of the Folktale*. University of Texas Press, Austin and London, June 1968.

[21] J. Rickel, editor. *Proceedings of the Workshop on Achieving Human-Like Behavior in Interactive Animated Agents*, Barcelona, Spain, June 2000.

[22] M. Scaife and the Puppet Project Team. Imagination, creativity and new forms of learning: Designing a virtual theatre for young children. In M. Caenepeel, D. Benyon, and D. Smith, editors, *Proceedings of the i3 Annual Conference*, pages 173–177, Siena, Italy, Oct. 1999.

[23] P. Sengers. Narrative intelligence. In K. Dautenhahn, editor, *Human Cognition and Social Agent Technology*, chapter 1, pages 1–26. John Benjamins Publishing Company, 2000.

[24] P. J. Sengers. Designing comprehensible agents. In D. Thomas, editor, *Proceedings of the 16th International Joint Conference on Artificial Intelligence (IJCAI-99-Vol2)*, pages 1227–1232, S.F., July 31–Aug. 6 1999. Morgan Kaufmann Publishers.

[25] N. M. Sgouros et al. A framework for plot control in interactive story. In *Proceedings of the AAAI*, pages 162–167, 1996.

[26] N. Szilas. Interactive drama on the computer: Beyond linear narrative. In Mateas and Sengers [15].

[27] R. Trappl and P. Petta, editors. *Creating Personalities for Synthetic Actors: Towards Autonomous Personality Agents*, volume 1195 of *Lecture Notes in Computer Science*. Springer-Verlag Inc., New York, NY, 1997.

The InViWo Toolkit: Describing Autonomous Virtual Agents and Avatars

Nadine Richard[1], Philippe Codognet[2], and Alain Grumbach[1]

[1] ENST
46 rue Barrault
75013 Paris, France
{Nadine.Richard, Alain.Grumbach}@enst.fr
[2] LIP6
8, rue du Capitaine Scott
75015 Paris, France
Philippe.Codognet@lip6.fr

Abstract. The INVIWO project aims at providing high-level intuitive tools to describe virtual worlds populated with "intelligent" creatures and avatars. For this purpose, we have defined the MARVIN language, which enables the high-level description of autonomous agent behaviours. In this paper, we present the underlying model we have designed, especially our agent and avatar architectures. We then present the main features of the MARVIN language and we introduce the use of constraints as powerful tools for describing and combining behaviours.

1 Introduction

1.1 Motivations

The INVIWO (*Intuitive Virtual Worlds*) project aims at providing high-level intuitive tools for describing inhabited virtual worlds, *i.e.* synthetic worlds where users can interact with objects and "intelligent" entities. A typical application area is entertainment worlds, such as the Diamond Park [35], a virtual leisure park where various virtual agents could either entertain users (*e.g.* circus agents) or assist them (*e.g.* bus drivers). A key point in the design of virtual worlds is the possibility to define autonomous entities that will "populate" the world and make it more attractive to the user.

Our objective is eventually to provide high-level tools, based on a specific language for agent behaviour description. This language, called MARVIN, enables the advanced user to define basic tasks such as goal-directed navigation or obstacle avoidance, by combining agent behaviours, triggering conditions and high-level goals in a simple way. MARVIN is essentially based on reactive rules, temporal control structures and constraints, and on the primitive actions an agent can perform.

The underlying agent model has been designed as a synthesis and a simplification of existing agent architectures, in order to present a minimal set of

A. de Antonio, R. Aylett, and D. Ballin (Eds.): IVA 2001, LNAI 2190, pp. 195–209, 2001.

components that could be easily manipulated by non-computer scientists. Multi-agent systems are currently widely used to simulate or control complex systems, as they take advantage of the robustness and the flexibility of collaborating, adaptive and autonomous entities. Our agent architecture is fully decentralized and homogeneous.

Figure 1 shows an example of INVIWO worlds: the inhabitants are rabbits moving on a chess board. Each rabbit has to reach several predefined target points. When a rabbit detects a collision risk with an obstacle, for instance when a static cube or another rabbit appears into specified boundaries, it will try to avoid the obstacle while trying not to go too far from its goal trajectory. On the screenshot, the sensibility boundaries are represented as transparent spheres around the characters.

Fig. 1. The autonomous rabbits, seen from the avatar point of view.

1.2   Organization of the Paper

This paper is organized as follows: first, we recall some background material on virtual agents and reactive architectures in section 2. Then section 3 details the model we have designed, *i.e.* the overall architecture we have chosen for inhabited virtual worlds, and the models we have defined for autonomous virtual agents and avatars. In section 4, we propose our approach to ease the description of agent behaviours: we describe our behaviour-based architecture for action selection, we present the MARVIN language and we introduce the use of constraints in our model. Before concluding this paper, we shortly describe the INVIWO toolkit in section 5.

2 Related Work

2.1 Behaviour-Based Architectures

Classical Artificial Intelligence considers cognitive agents, which have symbolic representations of their environment and reasoning capabilities, in order to plan long-term actions. R. Brooks opposes the so-called "new Artificial Intelligence" to the cognitive approach, because of the complexity of the external environment to be symbolically represented [7]. This bottom-up, reactive approach is strongly inspired by ethology and biology; it has been successfully applied to virtual creatures called animats [5,27,30,33] and to behaviour-based robotics [1,7,22]. As purely reactive agents lack of reasoning abilities and high-level, task-oriented behaviours, many authors have been advocating for hybrid agents that combine reactive and cognitive skills and that are thus able to have both reflex and deliberative reactions [1,12,20].

In behaviour-based architectures, sensing, action selection and acting are distributed among independent basic behavioural modules, that interact for achieving particular agent tasks (eating, mating, avoiding predators, *etc.*). The global behaviour of the agent emerges from the interaction of the concurrent modules. Behaviour-based architectures have been first investigated by R. Brooks and his well-known *subsumption architecture*, which consists in hierarchical layers of concurrent behaviours combined with inhibition mechanisms [6]. This architecture has been used for controlling robots that should quickly respond to dynamic and unpredictable environments.

2.2 Virtual Agents

The reactive approach has been extensively used to animate virtual creatures, especially for navigation, obstacle avoidance, schooling and pursuit simulation [23, 24]. A classical example is presented in [34]; the authors have produced realistic animations of artificial fishes by adding biomechanical models to a behavioural architecture. Behaviour-based animations are usually only aimed for spectators that cannot interact with the virtual entities. Yet, there is a strong need for highly-interactive agents, for example in MUD-like worlds, which are designed for gaming and chatting. In such environments, the user becomes a "spectactor" interacting with assistants like hosts and security guards [21], chatterbots like JULIA [17], artificial pets as in the ALIVE system [18] or virtual humans [3,31, 35].

2.3 Describing the Behaviour of Hybrid Agents

Finite-state automata are traditionally used to describe reactive behaviours. Game characters [15] or vehicle simulations [9,19] make use of hierarchical parallell automata, which reduce complexity when designing and executing concurrent behaviours. In particular, the PAT-NETS (*Parallel Transition Networks*) have been introduced for simulating virtual humans [2]. The main drawback of finite-state automata lies in their poor maintainability: a minor modification of the behaviour specification can lead to the complete redefinition of the automata.

Specific languages have been designed for high-level behaviour scripting [3, 16], in particular for reviving the cognitive approach in the field of computer animation [11]. The PAT-NETS have been recently extended with an abstract action model to provide high-level description and parametrization of generic actions [3]. Some efforts have also been made to propose intuitive graphical programming, for example in the VIRTUAL FISHTANK project [32].

3 The InViWo Model

3.1 InViWo Agents and Worlds

We focus on decentralized virtual worlds, where no entity is in charge of managing the world. Unlike in [14], where the authors distinguish virtual humans and smart objects, we have chosen an homogeneous approach: we consider any object as an agent because each object can possibly autonomously react to incoming events. An INVIWO world is therefore a uniform multi-agent system, and the environment of an agent is just the set of the other agents. An INVIWO world is basically a set of agents, with no specific organization; such a world evolves depending on the agent interactions, creations and destructions. INVIWO agents are fully autonomous: the internal state and the behaviour of an agent cannot be directly manipulated by an external entity (a scene manager or another agent). Simpler agents are reactive, but agents that have a structured memory can use it to build their own representation of the environment, in order to make temporal and spatial reasoning.

Our agents communicate with each other *via* what we call *stimuli*. Stimuli are typed messages, which can contain structured data. Interaction with the environment is thus achieved only through message-based communication, according to three modes: unicast, multicast and broadcast communication. The INVIWO world designer can define multi-level communication within the same virtual world by describing appropriate interaction protocols between agents.

3.2 Architecture of the InViWo Agents

An autonomous agent is a computational entity that is able to perceive its environment and act on this environment. It is autonomous since it decides what to do depending on the received stimuli, its own resources and its goals. The behaviour of an agent consists of a set of decision rules which lead to action selection. As shown in figure 2, an INVIWO agent is made of a set of attributes representing the characteristics of the agent (*e.g.* its shape, position, or mood) and its knowledge (*e.g.* a personal map of the world), sensors to perceive internal and external stimuli, effectors to perform internal and external primitive actions, and a decision process.

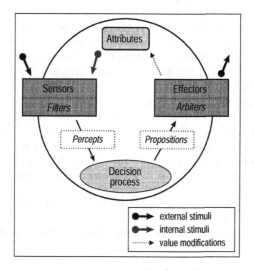

Fig. 2. Basic architecture of an INVIWO agent.

Effectors encapsulate abstract actions to be realized through combinations of primitive actions. Three primitive actions are available:

- Send an external stimulus (according to a specified communication mode).
- Modify the value of an attribute.
- Modify the agent structure by adding or removing a component. This kind of actions enables evolutive agents.

An internal state modification, either a structure or an attribute change, causes the appropriate internal stimulus to be generated. Sensors can receive both external stimuli from the environment and internal stimuli from inside the agent. Figure 2 only represents the attribute modification and reaction, for clarity purposes.

Sensors translate the received stimuli into percepts and send those percepts to the decision process, after a filtering step. Activation bounds can be specified in the sensors as facilities for external stimulus filtering. The decision process is made of independent decision-making units called behavioural modules, which run concurrently to select actions to be performed. A behavioural module is basically a set of rules activated on the received percepts, and that lead to action propositions made to the effectors (see section 4.1 for details). The arbiter associated with an effector should solve the conflicts between the requests from the concurrent behavioural modules when needed: the decision process of an agent is thus shared between the behavioural modules and the arbiters, as in the DAMN architecture [28]. The effectors finally perform the chosen actions.

3.3 The InViWo Avatars

Within a virtual world, the human operator (or user) is usually represented by an avatar, which is in charge of two separate tasks: it represents the user towards the other users, and it includes navigation and basic perception capabilities. In most cases, the object representing the user can move within the world and a camera gives him/her a subjective view of the 3D scene. The simplest way to integrate users into InViWo worlds is to consider the avatar as an agent, which both represents the user towards the other agents, and gives him a personal view of the environment with the capability to act on it: an InViWo avatar is a specific agent, which can be interactively controlled by a human operator. We thus prefer to refer to the InViWo avatar as a mediator of the user, rather than to his/her representation, since it is a bidirectional translator:

- It receives external stimuli, and it informs its user about its internal state and about the environment.
- It executes user commands by modifying its attributes and structure and by sending external stimuli into the environment.

As shown in figure 3, the interaction between the user and his/her avatar is realized by adding specific stimuli called *user stimuli*. The user interface should be able to send and receive user stimuli in order to communicate with the avatar. This model makes the user interface completely independent from the avatar; it also enables two original uses of avatars:

- A user can control several avatars in the same InViWo world, and thus be represented by different characters and perceive the world through different points of view, at the same time.
- An avatar can be controlled by several users, and thus become a "multi-user avatar".

In many existing systems, the user can have multiple views and perform actions in the virtual world, even if the avatar does not have the corresponding sensors and effectors. We think that a user should not be able to do more than his/her avatar can do: the user partly controls his InViWo avatar, but he/she can be constrained by its abilities. When autonomous enough, the avatar may assist the user by executing repetitive or high-precision tasks, like walking on an irregular ground or grasping a glass of water. Moreover, the avatar can have its own personality, and thus constrain the user in a role, in order to get a believable behaviour: for example, a user should not be able to control the lurching behaviour of his drunk avatar.

As an InViWo avatar is an agent, the avatar autonomy can be achieved with little effort: in the example of figure 1, the avatar is based exactly on the same behavioural modules as the rabbits. We just added the ability to take user

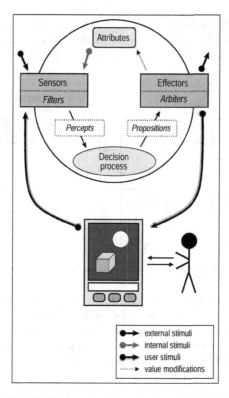

Fig. 3. The INVIWO avatar, the user interface and the user.

inputs into account by adding avatar-specific behavioural modules and the corresponding user stimuli: the user can request to go forward or backward, to turn right or left and to stop walking. Without having to program the corresponding behavioural modules twice, we obtain a semi-autonomous avatar, which avoids static and dynamic obstacles by itself. Conflicts between the autonomous part and the user-controlled part of the agent are solved by the arbiters in an homogeneous way.

4   Describing Virtual Agent Behaviours

4.1   The Behaviour-Based Architecture

Our behaviour-based architecture for action selection is strongly inspired from the principles of reactive synchronous systems, in particular from the ESTEREL language [4]. The INVIWO behavioural modules are reactive, concurrent units that should respond *instantaneously* to input signals by emitting output signals; it means that output signals should be produced in the same instant (timestep) as input signals. Signals are typed messages, which can contain structured values. The outputs of a module can be routed to the inputs of other modules, by creating specific channels; this connection is possible only if the linked ports have the same type. As shown on figure 4, the percepts built by the sensors are actually signals, as well as the action propositions received by the effectors.

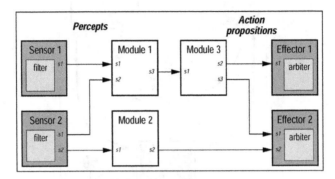

Fig. 4. Example of a behavioural network.

A behavioural module is basically made of a decision process, and possibly of internal variables and encapsulated subbehaviours. The decision process is roughly a set of decision rules, triggered when specific signals are received. The activation of a rule leads to the emission of output signals and possibly to the modification of internal variables. Sensors and effectors are similar to behavioural modules, with some differences:

- A sensor has no input signals, as it receives stimuli; its filter is able to translate the received stimuli into signals.
- An effector has no output signals, as it performs internal and external actions; its arbiter is able to perform primitive actions, such as sending an external stimulus or modifying the value of an attribute.

We have described a decomposition of the decision process into independent, concurrent behavioural modules. This decomposition enables modular programming (*e.g.* in MARVIN) as well as visual component-based description of the behaviour of an INVIWO agent.

4.2   The Marvin Language

The MARVIN language is clearly inspired from ESTEREL, with the addition of object-oriented and agent-oriented features. Agents and agent components are specific objects. Behavioural modules described in MARVIN are composed of an interface and a body: input and output signals are declared in the interface part, and the body part contains a composition of imperative and reactive instructions. A behavioural module can only modify its own state or emit output signals. Sensors and effectors are syntactically similar to behavioural modules, to keep an homogeneous description language.

The following example of a MARVIN description shows how we can describe the management of the agent energy level. This level decreases at each timestep of the agent or when the **Loose** signal is received. We assume that the attributes **energy** and **energy_step** do exist; those attributes can be read by using the **owner** keyword, which refers to the agent:

```
behaviour loose_energy
  in  Loose (int) ;
  out Reduce (int) combine with + ;

  body
    loop
      wait
        Tick -> emit Reduce (owner.energy_step)
      | Loose (a) with [ a > 0 ] -> emit Reduce (a)
      end wait
    end loop
  end body
end behaviour
```

The **Tick** signal, used in the first reactive rule, is a pure predefined signal corresponding to the internal clock; it doesn't need to be declared in the module interface. The second rule makes use of a guard concerning the received signal parameter; this guard ensures that the reaction will only lead to a decreasing of the energy level. Such a guard can also be applied to the agent attributes or to the internal variables of the module.

The two rules can be activated simultaneously if both signals are received at the same instant; those rules can thus emit simultaneous different values for the **Reduce** signal. To avoid inconsistencies, we have to define a combination method for this output signal; when both rules are triggered, the two emitted values are added (+) in order to get only one signal value for the current instant. The module we have defined should be linked with the appropriate sensors or other behavioural modules so it can be activated; it should also be routed to the appropriate effectors so it can have an effect on the **energy** attribute.

The next example describes a sensor, which supervises the energy level in order to warn the other behavioural components when its value falls below a specified threshold; we assume that this threshold is an agent attribute. This behaviour is realized by waiting for the internal stimulus **_energy**, with the appropriate guard:

```
sensor energy_sensor
  out Dead ;

  filter
    waitstim _energy
      with [ owner.energy < owner.min_energy ] -> emit Dead
  end filter
end sensor
```

In the following example, we describe an effector, which accepts two kinds of action propositions: adding or subtracting a given quantity to the **energy** attribute. The **set** primitive affects the given value to the attribute (known by its identifier) and then generates the associated internal stimulus:

```
effector energy_effector
  in Add (int), Subtract (int) ;

  method sum (l)
    q <- 0 ;
    foreach p in l do
      q <- q + p
    end foreach ;
    return q
  end method

  arbiter
    loop
      add <- 0 ; sub <- 0 ;
      wait
        all Add as propositions ->
          add <- sum (propositions.values())
      | all Subtract as propositions ->
          sub <- sum (propositions.values())
      end wait ;
      set (owner.energy.id, (add - sub))
    end loop
  end arbiter
end effector
```

The "**all** S **as** *var*" construction means that all the S signals received simultaneously will be placed in a dictionary called *var*. This construction enables the arbiter to process the multiple propositions made by the behavioural modules for the current instant. As an effector is an object, we can define a method **sum** for factorizing code.

4.3   Using Constraints

Constraint solvers for arbitration. A constraint is simply a logical relation between several variables, which restricts the degrees of freedom of the variables, that is the possible values the variables can take in their specific domain. A constraint thus represents some partial information relating the objects of interest. The whole idea of constraint solving is to start reasoning and computing with partial information, ensuring the overall consistency and reducing as much as possible the domains of the variables in order to prune the search space. Constraint Programming combines the declarativity of high-level languages with the efficiency of specialized algorithms for constraint solving, sometimes borrowing techniques from Operations Research and Numerical Analysis [29]. It has proved to be very successful for Problem Solving and Combinatorial Optimization applications. While constraint solvers can be enhanced by using agent-based approaches, multi-agent systems can take advantage of the constraint computation paradigm [10].

In the INVIWO framework, constraint solvers can be used in the arbiters, in order to choose the actions to perform according to the propositions given by the behavioural modules. Classical constraint solvers can combine non-contradictory actions to get emergent behaviours. For example, a left move combined with a right move will lead to go straight. To handle possibly contradictory actions, we need to use *soft constraints* solvers, as detailed in [13]. Soft constraints are no more simple boolean logical relations, but are valued in a semi-ring structure. For instance, fuzzy constraints are valued in the set [0..1] equiped with *max* and *min* as additive and multiplicative operations.

Goal constraints and adaptive search. Constraints can also be used to express high-level goals in a declarative way: we call *goal constraint* a relation that the agent should try to achieve whenever it is not satisfied. We cannot consider classical Constraint Programming to handle dynamic and unpredictable environments: we therefore propose a new solving method called *adaptive search* to iteratively select actions that will eventually lead to the satisfaction of the goal constraints [8].

At each timestep, the agent should select the best action, in order to reduce the discrepancy between its current state and the overall satisfaction of the set of goal constraints. It is thus possible to reactively adapt the agent behaviour to a changing environment. It is worth noticing that behaviours are stated in an implicit way by giving a set of constraints and not in an explicit way, for example by giving a precise trajectory. Our framework can be used as a motivation architecture for virtual creatures, by considering constrained variables for denoting internal states (*e.g.* energy level or thirst), and goal constraints for defining internal needs (*e.g.* the energy level should stay above a given value), routine behaviours (*e.g.* if the energy level is too low, go for food) or external desired properties (*e.g.* stay away from predators).

We need the ability to handle internal variables, parametrized inputs and dynamic representations of goals to be achieved. Constraints are used to state goals, or more precisely partial goals, that the agent has to achieve. The primitive spatial constraints for autonomous navigation are:

- *in(region)*: stay within the zone defined by *region*
- *out(region)*: stay outside the zone defined by *region*
- *go(object)*: move towards the location of *object*
- *away(object)*: move away from the location of *object*
- *attraction(stimulus)*: move towards the source of *stimulus*
- *repulsion(stimulus)*: move away from the source of *stimulus*

These declarative constraints will reduce to some arithmetic constraints. For a circle *region*, the *in(region)* constraint will for instance reduce to:

$$agent.position - region.center < region.radius$$

It is clear that a combination of such goal constraints could produce quite complex behaviours: a following behaviour can be simply obtained by combining a *go* constraint and an *out* constraint, in order to move towards the followed object but not too close. The limited set of primitive goal constraints has been chosen because efficient methods can be designed to solve them. Indeed, one can define a *repair* mechanism for each constraint: this mechanism will propose an action that could reduce the degree of violation of the constraint whenever the constraint is not satisfied. For example, the repair action for a *go* constraint could perform the following navigation step in the direction of the target *object*:

$$agent.position = agent.speed \times \|object.position - agent.position\|$$

Let us now detail how to solve a combination of goal constraints by choosing the most appropriate repair action. Local search methods, such as simulated annealing or genetic algorithms, are working by iterative improvement over an initial state and are thus well-suited to reactive environments. The basic algorithm consists in starting from a random configuration, explore the neighbourhood and then move to the best candidate; this process will continue until a satisfactory solution is found.

In our framework, we select the adequate repair action whenever goal constraints are not fully satisfied. The input of the method is a set of variables V, a set of constraints C over V, and a cost function F to be minimized (for example, the number of violated constraints). For each constraint, we need also an *error function* giving an indication on how much the constraint is violated. Adaptive search seeks to reduce the error on the worse variable. It also include an adaptive memory module to prevent being trapped by local minima, like in the Tabu search method: each variable leading to a local minimum is marked and cannot be chosen for new iterations. The algorithm starts from a random assignment of the variables in V, and then repeats the following steps until a solution is found or the maximal number of iterations is reached:

1. **Compute scores** of constraints in C and combine scores on each variable.
2. **Select variable** X with highest score and evaluate cost of all possible moves from X.
3. **If** no better move **then** mark X tabu **else** select the best move and change the value of X accordingly.

This very simple method is surprisingly efficient to solve complex combinatorial problems such as the well-known "magic square" puzzle (see [8] for details). This framework also naturally copes with over-constrained problems. As defined above, this method does not perform any planning, as it only computes the next move out of all possible current moves. A simple extension would be to allow some limited planning by considering not only the immediate neighbours but all configurations on paths up to a given distance, and then choose to move to the neighbour in the direction of the most promising node. Therefore the method can plan for the best trajectory in a limited time-window. Goal constraints are expressed in MARVIN as specific entities, based on behavioural modules.

5   The InViWo Toolkit

The current prototype of the INVIWO toolkit is developed in Java, to be portable and to take advantage of simple GUI design. We use the Java3D API for displaying the 3D view of avatars.

The low-level library implements a programming interface and an execution platform. The platform is in charge of executing agent behaviours and of handling the communication between entities. The API provides the basic generic agent and avatar components we described in sections 3.2 and   3.3. Programmers can easily extend our model and develop new components. No interpreter for the high-level language is available at the moment: MARVIN descriptions are specifications that we manually translate into Java programs, which make use of the INVIWO API.

6   Conclusion

We have proposed a multi-agent model for inhabited virtual worlds, *i.e.* worlds populated with autonomous agents and avatars. We have designed a synthetic agent architecture, in order to ease the description of virtual creatures. We have extended this architecture to integrate avatars while keeping an homogeneous model; moreover, avatars can be partly autonomous and thus have their own behaviour or personality.

The control architecture of our hybrid agents is a behaviour-based model, where concurrent behavioural modules propose actions and where arbiters select final actions to be performed among those propositions. Behavioural modules can be spcified in the high-level language MARVIN, inspired from ESTEREL. The use of constraints extends the expressivity of our language, and makes it possible to add some planning capabilities to the INVIWO agents.

References

1. R. ARKIN. *Behavior-based Robotics*. MIT Press, 1998.
2. N. BADLER, C. PHILIPS, B. WEBBER. *Simulating humans: computer graphics, animation, and control*. Oxford University Press, 1993.
3. N. BADLER ET AL. *Real Time Virtual Humans*. International Conference on Digital Media Futures, Bradford (UK), April 1999.
4. G. BERRY *The* ESTEREL *v5 language primer*. Technical Report, Centre de Mathématiques Appliquées (INRIA et École des Mines de Paris),1999.
5. B. BLUMBERG, P. TODD, P. MAES. *No bad dogs: ethological lessons for learning in Hamsterdam*. From Animals to Animats 4, Cape Cod (USA), September 1996.

6. R. BROOKS. *A robust layered control system for a mobile robot.* IEEE Journal of Robotics and Automation, April 1986.

7. R. BROOKS. *Cambrian Intelligence: the early history of the new AI.* MIT Press, 1999.

8. P. CODOGNET. *Declarative behaviors for virtual creatures.* ICAT'99, 8th International Conference on Augmented Reality and Tele-existence, IOS Press 1999.

9. S. DONIKIAN, E. RUTTEN. *Reactivity, concurrency, data-flow and hierarchical preemption for behavioural animation.* Eurographics Workshop on Programming paradigms in Graphics, Maastricht (The Netherlands), September 1995.

10. P. EATON, E. FREUDER, R. WALLACE. *Constraints and agents.* American Association for Artificial Intelligence, Summer 1998.

11. J. FUNGE, X. TU, D. TERZOPOULOS. *Cognitive modeling: knowledge, reasoning and planning for intelligent characters.* SIGGRAPH'99, Los Angeles (USA), August 1999.

12. E. GAT. *Reliable goal-directed reactive control for real-world autonomous mobile robots.* Ph. D., Virginia Polytechnic Institute and State University, 1991.

13. Y. GEORGET AND P. CODOGNET. *Compiling Semiring-based Constraints with clp(FD,S).* CP'98, 4th International Conference on Constraint Programming, Pisa (Italy), Lecture Notes in Computer Science, Springer Verlag 1998.

14. M. KALLMAN, D. THALMANN. *A behavioral interface to simulate agent-object interactions in real time.* Computer Animation'99, Geneva (Switzerland), May 1999.

15. Y. KOGA, C. BECKER, M. SVIHURA, D. ZHU. *On intelligent digital actors.* Imagina'98, Monte-Carlo (Monaco), 1998.

16. B. LOYALL, J. BATES. *Real-time control of animated broad agents.* 15th Annual Conference of the Cognitive Science Society, Boulder (USA), June 1993.

17. P. MAES. *Artificial Life meets entertainment: lifelike autonomous agents.* Communications of the ACM, Special Issue on New Horizons of Commercial and Industrial AI, 38(11), November 1995.

18. P. MAES ET AL. *The ALIVE system: wireless, full-body interaction with autonomous agents.* Technical Report of the MIT Media Laboratory Perceptual Computing, November 1995.

19. G. MOREAU, S. DONIKIAN. *From psychological and real-time interaction requirements to behavioural simulation.* Workshop on Computer Animation and Simulation'98, Lisbon (Portugal), September 1998.

20. J. MÜLLER. *Control architectures for autonomous and interacting agents: a survey.* Intelligent Agent Systems (Theoretical and Practical Issues), Springer-Verlag, 1997.

21. C. PAUL, R. PETERS, A. GRAEFF. *Agents in multi-user virtual environments.* Eurographics'98 short paper session, Lisbon (Portugal), September 1998.

22. R. PFEIFER AND C. SCHEIER. *Understanding Intelligence.* MIT Press, 1999.

23. C. REYNOLDS. *Flocks, herds, and schools: a distributed behavioral model.* SIGGRAPH'87, Anaheim (USA), July 1987.

24. C. REYNOLDS. *Steering behaviors for autonomous characters.* Game Developers Conference, San Jose (USA), March 1999.

25. N. RICHARD, P. CODOGNET, A. GRUMBACH. *Constraints to describe high-level behaviours in virtual worlds.* Eurographics'98 short-paper session, Lisbon (Portugal), September 1998.

26. N. RICHARD, P. CODOGNET, A. GRUMBACH. *The INVIWO virtual agents.* Eurographics'99 short-paper session, Milano (Italy), September 1999.

27. H. ROITBLAT AND J-A. MEYER (Eds.). *Comparative approaches to cognitive science*. MIT Press, 1995.

28. J. K. ROSENBLATT *DAMN: a Distributed Architecture for Mobile Navigation*. Ph. D. thesis, Robotics Institute, Carnegie Mellon University, 1997.

29. V. SARASWAT, P. VAN HENTENRYCK, P. CODOGNET ET AL. *Constraint Programming*. ACM Computing Surveys, 28(4), December 1996.

30. N. SCHMAJUCK (Ed.). *Special issue on biologically-inspired models of navigation*. Adaptive Behavior, 6(3/4), Winter/Spring 1998.

31. D. THALMANN, H. NOSER. *Towards autonomous, perceptive, and intelligent virtual actors*. Artificial Intelligence Today, Lecture Notes in Artificial Intelligence, 1600, Springer, 1999.

32. M. TRAVERS. *Behave! A visual behavior language*. `http://xenia.media.mit.edu/~mt/behave/behave.html`.

33. O. TRULLIER AND J-A. MEYER. *Biomimetic navigation models and strategies in animats*. AI Commmunications, vol. 10, no. 2, 1997.

34. X. TU, D. TERZOPOULOS. *Artificial fishes: physics, locomotion, perception, behavior*. SIGGRAPH'94, Orlando (USA), July 1994.

35. R. WATERS ET AL. *Diamond Park and Spline: a social Virtual Reality system with 3D animation, spoken interaction, and runtime modifiability*. Technical report of the Mitsubishi Electric Research Laboratory, November 1996.

SimHuman: A Platform for Real-Time Virtual Agents with Planning Capabilities

Spyros Vosinakis and Themis Panayiotopoulos

Knowledge Engineering Laboratory, Department of Informatics, University of Piraeus, 80
Karaoli & Dimitriou str., 18534, Piraeus, Greece
`spyrosv@unipi.gr, themisp@unipi.gr`

Abstract. In this paper, we present SimHuman, a platform for the generation of
real-time 3D environments with virtual agents. SimHuman is highly dynamic
and configurable, as it is not based on fixed scenes and models, and has an
embedded physically based modelling engine. Its agents can use features such
as path finding, inverse kinematics and planning to achieve their goals. The
paper explains in detail design and implementation issues and presents the
architecture of the system as well as an illustrative example.

Keywords: virtual agents, believable agents, autonomous virtual humans,
virtual environments, real-time animation, planning, simulation

1   Introduction

A virtual agent can be defined as an autonomous entity in a virtual environment. It
should not only look like, but also behave as a living organism (human, animal or
other fictional character) in a synthetic three-dimensional world, and be able to
interact with it and its inhabitants. These could be either real users in the form of
avatars, or other virtual agents.

There are numerous applications that would require some form of virtual agents in
their environments, especially in fields such as entertainment, education, virtual
environments, simulation, etc. [5]. There is, nevertheless, no standard definition of
how such an 'entity' is to be implemented and this is due to the fact that different
applications focus on different characteristics of such synthetic creatures. A game, for
example, focuses mainly on appearance and behaviour, because the agents should be
believable, while a simulation system aims at higher accuracy.

In this paper we present a system called SimHuman, which is our approach
towards the generation of real-time virtual environments with intelligent virtual
agents for desktop VR applications. This system can use any 3D model for agents,
avatars and other virtual objects and is therefore highly dynamic and configurable. It
has an embedded physically based modelling engine, and its agents can use features
such as path finding, inverse kinematics and planning to achieve their goals. The
system is designed in such a way that it maintains a balance between performance,
autonomy and believability and can be used as a basis for real-time virtual
environments and simple simulation systems.

A. de Antonio, R. Aylett, and D. Ballin (Eds.): IVA 2001, LNAI 2190, pp. 210-223, 2001.

The paper is structured as follows: In section 2 we present the related work in the field of virtual agents. The design issues of simulated humans for virtual environments are discussed in section 3, while the architecture of the SimHuman system is the subject of section 4. The next section presents an illustrative example of an application generated with SimHuman. Section 6 is concerned with the implementation issues, and in the last one we state our conclusions and possible extensions of this system.

2   Background

There has been a great amount of research in the field of virtual agent display, motion and behaviour, and a number of different systems and approaches have been proposed. Each of them varies in appearance, function and autonomy according to the application field and the required detail and accuracy.

The process of displaying and animating a virtual human involves three different stages. The most primitive one is the visualisation of the body, which is the same process as modelling any other 3D object. The next stage is the modelling of the skeleton, which defines the moving parts of the body and the type of motion that they can perform, and the last one is the modelling of skin and clothes, so as to move in a natural way [12]. The calculation of the skin and cloth motion is the most computationally intensive task, which is why it is not suitable for real-time animation.

Believable human body animation is a surprisingly hard task. The animation techniques fall into three basic categories: *keyframing, motion capture* and *simulation* [8]. All three involve a trade-off between the level of control that the animator has over the fine details of the motion and the amount of work that the computer does on its own.

In keyframing, the animator has to specify critical, or key, positions for the body parts, and the computer fills in the missing frames by smoothly interpolating between those positions. Body postures can be defined either with the low-level *forward kinematics* approach, or with the more elegant *inverse kinematics* one [29]. On the other hand, motion capture involves measuring a real person's / object's position and orientation in physical space, and then recording that information in a computer-usable form. [23].

Unlike keyframing and motion capture, simulation uses the laws of physics to generate motion of figures and other objects. Virtual humans are usually represented as a collection of rigid body parts. Although the models can be physically plausible, they are nonetheless only an approximation of the human body, because they ignore the movement of muscle mass relative to bone. Recently, researchers have begun to build more complex physical models based on bio-mechanical data, and the resulting simulations are becoming increasingly lifelike [10].

There have been some significant approaches towards the generation of synthetic figures in virtual environments, such as the work of Kalra et al.[11], which describes an interactive system for building realistic virtual humans for real time applications, and that of Aubel et al. [1], which presents techniques for rendering and animating a multitude of virtual humans in real-time.

One important application that utilises many aspects of human motion and simulation is a commercial system called Jack, developed at the University of

Pennsylvania [3]. It contains kinematic and dynamic models of humans based on biomechanical data and displays several built-in behaviours including balance, reaching and grasping, walking and running. A similar environment is HUMANOID [7], which is additionally using metaballs for a more realistic representation of the skin and muscles. VLNET [19, 18] is a networked multi-user virtual environment that is using HUMANOID's articulated body model as a basis for virtual human display and motion.

A synthetic human should not only be capable of animating its body and applying forces on other objects, but also be able to interact with a dynamic environment and exhibit some form of behaviour. Borrowing the theory from the field of Intelligent Agents [30], a Virtual Agent should be able to sense the environment and decide on its actions according to its predefined goals. One important decision technique for dynamic environments is planning [15, 17, 27] and there are a number of different systems that use planning for the behavioural control of virtual agents.

N. Badler and B. Webber propose an architecture [4] that is providing high level control of a Virtual Human with planners and parallel state-machines, and low level one with Sense-Control-Act loops. On the other hand, A. Caicedo and D. Thalmann present a complex behavioural engine for autonomous virtual agents with trust models and beliefs about other agents [9].

One interesting application towards a 3D environment with intelligent virtual agents are the Virtual Teletubbies [2]. The system uses a simple physics model to simulate gravity and the agents' personality is based on a novel behavioural architecture, the Behavioural Synthesis Architecture [6]. Agents with personality are also the main subject of the work of D. Silva et al [26]. They propose a Synthetic Actor model that connects emotions and social attitudes to personality, providing a long-term coherent behaviour. They present two games as case studies to their proposed architecture.

The EXCALIBUR project [16] uses a generic architecture for autonomously operating agents that can act in a complex computer-game environment. The agents use planning in a constraint programming framework and the behavioural model is able to handle incomplete knowledge and information gathering. Another interesting system for the creation of real-time behaviour-based animated actors is Improv [21]. It consists of an Animation Engine that uses procedural techniques to generate layered, continuous motions and transitions between them, and a Behaviour Engine that is based on rules governing how actors communicate and make decisions. The combined system provides an integrated set of tools for authoring the 'minds' and 'bodies' of interactive actors.

Lokutor [14] is an agent prototype with an embededded behaviour system for use in 3D virtual environments. It takes advantage of speech synthesis and recognition techniques to interact with the user and uses Web-based technology, such as Java3D, VRML and H-Anim [24] for portability.

There may be a considerable amount and variety of research going on in the field of intelligent virtual agents, but not all the aspects of the problem have yet been explored. Applications like Jack mainly focus on the accuracy of the simulation and include far too many details on human body structure, because their main target is the field of industrial design (and similar fields that need detailed results), while others emphasise too much on personality and behaviour. On the other hand, applications such as Virtual Environments and simple Simulation Systems do not need 100% accuracy. They require natural looking motion, as well as acceptable execution speed and this is the aspect that our approach is focusing on. The aim of our system is to combine simple yet effective design algorithms and implementation techniques for the creation of synthetic humans with planning capabilities that focus on real-time desktop VR applications.

3   A Simulated Human for Real-Time Environments

The SimHuman system is a platform that allows the user to define three-dimensional scenes with an arbitrary number of virtual agents and user-controlled avatars, and serves as a basis for applications such as virtual environments and simulation systems. In this section we will focus on the design issues and functionality of the virtual agents that are implemented in the SimHuman environment. We will present issues such as motion, collision detection, inverse kinematics and planning.

3.1   Display and Primitive Motion

In the SimHuman environment all objects of the scene (including virtual agents' bodies) are defined in terms of 3D Polygons. Agents are not based on a fixed model, but the system is able to load models dynamically, from a *geometry file* that contains the details of their appearance. Additionally, some skeletal information is necessary, to define how the body segments are going to be transformed. This is loaded from a supplementary file, called *hierarchy file* which includes the joint hierarchy and the position and limits of each joint. Virtual agents can have an arbitrary number of joints and segments and any possible hierarchy tree to connect them. This gives the user / programmer the ability to load various models and adjust the program to the needs of different applications having the required level of detail.

A classic problem of articulated figures is that the rotation of a segment causes a crack around the joint, because the faces of adjacent segments are not adjoining anymore. One way to deal with it is to have fixed primitives (usually spheres) on the joints, but one drawback is the fact that these primitives do not always fit perfectly with the model's meshes, thus distorting the appearance of the model. Another problem is that they add a lot more polygons to the scene and decrease the performance significantly.

In our system we have the ends of adjacent segments always connected with each other and, whenever a segment is rotated, the vertices that are common with any adjacent segment are not transformed. The effect of this method is demonstrated in figure 1.

The SimHuman system is using keyframing as the basis of all animation sequences. This generates a smooth transition between two states (poses). With this simple process of keyframing, we can load various body postures stored in an *animation library* and use them to produce more complex animation sequences, such as walking.

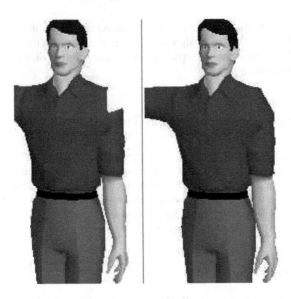

Fig. 1. Shoulder rotation without and with common vertices

3.2   Physically-Based Modelling, Collision Detection, and Response

In our system there is a physically based modelling engine that is used to increase the believability of the animation. The physical simulation is conducted in discrete timesteps. Each object has its own mass, position and velocity and in each timestep its position and velocity are recalculated following the laws of kinematics and collision.

In a simulated environment all objects have to behave as rigid bodies, i.e. no object should be allowed to penetrate another. The process of *collision detection* is to examine if the whole or part of the geometry of an object is within another. Associated with this is another equally important process, that of *collision response*, which should determine the new position and velocity of the two (or more) objects that collided.

Calculating an accurate collision detection and response for a human body mesh is not an easy task. The program has to check each polygon of the mesh against all the other objects of the scene and determine if it is penetrating another polygon. The approach that we use in our system is somehow different. We use bounding primitives around the human body segments and perform all collision detection checks with them. This reduces the computational time significantly, making it possible to run in acceptable speeds in real-time systems. The primitives that we have chosen are cylinders, mainly because their geometry is more symmetrical compared to bounding boxes and they still fit well around the human body (figure 2).

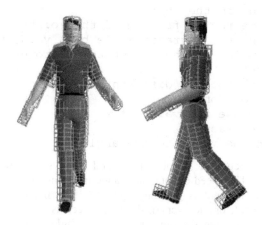

Fig. 2. A human body mesh covered with bounding cylinders

3.3   Dynamic Actions

Dynamic actions are those actions executed by a virtual agent that are not predefined (such as an animation sequence), but adapted to an ever-changing environment. This is, therefore, a very important issue for simulation systems, because, in most of the cases, their objects / creatures have to act in a dynamic environment. In our system, the physically based modelling engine as well as the co-existence of more than one agents and avatars inevitably 'generate' a dynamic environment, and a virtual agent has to be able to execute dynamic actions to interact with it.

Such actions are path planning and obstacle avoidance, i.e. the ability to move to a specified target without bumping into other objects. To execute these actions, the virtual agent has a 'sensing' mechanism, which enables it to have a limited view of the environment. This mechanism is based on *ray casting*. Whenever the agent 'looks', it casts a number of rays into the scene, and reads the objects that these rays intersect with. With this mechanism the agent is able to know the position, size and type of the objects that are in its field of view, and use this information to avoid obstacles and plan its path to the target. The agent keeps its own, internal map of the scene, which is the agent's 'memory' and is updated after every 'look' process. The agent uses this map to calculate a safe path to the target.

More complicated dynamic actions involve catching a moving object, hitting it, or leaving an object on a specified location. These actions must use a form of inverse kinematics, because they involve more than one joints that have to be coordinated to succeed. Instead of using a generic inverse kinematics solver, a different approach is introduced. This approach tests at every step the best rotation for each joint to achieve the target.

The set of joints (or the joint chain) that is going to be used by the system is first defined. Then, a function has to be assigned and return on how close to the target is the current state of the virtual human. The process (in pseudocode) is:

```
For each joint in the chain
    For each degree of freedom of the joint
        increase and decrease angle by a value v
        check which of the two states improves the
            function
        if that state is different from the
            previous one
            decrease the value of v
        else increase it
        assign the value to the angle
```

This process is repeated in each frame and the system always corrects itself towards the target. The speed of rotation change per joint depends on the success of the move. If one segment is 'shaking' (the angle is increased in one step and decreased in the next, or vice versa), the joint speed is decreased to provide finer approach to the target. On the other hand, if an angle change is always heading towards the correct direction, the speed is increased until it reaches the maximum value.

3.4   Behavioural Control

What we have presented so far is a human model, which can execute various actions in a 3D environment. These features may be enough for avatars, but a virtual agent should also have a mechanism to select actions and execute them in order to achieve its goals. This is the agent's 'mind', which defines its behaviour, and in the SimHuman system it is implemented with the use of a *planner*. Therefore, we can say that the agent consists of two parts, the motion controller and the behavioural controller.

The agent's behavioural control unit works with a symbolic representation of the world, just like a human's mind does not think in terms of 3D coordinates and geometry, but in rather abstract terms. Procedures such as walking towards a target, avoiding obstacles and grasping objects are not calculated at the high-level declarative part of the 'mind' but are part of the agent's functionality as standard actions. Otherwise, the planning time needed to execute those actions would slow down significantly the system's performance. A real-time system with good performance should use planning only at a higher level, while the real time activities should be implemented with standard algorithms (such as path finding, collision avoidance, inverse kinematics, etc). Nevertheless, this approach poses a very important problem: how to represent the world in abstract terms and how to maintain its integrity.

Just like an intelligent agent might be based on a sense – decide – act loop, our virtual agents have equivalent methods for sensing, deciding and acting. Nevertheless, these three processes are not executed sequentially, but in parallel. One action might take a significant amount of time to be executed (e.g. walk to a very distant target) and the decide() process might also take some time, because planning is not a simple task. Therefore it is much more efficient to let them work in parallel, e.g. while the agent is walking it can also think of its next actions. The sense() process is executed very frequently, because the agent is always sensing (looking) the place. Based on the sensed data, the decide() process is trying to compute a plan for the agent's actions using symbolic information of the world. This plan is a sequence of actions executed by the `act()` process. This coordination between sensing, deciding and acting becomes more complex in dynamic worlds where the state of the world can change arbitrarily (due to other agents' or avatars' actions). In such cases the `decide()` process should also check whether the plan it has generated is still applicable, or if a change in the world's state prohibits the agent from reaching its goals. In the second case a new plan has to be computed and the action queue is not valid.

When the agent senses, it 'scans' the 3D world and 'reads' the objects. There is a list, which holds all the objects that the agent has 'seen' during its last sensing process (the agent's memory), namely the name and type of each object together with its attributes (position, orientation, size and other object-specific attributes). Nevertheless, the information stored in that list is of no use to the decision process, because the planner works with an abstract representation of the world and its objects. For example, it would need information such as 'the ball is on the table' instead of 'the ball's position is (5.3, 3.2, 3.1) and the table's position is (4.1, 1.0, 4.0)'. Therefore, there is a module that generates the abstract definition of the world and the spatial relationships between the world's entities.

As stated before, the `decide()` process uses planning to generate an action sequence that should achieve the agent's goals. First of all, the agent should have a clearly defined *goal state*, a set of objects' attributes and relationships that the agent aims for. Additionally, the planning process also needs the set of all the possible actions that the virtual agent is able to perform, and each of these actions should also state its preconditions and its effects in abstract terms. For example an action such as 'put object A on object B' has the precondition that the agent is holding object A and the effect that object A is on object B.

The sensing process stores a list of objects and their attributes, and can therefore generate an abstract world representation with all possible relationships between the objects. This set of terms that represent the world in an abstract way are the agent's *beliefs*, on which the planner is based to generate an action sequence that will lead the agent to its goals. Nevertheless, it might be possible that the planner has worked out a solution, but, during the execution of an action, the state of the world has changed in such a way that the plan is not going to succeed. This can simply be determined by comparing the set of beliefs to the actual state of the world as it is perceived by the sensing process. If the 'expected' state does not match the actual one, the plan has to be recalculated. Of course, after any successful execution of an action by the agent, this 'expected' state has to be updated as well (by applying the effects of the action to the agent's beliefs). If a new plan has been generated, all remaining actions in the action sequence are deleted and the agent starts over with a new set of orders. The `decide()` function expressed in pseudocode is:

```
bool decide() {
    if(beliefs_match_sensing_data) {
        if(goals_match_beliefs) {
            // the plan is applicable and has succeeded
            clear(action_queue);
            return true;
        }
        // else: the plan is still applicable, but has
```

```
not
    succeeded yet
    return false;
}
// the plan is not applicable, it has to be
recomputed
clear(action_queue);
update(beliefs);
recompute(plan);
update(action_queue);
}
```

4   The Architecture of SimHuman

SimHuman consists of two basic modules: the 3D Visualization, which renders the scene, and the physically based modelling, which applies the laws of physics. Each scene can have an arbitrary number of passive objects, virtual agents and avatars (figure 3). During each timeframe, the physically based modelling part applies forces, checks for collisions between objects and handles their motion. The 3D Visualization part then uses the final positions of the world's entities and displays the scene on the screen.

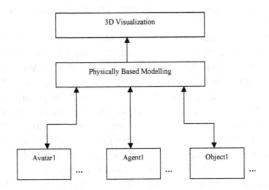

Fig. 3. The general architecture of SimHuman

Both virtual agents and avatars are articulated figures (humans or other lifelike characters) and use therefore a geometry file, a joint hierarchy file and an animation library to execute their actions. All the other objects of the scene are described by simple geometry files. A virtual agent consists of a motion controller, which is able to execute simple and dynamic actions, and a behavioural controller, which decides for the agent's behaviour in the virtual space. On the other hand, an avatar has a motion controller with the same structure, but its behaviour is determined directly from the user. Figure 4 shows the architecture of an agent and an avatar. Boxes stand for modules and drums for data

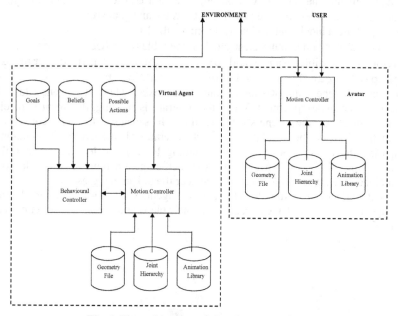

Fig. 4. The architecture of virtual agents and avatars

5   An Illustrative Example

In this section we will present a sample application that has been created with SimHuman. It is the typical planning problem of blocks world: there is a set of boxes on a table and the agent's task is to move the boxes and achieve a specific arrangement. One example is that of figure 5.

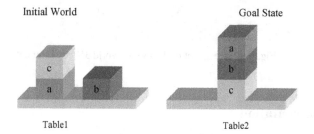

Fig. 5. A blocks world example

In this example, one symbolic representation of the initial world is { on (a,table1), on(c,a), on(b,table1), clear(c), clear(b) } and of the goal state { on(c,table2), on(b, c), on(a, b) }, where on(A,B) means that object A is on object B and clear(X) means that there is nothing on top of object X. The possible actions for an agent are:

- to pick up a block that is clear (pickup(Obj))
- to put a block on another clear block or the table (put(Obj, Location))

Therefore, a possible plan would be { pickup(c), put(c, table2), pickup(b), put(b, c), pickup(a), put(a, b) }.

We use a scene with two tables and three boxes, where the agent's task is to achieve a specific arrangement. When the program is running, the agent is receiving information about the scene's objects through sensing. It, then, converts this information into symbolic relations (e.g. it generates all the on(X,Y) relations by comparing the objects' positions and bounding boxes) and lets the planner find a solution. This solution is then converted to specific agent actions (e.g. in order to pick up an object, the agent has to go to a place near the object and grasp it).

An extension of this example is to have two agents with contradicting goals. In this case, agents will always have to recompute their plans and follow a new set of actions (figure 6).

Fig. 6. A screenshot of the blocks world 3D environment

6   Implementation

We have implemented the SimHuman system as a set of C++ classes, using OpenGL for the 3D visualization. We have created a semi-automated platform in Microsoft Visual C++, which demonstrates the capabilities of the SimHuman system in a simulated physical environment and allows the development of 3D environments with virtual agents [28]. The geometry models for virtual humans can be directly imported from Curious Labs Poser [22], provided that they have been exported as VRML 97 files, due to an embedded VRML parser that is used by the program. Therefore there is practically no limitation on the number of different models that can be used by our system. The SimHuman platform automatically generates the bounding cylinders of the body and, together with a hierarchy file and an animation library, uses the 3D model as a representation of an agent or avatar.

Our planner is implemented in Prolog. The planner itself as well as the abstract action definition are precompiled in SICStus Prolog [25], while the current world state and goals are dynamically passed as arguments whenever the agent has to calculate a new plan. The ability to call SICStus Prolog queries from a C program allows SimHuman to use the planner dynamically while running.

7   Conclusions and Future Work

In this paper we have presented a design and implementation approach for virtual agents, which can be used in real-time systems. The field of human modelling, simulation and behaviour is an area of continuous research and a lot of different approaches have been proposed. In the SimHuman system, we have tried to balance between efficiency and accuracy in order to produce believable human motion in real-time environments. Possible applications include simulated worlds that demonstrate human action, virtual environments with avatars or other computer controlled human models, educational applications, etc.

There are, nevertheless, a lot of issues that need to be solved, such as handling of uncertainty, execution of parallel actions, hierarchical planning, etc. We are working on integrating spatio-temporal reasoning and planning techniques into SimHuman's behavioural control and on allowing concurrent execution of agents' actions. In order to do this, we intend to follow the paradigm of Advisor [13] and TRL-tutor [20], temporal planners developed by members of our research team. Additionally, we are working towards a generic visual tool for the set up of a scene and the description of agents' behaviour to serve as a basis for the automatic generation of virtual environments with believable agents.

Acknowledgements. This work has been supported by the Greek Secretariat of Research and Technology under the PENED'99 project entitled "Executable Intensional Languages and Intelligent Multimedia, Hypermedia and Virtual Reality applications", Contract No. 99ED265.

References

1.   Aubel, A., Boulic, R., Thalmann, D.: Real-timeDisplay of Virtual Humans: Level of Details and Impostors. IEEE Trans.Circuits and Systems for Video Technology, Special Issue on 3D Video Technology
2.   Aylett, R., Horrobin, A., O'Hare, J., Osman, A., Polshaw, M.: Virtual Telebubbies: reapplying a robot architecture to virtual agents. In Proceedings of the Third International Conference on Autonomous Agents. New York: ACM Press (1999) 514-515
3.   Badler, N., Phillips, C., Webber, B.: Simulating Humans: Computer Graphics Animation and Control. Oxford University Press (1993)

4.   Badler, N., Webber, B., Becket, W., Geib, C., Moore, M., Pelachaud, C., Reich B., Stone, M.: Planning and parallel transition networks: Animation's new frontiers. In: S. Y. Shin and T. L. Kunii (eds.), Computer Graphics and Applications: Proc. Pacific Graphics '95, World Scientific Publishing, River Edge, NJ. (1995) 101-117
5.   Badler, N.: Virtual humans for animation, ergonomics, and simulation. IEEE Workshop on Non-Rigid and Articulated Motion. Puerto Rico (1997)
6.   Barnes, P.: A behaviour synthesis architecture for cooperant mobile robots. Advanced Robotics and Intelligent Machines. J.O. Gray, D.G. Caldwell (eds). IEE Control Engineering Series 51 (1996) 295-314
7.   Boulic, R., Huang, Z., Shen, J., Molet, T., Capin, T., Lintermann, B., Saar, K., Thalmann, D., Magnetat-Thalmann, N., Schmitt, A., Moccozet, L., Kalra, P., Pandzic, I.: A system for the parallel integrated motion of multiple deformable human characters with collision detection. Computer Graphics Forum 13(3). (1995) 337-348
8.   Brogan, D., Metoyer, R., Hodgins, J.: Dynamically Simulated Characters in Virtual Environments. IEEE Computer Graphics and Applications. September/October 1998, Volume 15 Number 5 (1998) 58-69
9.   Caicedo, A., Thalmann, D.: Virtual Humanoids: Let Them be Autonomous without Losing Control, Proc. 3IA2000, Limoges, France (2000)
10. Hodgins, J., Wooten, L.: Animating Human Athletes. In Robotics Research: The Eighth International Symposium. Y. Shirai, S. Hirose (eds). Springer-Verlag: Berlin (1998) 356-367
11. Karla, P., Magnenat-Thalmann, N., Moccozet, L., Sannier, G., Aubel, A., Thalmann, D.: Real-time Animation of Realistic Virtual Humans. IEEE Computer Graphics and Applications, Vol.18, No.5. (1998) 42-55
12. Magnetat-Thalmann, N., Carion, S., Courchesne, M., Volino, P., Wu, Y.: Virtual Clothes, Hair and Skin for Beautiful Top Models, Computer Graphics International '96, Pohang, Korea (1996) 132-141.
13. Marinagi, C.C., Panayiotopoulos, T., Vouros, G.A., Spyropoulos, C.D.: Advisor : A knowledge-based planning system. International Journal of Expert Systems, Research and Applications, Vol.9, No.3. (1996) 319-355
14. Milde, J.: Lokutor: Towards a Believable Communicative Agent, AGENTS 2000 Workshop, Barcelona (2000)
15. Nareyek, A.: A Planning Model for Agents in Dynamic and Uncertain Real-Time Environments. Workshop on Integrating Planning, Scheduling and Execution in Dynamic and Uncertain Environments at the Fourth International Conference on Artificial Intelligence Planning Systems (AIPS-98), Technical Report, WS-98-02, 7-14. AAAI Press, Menlo Park, California (1998)
16. Nareyek, A.: Intelligent Agents for Computer Games. In Proceedings of the Second International Conference on Computers and Games (2000)
17. Panayiotopoulos, T., Katsirelos, G., Vosinakis, S., Kousidou, S.: An Intelligent Agent Framework in VRML worlds. Advances in Intelligent Systems : Concepts, Tools and Applications, S. Tzafestas (ed.), Kluwer Academic Publishers (1999) 33-43
18. Pandzic, I. , Capin, T., Magnenat Thalmann, N., Thalmann, D.: Motor functions in the VLNET Body-Centered Networked Virtual Environment, Proc. 3rd Eurographics workshop on Virtual Environments, Monte Carlo, Virtual Environments and Scientific Visualization '96, Springer,Wien. (1996) 94-103
19. Pandzic, I., Capin, T., Magnenat Thalmann, N., Thalmann, D.: VLNET:A Networked Multimedia 3D Environment with Virtual Humans. Proc. Multi-MediaModeling MMM '95, Singapore. (1995) 21-32
20. Payiotopoulos, T., Avradinis, N., Marinagi, C.C.: Using Forward Temporal Planning for the production of Interactive Tutoring Dialogues. Advances in Intelligent Systems : Concepts, Tools and Applications, (S. Tzafestas ed.), Chapter 20, Kluwer Academic Publishers, Netherlands. (1999) 219-230.

21. Perlin, K., Goldberg, A.: Improv: A system for scripting interactive actors in virtual worlds. In ACM Computer Graphics Annual Conf. (1996) 205-216
22. Poser 4: http://www.curiouslabs.com/ products/poser4, Curious Labs
23. Pourazar, G.: A method to capture and animate the dynamics of human motion. COMPUGRAPHICS '91, I (1991) 181-197
24. Roehl, B.: Specification for a standard humanoid [Online]. Available: http://ece.uwaterloo.ca/~h-anim/spec1.1/
25. SICstus Prolog: http://www.sics.se/sicstus
26. Silva, D., Siebra, C., Valadares, J., Almeida, A., Frery, A., Ramalho, G.: Personality-Centered Agents for Virtual Computer Games, Virtual Agents 99, Workshop on Intelligent Virtual Agents, Salford, UK (1999)
27. Vosinakis, S., Anastassakis, G., Panayiotopoulos, T.: DIVA: Distributed Intelligent Virtual Agents, Workshop on Intelligent Virtual Agents, Virtual Agents 99 Salford (1999) 131-134
28. Vosinakis, S., Panayiotopoulos, T.: Design and Implementation of Synthetic Humans for Virtual Environments and Simulation Systems. 5th WSES/IEEE WORLD MULTICONFERENCE ON Circuits, Systems, Communications & Computers (CSCC 2001), to be presented (2001)
29. Welman, C.: Inverse Kinematics and Geometric Constraints for Articulated Figure Manipulation. MSc Thesis, Simon Fraser University (1993)
30. Wooldridge, M., Muller, J., Tambe, M., editors: Intelligent Agents II, Agent Theories, Architectures and Languages. Volume 1037 of Lecture Notes in Artificial Intelligence, Springer-Verlag (1996)

MAgentA: An Architecture for Real Time Automatic Composition of Background Music

Pietro Casella[1] and Ana Paiva[1,2]

[1] IST, Av. Rovisco Pais, 1049-001 Lisboa, Portugal
[2] INESC, Rua Alves Redol 9 Apartado 13069, 1000-029 Lisboa, Portugal
pcas@mega.ist.utl.pt, ana.paiva@inesc.pt

Abstract. This paper describes MAgentA (Musical **Agent** Architecture), which is an Agent that automatically composes background music in real time using the emotional state of the environment within which it is embedded. Its goal is to generate a "film-like music " output for a virtual environment emphasizing the dramatic aspects of such environment.

The approach followed in MAgentA is that of dynamically choosing an appropriate composition algorithm, among several others stored in a database, which were previously processed and duly associated to a particular emotional state.

MAgentA is in the process of being integrated from an abstract level in the FantasyA Virtual Environment, a wide scale virtual environment game currently being researched with INESC.

1 Introduction

The growing interest in Intelligent Virtual Environments (IVE), on areas of application such as games, has raised the demand for adequate background music in order to respond to the ever more demanding gamer. The main reason for this is the long known ability of music to induce certain emotional states in its listener, and as such providing sustainable immersion.

The composition of music for both IVE and Film Music is similar in many ways. The major difference is that while composing film music, the composer has access to the film script, thus having prior knowledge of the evolution of the emotional state of each scene. In an IVE where the agents have autonomous behaviors, and in some cases where the user's behavior is unpredictable, this evolution becomes unknown (i.e. there is no script), making it difficult to pre-compose contextualized music.

In general the approach followed by developers, in the game industry for example, is to loop pre-composed tracks which are attached to particular locations or events within the maze and faded at pre defined moments. One problem with this approach is that the users get accustomed of listening to the same music over and over again. Another problem is that the user associates music to events, predicting what is going to happen next and spoiling the overall experience.

A. de Antonio, R. Aylett, and D. Ballin (Eds.): IVA 2001, LNAI 2190, pp. 224–232, 2001.

Only more recently some commercial sound engines started to include technology to increase music diversity. Microsoft' DirectMusic[6] provides the possibility to compose several "interchangeable" pieces of music which are randomly arranged at run time, but still does so in response to some specific events.

The available literature on Agents that compose music based on the observation of the environment is scarce. One important step in this field is the work of Mark Downie [2] where Music Creatures were created following a reactive, behavior-based AI approach. Nakamura et al. [3] implemented a prototype system that generates background music and sound effects for short movies, based on Actors' Emotions and Motions. Some work has also been done at the University of Edinburgh, in particular [4] describes a system that generates atmospheric music in real time to convey fear using suspense and surprise. The system's parameters are controlled by a human director, that analyzes the flow of the narrative.

The MAgentA architecture generates appropriate background music, by choosing in real-time the algorithm that matches the current mood of the environment. The implemented algorithms are previously attached to a particular mood by a human using empirical evaluation. Future work includes the creation of rules to do so automatically, using some theory of emotions and music.

This document follows with an analysis of some of the involved areas of research. Section 3 describes in more detail the MAgentA architecture, in particular it's integration with the FantasyA Virtual Environment. The analysis arising from this document gives room for conclusions as well as some further discussion, which ultimately are the first milestone towards a more elaborate research project that shall follow suit.

2   Background Research

Building an agent capable of composing music in real time, based on the emotional state of the environment involves several areas of research which are described briefly in the following subsections.

2.1   Cognitive Psychology

Cognitive Psychology handles the problem of directly associating emotions to specific musical structures, which necessarily imply an understanding of how this interaction occurs, and how one is able to create rules that explain the phenomena of inducing emotions through music. However most of the research is, by necessity, highly theoretical, and generally disconnected from practical issues of performance and acoustic realization. One particularly interesting result is that of North and Hargreaves [1] in which they discuss and evaluate the possibility of fully describing the emotions evoked by music through a combination of the degree of "liking" and the degree of "arousal potential".

Context dependency is also described as being able to further enhance the granularity of music. Considering the example of one scene with two different tracks, the emotions transmitted can be quite different. While on the other hand the opposite is also true in that two different scenes with the same track can have different emotional effects on the viewer.

Yet another primitive is that any symbolism associated with music is highly culture dependent, thus constraining the applicability of any generalization made. The major organizing force in modern thinking on emotion and music was the work of L. B. Meyer [5], where the central thesis of the psychological theory of emotions (i.e. Emotion or affect is aroused when a tendency to respond is arrested or inhibited) is used to explain the interaction between emotion and music.

2.2   Automatic Composition

The problem of teaching a computer how to compose or play music has for long been a known Computer Music issue. The challenge is of creating algorithms able to generate an output that can be classified as music, when judged by an average human listener. The conducted research in Computer Music thus far has produced some interesting music pieces, however, real time composing systems are still rare (ex. [8]). An enduring milestone survey by Curtis Roads[7] argues that the main problem causing paucity is that it is still hard to compose computer music, in the sense that the currently existing programming languages are yet far of naturally expressing musical knowledge. Some work has been done but generally non real-time fixed compositional strategies were used. Roads concludes calling upon the necessity for interactive systems that allow for flexibility and as such avoiding the above mentioned fixed compositional strategies.

3   Architecture

One general definition of an Agent is an entity that interacts with the environment through perceptions and actions. The perceptions are the input and the actions are the output. More specifically, the agent described in this document perceives the emotional state of the environment, and acts upon it by producing music.

A typical environment in which such an agent could be placed would be a virtual theater or a computer game, where emotions are present and constantly changing. FantasyA qualifies as such an environment and is briefly described next.

3.1   Integration with FantasyA

Figure 1 shows how MAgentA is integrated with FantasyA. At the top of the figure we have the user input and the scene representation which is rendered to the screen. Low level modules control for example the physical position of objects in the scene, frame by frame. They also have access to the user inputs. High level modules control the low level modules. For example the mind module of each

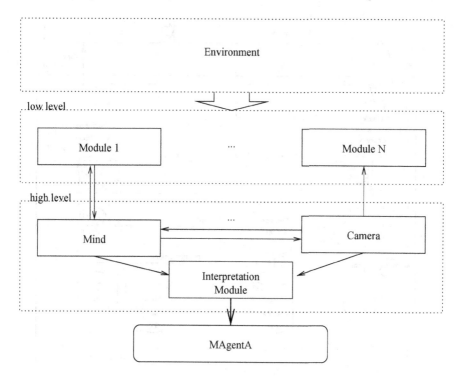

Fig. 1. Integration with FantasyA Architecture

agent controls its body (low level module). The behavior of the mind module is influenced by the emotions of the agent. High level modules can interact. The mind module of an agent can notify the camera module about some important action. At this level there is a module that gathers information about the scene, which is then interpreted, and ultimately transmitted in the form of emotions, upon request, to MAgentA. The interpretation criteria can be either the application of some theory of narrative, or it can come directly from a director agent. Note that from MAgentA's point of view, the environment can return emotions, i.e. the decision of what is the current scene's emotion is external to the Musical Agent.

3.2   Architecture Description

The MAgentA architecture is by nature flexible/adaptative, and as such, it should be robust and easily modifiable. The bottom line is that every time a new musical composing algorithm is drafted, or whenever one wants to try out a new sound API, the modifications in the Agent's source code are to be kept to a minimum and thus be straightforward. To that effect while conceptualizing the architecture, modularity has been a primary concern.

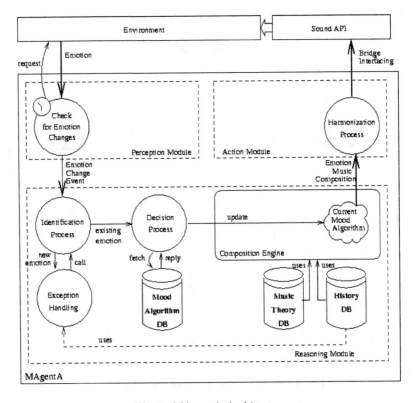

Fig. 2. MAgentA Architecture

The MAgentA architecture is comprised by three main modules, namely the Perception Module, the Reasoning Module, and the Action Module. The Figure 2 describes each of these modules and how they interact between themselves as well as with the environment itself.

An underlying assumption of the MAgentA architecture is that the existing "Mood Algorithm Database", duly supports the set of emotions present within the environment. However should a non-specified emotion occur within the environment the architecture triggers a default Exception Handling Mechanism (described along with the Reasoning Module) and thus still be able to generate a smooth and appropriate composition.

The Perception Module has a regular time frame functionality of checking for any emotional changes in the environment. The attributed frame length depends on the granularity of the generated output. i.e. if the algorithm only produces one note each second there is no need to analyze the environment in more detail. When a change is detected an Emotion Change Event containing the newly detected emotion is generated.

The Reasoning Module listens to any event generated by the Perception Module and when one emerges the algorithm selection mechanism is triggered.

Firstly there is an Identification Process that concludes whether or not the changed emotion is supported by the architecture:

– if the emotion is indeed supported the Mood Selection Process determines the corresponding stored Mood within the Mood Algorithm Database which is then fed to the Composition Engine. However one must not forget that there are occasions where one particular emotion may have several Mood Algorithms associated to it. The selection process is stochastic (i.e. one algorithm is randomly selected from the relevant subset of algorithms, all of which with equal probabilities). Thus unlike before there is non-deterministic music composition patterns. This mechanism gives room for further intricate thinking that can be found in the Discussion section
– Otherwise, if the emotion is not currently supported by the architecture a default Exception Handling Mechanism is triggered. This mechanism makes use of the run time created History Database so that upon analysis it is able to determine the most appropriate available algorithm for the new emotion. Once a Mood Algorithm is determined for the new emotion two separate steps occur: firstly the Learning Process which consists of the Mood Algorithm Database being updated to include the support of the new emotion (i.e. next time it occurs it will not be a new emotion any longer). Secondly the Identification Process is called with a no longer new emotion.

Please refer to the Discussion section for more relevant detail on the specific metrics adopted in the analysis process.

Once the Composition Engine is fed with the selected algorithm to handle the emotion change it initiates the composition process, which consists in running the actual algorithm. Each algorithm in itself "knows" how to use the individual building blocks and their connective rules as described in the Music Theory Database. The lastly mentioned database describes a standard definition for all existing musical structures and their manipulation primitives inherently inscribed in a particular musical system. The Emotional Music Composition output from the Composition Engine is then directed to the Action Module, and stored in a History Database kept within the Reasoning Module.

The Action Module is an abstract layer that acts as an interface bridge to all external devices (i.e. Sound API), which intend to sit upon the MAgentA architecture, thus ensuring its full usability and portability

3.3 Composition Algorithms

Questions yet to be answered:

– how to compose music that induces specific emotions?
– how to compose real music automatically?

The first question concerns the trends presented by Cognitive Psychology. The MAgentA approach presented has been that of creating a framework that enables the empirical testing of new structures by listening and fine-tuning parameters, postponing any decision about music, emotion and meaning relationships to future research. To support this choice the architecture presented was conceived to be modular and customizable to the extent of allowing for any individual composer's music taste while integrating MAgentA into his own particular system. Also to further help this process a tool was developed so as to provide a test bed for Mood Algorithm candidates, which once successful are identified with a particular emotion and finally cataloged in the Mood Algorithms Database. At this stage the concern is to generate an initial database to start off the architecture.

Hence a typical session begins by starting the music output, and then changing instruments, scales, chords, algorithms, or any other specific parameter. In the case of a new idea emerging, a new algorithm is programmed, and then added to its corresponding package (manually) and the next time the tool is ran the new algorithm is already available for testing.

To answer the second question, a straightforward approach was followed. The composition algorithms implemented map the authors own heuristic knowledge about music. As an example, one such algorithm consists of three concurrent processes one for the harmony, one for the bass line and one for the melody. Each process consists of a cycle where some notes are started, an arbitrary time is waited, and those notes are stopped. The choice of notes, the time waited (i.e. duration of notes) and the instruments are parametererized. Particular instantiations of those parameters produce particular results. Future work includes the dynamic adaptative control of these parameters, and the investigation of different composition paradigms.

4   Discussion

In this section some issues are discussed concerning relevant future modifications and/or extensions to the MAgentA.

One important question about MAgentA in the context of the current solutions to the problem of creating music for dynamic environments, is in what way the music output is dynamic and non-repetitive? There are two separate mechanisms that make it possible. The first one is located within each Mood Algorithm, in the sense that the algorithm should be highly dynamic and sufficiently creative to provide different and interesting music for a large period of time, while satisfying the emotional requisite. The second mechanism is the Selection Process that selects one of the several available and relevant algorithms to the particular emotion. This mechanism can have several increasing levels of complexity. As explained in Section 3, the suggested implementation is a random choice between available algorithms. A more sophisticated choice would analyze the History Database and choose according to a different distribution implied by a "maximization of diversity" criteria, assigning probabilities to each algorithm proportionally to the distance to past choices or frequency of occurrence.

Another important issue resides on the exception handling mechanism. The choice of which algorithm best represents an unknown emotion is not trivial, and any choice has both its pros and cons. The more simple mechanisms are:

- choose randomly between all available algorithms
- or to behave as if no emotion change occurred.

More ambitious choices would try to predict the meaning of this emotion by analyzing the History database. For example a clustering algorithm could detect some sort of repeating pattern that would make the choice obvious if that were the case.

The exception handling mechanism has yet another interesting aspect which is the updating of the Mood Algorithm Database, which is itself a form of learning. The storage method can be one of two:

- the first one is to store the new emotion/algorithm association like any other entry
- the second method is to store this emotion tagged as a special emotion, allowing future belief revision mechanisms to change this choice, providing a continuous learning scheme.

The transition between moods has to be smooth. The responsibility for such smoothness relies on each mood algorithm's particular implementation. This choice allows full "encapsulation" of the algorithm in the sense that each and every note played is the creation of one algorithm. So the mood algorithm programmers should have in mind the specific goals and context of the architecture.

One last issue that is worth mentioning is that of the History Database flushing. This mechanism is responsible for keeping the size of the database at reasonable levels. If the agent is to be running for a large period of time, the constant size of the database is proportional to the specified "horizon".

5   Conclusions

As any other system architecture, extensibility and robustness have been prime concerns while conducting analysis and design. In order for one to create interesting music, diversity has to be given deserving attention. Hence it was vital that the architecture allowed for many different composing algorithms to be added with minor effort.

Evaluating the results is difficult because music is inherently subjective, and there is a strong correlation between what is seen and what is heard. Since the FantasyA is not yet fully implemented, the full evaluation phase was postponed to future work. Also the current implemented algorithms reveal lack of expressive power, namely they sound too "melancholic" or "enigmatic" as described by the first listeners of MAgentA. This suggests that the more complex musical constructions must be used in the algorithms. Future work also includes more research in this area.

All in all valuable results have been attained given that they enlighten the existing research area and help eliminate some of the established panaceas with the focused aim of obtaining ever evolving and accurate emotional composition Agents.

References

1. North A. and Hargreaves D. Liking, arousal potential and the emotions expressed by music. *The Scandinavian Journal of Psychology*, (38):45–53, 1997.
2. Mark Downie. Behavior, animation, music: the music and movement of synthetic characters. Master's thesis, MIT, 2001. Preliminary Version.
3. Nakamura et al. Automatic background music generation based on actor's emotions and motions. In *Proceedings of First Pacific Conference on Computer Graphics and Applications*. World Scientific Publishing Co., 1993.
4. T. Stapleford J. Robertson, A. Quincey and G. Wiggins. Real-time music generation for a virtual environment. In *Proceedings of the ECAI 98 Workshop on AI/ALife and Entertainment, Brighton*, 1998. Dep. of Artificial Intelligence, University of Edinburgh.
5. Leonard Meyer. *Emotion and Meaning in Music*. The Oxford University Press, 1956.
6. Microsoft. Directmusic. http://www.microsoft.com/DirectX.
7. Curtis Roads. Research in music and artificial intelligence. *ACM Computing Surveys*, 2(17), 1985.
8. Chong Yu. Computer generated music composition. Master's thesis, MIT, 1996.

Agent Oriented Simulation with OOCSMP. An Example in Evolutionary Ant Colonies

Juan de Lara[1,2] and Manuel Alfonseca[2]

[1] School of Computer Science
McGill University
3480 University Street
Montrèal, Quebèc, H3A 2A7, Canada
Juan.Lara@ii.uam.es

[2] Dept. Ingeniería Informática, Universidad Autónoma de Madrid
Ctra. De Colmenar, km. 15, 28049 Madrid, Spain
Manuel.Alfonseca@ii.uam.es

1. Introduction

Agent-based simulation [1] is a powerful and natural way to carry out complex simulation experiments, in which many autonomous and interacting entities take part. The key abstraction in this methodology is the autonomous agent, which interacts with other agents via discrete events.

OOCSMP [2] is an object oriented continuous simulation language. A compiler (C-OOL) was built for this language to produce C++ code or Java applets from the simulation models. This approach simplifies the generation of simulation based web courses. We have generated a number of courses in this way, which can be accessed at http://www.ii.uam.es/~jlara/investigacion.

Although it was conceived as continuous, OOCSMP has features that allow a certain degree of discretization, such as handling discrete events, or iterating over matrix and vector indexes and blocks to transform continuous to discrete values.

2. Extending OOCSMP for Agent-Oriented Simulation

Several extensions have been added to OOCSMP in order to perform agent-oriented simulation, such as: multiple object constructor invocation; objects can be erased from the simulation; a new output form represents the position and the state of the agents; multicast and broadcast message-passing mechanisms: methods can be invoked on objects (point-to-point), classes (broadcast) or collections of objects (multicast). The elements in a class/collection can be accessed sequentially (first to last or last to first), randomly, or in any order, specified as a vector. This makes it possible to avoid phenomena that may arise due to accidentally imposed inter-agent correlation.

A. de Antonio, R. Aylett, and D. Ballin (Eds.): IVA 2001, LNAI 2190, pp. 233-234, 2001.
© Springer-Verlag Berlin Heidelberg 2001

3.   An Example: Simulation of an Evolutionary Virtual Ant Colony

Our *vants* (virtual ants) communicate directly with other vants when they are near, rather than by dropping pheromones. They live in a two-dimensional grid and their objective is to find food. When they find it, they eat a portion (which extends their life span), and take another portion to the nest. This may be repeated until the food is depleted. Several locations with food may exist at the same time. When a vant arrives at the nest, it rests there for some time. When two agents meet outside the nest, they can exchange their knowledge about the food position. If a vant does not find food during a certain period of time, it returns to the nest.

A vant has several parameters that control its behaviour: *Activity* defines its speed; *Communicative* controls if it will communicate with another agent when they meet; *Scepticism* its credulity; *Lie* controls if it will lie or tell the truth when informing the others of the food position; *Memory* gives the probability of forgetting the food position. The five parameters are encoded in binary and concatenated, making a genotype. When two agents meet at the vant-hill, they can reproduce if there's enough food in the nest. In each reproduction, two new agents are created, with *'genetic'* information resulting from their parents genomes after the operations of mutation and crossing-over have been applied to them, a typical procedure with genetic algorithms.

4.   Conclusions

The *Activity* and *Memory* parameters in the population grow quickly to their maximum. The other parameters may oscillate. When food is scarce, agents compete between themselves and liars proliferate. As this parameter goes up, scepticism also grows. When there's plenty of food, it's better for vants to co-operate, and liars and sceptics may disappear quickly. This is an interesting emergent behaviour of the system.

Acknowledgment. This paper has been sponsored by the Spanish Interdepartmental Commission of Science and Technology (CICYT), project number TEL1999-0181

References

1. Wooldridge, M. 1999. *"Intelligent Agents"*. In *"Multiagent Systems. A modern approach to Distributed Artificial Intelligence"* (Weiss ed.). pp. 27-77, The MIT Press.
2. Alfonseca, M., de Lara, J., Pulido, E. *"Semiautomatic Generation of Web Courses by Means of an Object-Oriented Simulation Language"*, special issue of "SIMULATION", Web-Based Simulation, Vol 73, num.1, July 1999, pp. 5-12.

The Lexicon and the Alphabet
of Gesture, Gaze, and Touch

Isabella Poggi

Dipartimento di Scienze dell'Educazione - Università Roma Tre
Via del Castro Pretorio 20 - 00185 Roma, Italy
poggi@uniroma3.it

Abstract. The paper argues that to build Multimodal IVAs it is necessary to provide them with the lexicons and alphabets of different communication systems, and it presents some attempts to find them out in symbolic gestures, gaze and touch.

1 Communication Systems in Different Modalities

A Human Agent uses several communication systems, residing in different body organs. The head produces head movements, the eye region (eyebrows, eyelids, eyes), gaze, the mouth words and prosody (acoustically) and visemes, smiles, grimaces (visually); shoulders, arms and hands produce gestures, trunk and legs postures, movements, orientations, proxemic signals. And a Human Agent can also communicate by touch and smell.

Communication systems may be either "lexical" or "creative". A "lexical" system is one where several signal-meaning pairs are coded in memory (like words or symbolic gestures). In a "creative" system, what is coded in memory are only a few generative rules to create new signals for given meanings or retrieve meanings from new signals (iconic gestures) [2].

I think that not only words or symbolic gestures, as it is generally accepted, but also other kinds of gestures and even gazes, facial expressions, posture shifts, are "lexical" systems: if they did not have each a precise meaning coded in our memory, we could not understand each other. To the objection that nonverbal signals are the domain of homonymy, polysemy and vagueness, I counterargue that also for apparently very diffent meanings of the same signal a common core meaning can be found in all its occurrences [1], [3].

To build an Intelligent Multimodal Virtual Agent that communicates multimodally, a necessary condition is to provide it with signals in different modalities and with their meanings; that is, to find out, for each modality, its *mode-specific lexicon and alphabet*: 1. the coded list of signal-meaning pairs and 2. the set of sublexical components of signals that, variously combined symultaneously or in sequence, form all the possible signals in that modality.

In this work I present current research on the lexicons and alphabets of gaze, touch and italian symbolic gestures.

A. de Antonio, R. Aylett, and D. Ballin (Eds.): IVA 2001, LNAI 2190, pp. 235-236, 2001.

2 The Alphabets of Gesture, Gaze, and Touch

In order to find out the sublexical components of gestures, gaze and touch, I started from the notion of formational parameters, proposed by Stokoe [5]. Any signal (gesture, gaze or touch) can be described as the combination of specific values on a small set of parameters. Each value in each parameter of a gesture, gaze or touch has a "phonological" status, since if we change that value on that parameter the item shifts either from one signal to another signal or from a signal to a non-signal.

At the University Roma Tre the "Italian Gestionary" is being compiled, a lexicon of symbolic gestures of Italian hearing people. The alphabet of *gestures* is described in terms of their formational parameters: handshape, location, orientation and movement. 250 Italian symbolic gestures were analysed in terms of four parameters (Romagna, 1998), and the following values were found: 40 handshapes, 33 locations, 6 orientations. Movement was distinguished into subparameters: 10 directions, 7 paths, 4 parts of the hand, 4 tensions, 3 impacts, and tempo, distinguished into duration, speed, repetition.

Formational Parameters has also usefully applied also to *gaze* [4]. Some parameters are parts of the eye region (brows, eyelids, wrinkles), others are traits, movements and other aspects of the eyes (humidity, reddening, pupil dilation, direction, movement).

Finally, in the alphabet of *touch*, the relevant parameters are: touching and touched part, pressure, location, movement before and during touch

3 The Lexicons of Italian Symbolic Gestures, Gaze, and Touch

In the "Italian Gestionary", for 250 symbolic gestures it was found out a verbal paraphrase, its gestural synonyms, possible contexts, the core meaning of the gesture in all of them, and possible rhetorical uses (metaphorical, ironic...) [3]. 82 gestures of touch were collected and their meanings were hypothesised. Both meanings and contexts of use (formal-informal, sex, age) were assessed through questionaries.

As for gaze, a number of semantic categories were found out that can be conveyed by eye communication: deictic, physical properties, degree of certainty, source of mentioned knowledge, performative, emotion, topic-comment marking, metatextual information, turn-taking and back-channel signals [4]. All these types of gaze have been also simulated in Animated Agents.

References

1. Kendon, A.: Gestures as illocutionary and discourse structure markers in Southern Italian conversation. Journal of Pragmatics 23 (1995) 247-279.
2. Magno Caldognetto, E., Poggi, I.: Creative iconic gestures: some evidence from Aphasics. In: Simone, R. (ed.): Iconicity in Language. John Benjamins, Amsterdam (1995).
3. Poggi, I.: The italian gestionary. meaning representation, ambiguity, and context. In: Mueller, C., Posner, R. (eds.): The Semantics and Pragmatics of everyday Gestures. Berlin Verlag Arno Spitz, Berlin (2001).
4. Poggi, I., Pelachaud, C., de Rosis, F.: Eye communication in a conversational 3D synthetic agent. AI Communications 13 (2000) 169-181.
5. Stokoe, W.C. Sign Language Structure: An Outline of the Communicative Systems of the American Deaf. Linstock Press, Silver Spring (1978).

Extraction and Reconstruction of Personal Characters from Human Movement

Junichi Hoshino

University of Tsukuba, College of Engineering Systems
jhoshino@computer.org

Abstract. We propose a new method for extracting personal characteristics from 3D body movement for intelligent virtual agent. We introduce the eigen action space to represent and reconstruct the personal characteristics.

1. Introduction

Estimation of the personal characteristics from the body movement is important for building virtual actors. For example, if we can represent the personal characteristics of body movement in a few parameters, we would be able to synthesize human actions with various characteristics.

In this paper, we propose a new method for extracting personal characteristics from 3D body movement. We introduce the eigen action space to represent the personal characteristics. First, we estimate the average action from a set of 3D pose parameters from different people. Then we created the eigen action space from the covariance matrices of 3D pose parameters using KL transform. Because the eigen action space consists of orthogonal base vectors, 3D pose parameters of a person is represented as a point. Actions with new personal characteristics can be reconstructed by sampling new points in the eigen action space.

2. Eigen Action Method

First, we estimate 3D pose data of human from video. We use 3D human model estimate the pose parameters of each parts. We represent a human body by an articulated structure consisting of 10 rigid parts corresponding body, head, upper arms, under arms, upper legs, under legs. The motion parameters are estimated using the spatial-temporal gradient method, and automatic initial registration with silhouette [1].

Then, we estimate the personal characteristics of the 3D pose parameters. Let the 3D pose parameters xp of person p be a vector $x_p = [\psi_0^p, \psi_1^p, \psi_2^p, ... \psi_l^p]^T$ where l is the number of frames. The size of the pose parameters xp is k*l where k is the number of the pose parameters. The difference action Dp can be written as $D_p = x_p - c$ where C is the average action. The covariance matrices of the pose parameters Q is $Q = XX^T$ where $X = [D_1, D_2, ... D_p]$. Eigen vector and eigen value can be obtained from the equation $Qu_k = \lambda_k u_k$.

Because the eigen action space consists of orthogonal base vectors, 3D pose parameters of each persons are represented as a point. The personal parameters g_p can

A. de Antonio, R. Aylett, and D. Ballin (Eds.): IVA 2001, LNAI 2190, pp. 237-238, 2001.

be estimated as $g_p = [u_1, u_2, ...u_k]^T (x_p - c)$. 3D pose parameters can be reconstructed from a point in the eigen action space. The 3D pose parameters x_p of the personal parameter g_p are $x_p = \sum_{i=1}^{N} g_p u_i + c$. The personal parameter g_p can be any points in the eigen action space. Therefore we can synthesize the new 3D action with the different personal characteristics from that of training actions.

3. Experiments Using Video Sequences

We select one typical action from the gymnastic exercises (stretching). Fig.1 shows the example input images and tracking results. We collected the samples of the same action from the eight different people to generate eigen vectors. Fig2 shows the largest two eigen vectors. Fig.3 shows the result of projecting each person's motion into action eigen space. Fig. 4 shows the average action and the example of the reconstructed action from the eigen vectors.

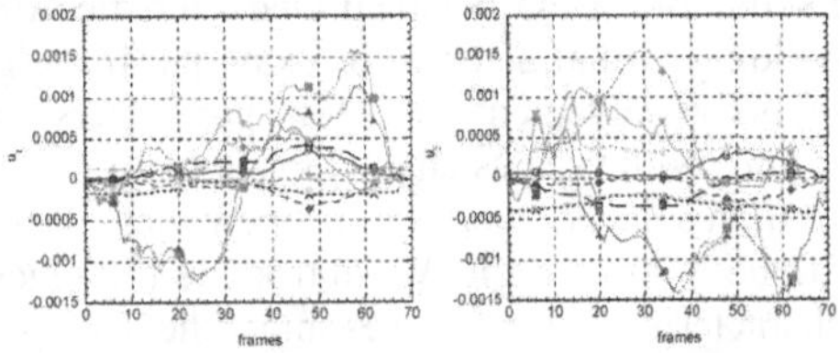

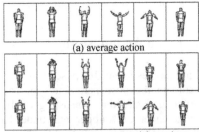

Fig. 2. Largest two eigen vectors

Fig. 1. Estimation of 3D pose from video

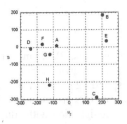

Fig. 3. Projection onto the action eigen space

(a) average action

(b) new action reconstructed from eigen-vectors

Fig. 4. Example of average action and reconstructed action using the eigen vectors

References

[1] J. Hoshino, H. Saito:"A Match Moving Technique for Human Body Sequences", ICASSSP2001, IMDSP-P3.1, 2001

The Origin of the Speeches: Language Evolution through Collaborative Reinforcement Learning

Ray Walshe

Artificial Intelligence Research Group
Dept. of Computer Applications, Dublin City University, Ireland
Ray.Walshe@CompApp.DCU.ie http://www.compapp.dcu.ie/~ray

Abstract. This research focuses on the artificial creation of the conditions that were necessary or facilitated language in its evolution. I propose a model for a system that has the capability to allow a complex communication protocol to evolve. In human language learning, the adult humans have already mastered the language and use their knowledge to teach infant humans. 50.000 B.C. (or whenever) when there were no adult masters of language, what conditions were necessary for the language-less homo sapiens to start developing the first language? Can machines evolve a language in a similar manner across generations? This research deals with facilitating the genesis of a communication system using evolutionary computation and reinforcement learning when initially none of the conspirators have mastered the system.

1 The Model for Language Evolution

Task Orientated Networked environment for the Acquisition of Language (TONAL) consists of a World where Agents exist and the Agents themselves. The World(s) and Agent(s) themselves are servers that can exist geographically anywhere on the Internet where there is WWW connectivity. Agents can travel to the World across the Internet while their minds remain where they are hosted [1]. The World has contained within it food cells, a nest and Agents. The World monitors the behavior of the Agents and provides some rewards depending on the outcome of actions that the Agent takes. The World server responds to some action by an Agent by updating the state of the World and sending the new state back to the Agent. The Agent(s) respond to the current state of the World by selecting an action to be taken and sending this new action to the World. If the Agent specifies an action that results in the Agent arriving at a Food Cell, then the Agent will receive a reward from the World and information pertaining to the new state of the World. If the Agent specifies an action in the World that results in the Agent arriving at the Nest, this will also result in the World rewarding the Agent. The World will respond with a Zero reward to the Agent, (that is the equivalent of punishment), when the Agent has specified an action to perform in the World which when enacted by the World does not result in (a) finding food or (b) returning to the nest. This environment is similar to that used by Humphrys [2][3] with the exception that there is also communication between agents. In order for this to be a true communications system rather than an information extraction system then the sending agent (Instructor/Speaker) must obtain some

A. de Antonio, R. Aylett, and D. Ballin (Eds.): IVA 2001, LNAI 2190, pp. 239–241, 2001.

reward that would not otherwise have been obtained [4]. There must be some sense of fairness built into this system where cheating is not rewarded (but is allowed) otherwise the population could never learn. Conflicts between rewards that come from the World and rewards that come from obeying the other Agents must be resolved to allow the system to evolve. This can be achieved by summing coincidental rewards from both World and Speaker or also by weighting the rewards accordingly.

The agent performs random acts until their Reinforcement Learning Network brain has developed so that learned actions can be performed. After they have visited a cell more than once they can "decide" whether an action should be taken or not depending on the Agents estimated reward for that action. Q Learning deals with delayed reinforcement and is described in [3]. In summary if a transition leads to a reward, then the Q values of intermediate steps that are taken which lead to this state are also increased but not by the same amount. This diminished reward decreases the further the intermediate steps are away from the rewarding state. Linguana acting under instruction, the acting Linguana (Hearer) carries out an action based on what the instructing Linguana (Speaker) has told it to do. If the Hearer Linguana performs the correct action (as instructed by the Speaker Linguana) then the Speaker Linguana rewards the Hearer. If, as result of this action, food is found or the nest is located, then the Environment rewards the Hearer Linguana. The Speaker constructs a "token-action" pair to map the instruction to an action and stores this mapping in a table. The Hearer receives the token and checks to see if it already has an action (meaning) linked to that token in its own table. If a mapping exists on the Hearers end then it performs the associated action, otherwise it selects an action which will be linked to the token if it elicits a reward from the Environment and the Speaker.

This symbiotic relationship between the Speaker and Hearer reinforces truthfulness as the reward functions for instructor actions only provide positive feedback when the outcome of the action benefits the actor. This means that only the instructions from the Speaker, which result in a reward for both Hearer and Speaker persist and malicious or random instructions are not rewarded. It is not in the Speakers interest to instruct the Hearer Linguana on a "fools errand" as the Speaker receives a punishment (zero reward) in this case. (Although initial instructions by the Speaker are random and can be termed malicious, they may result in random environmental rewards for the Hearer which in turn results in Lingua rewards for the Speaker). Malicious instructions are however permitted as the model better reflects real world communication.

Humphrys architecture of the WWM separates the Agent from the Environment and allows multiple agents to have their own view of the World [5]. It also facilitates inter-agent communication through actions in the world. Although the TONAL implementation of the WWM only requires a subset of its capabilities, the architecture model lends itself to many types of distributed intelligence and collaborative agent projects. The capacity to embed "foreign" language learning agents in the Environment can be used to test for noise, dialects and robustness of system where multiple tokens map to the same action.

References

[1] Humphrys, Mark (to appear), Distributing a Mind on the Internet: The World-Wide-Mind, to appear in *ECAL-01*, Prague, Czech Republic, September 10-14, 2001

[2] Humphrys, Mark (1996). Action Selection Methods using Reinforcement Learning. *SAB '96*. http://www.compapp.dcu.ie/~humphrys/

[3] Humphrys, Mark (1997) Action Selection Methods using Reinforcement Learning. PhD thesis, Cambridge University. http://www.compapp.dcu.ie/~humphrys/PhD

[4] Burghardt, G. M. (1970). Defining 'communication.'. *In Johnston, J., Moulton, D., and Turk, A., editors, Communication by Chemical Signals, pages 5--18*, New York. NY: Appleton-Century-Crofts.

[5] Walshe, Ray and Humphrys, Mark (to appear), First Implementation of the World-Wide-Mind, poster to appear in *ECAL-01*, Prague, Czech Republic, 2001.

Fanky: A Tool for Animating Faces of 3D Agents

Aldo Paradiso[1], Fabio Zambetta[2], and Fabio Abbattista[2]

[1]GMD - German National Research Center for Information Technology Institute (IPSI)
D-64293 Darmstadt, Germany
paradiso@darmstadt.gmd.de

[2]University of Bari
Dipartimento di Informatica
Via Orabona, 4
I-70125 Bari, Italy
fzambetta@programmers.net, fabio@di.uniba.it

Abstract. We propose the Fanky system, a facial animation tool applied to faces of 3D agents. The tool is based on an object-oriented architecture, where the face is subdivided into a set of regions called Standard Anatomical Components, each provided with its own deformation and animation parameters. The deformation algorithm of Fanky is mainly founded on a FFD based technique for the facial deformation of the character. We adopt the MPEG-4' Facial Animation Parameters as a description format for facial expressions and animations.

1. Introduction

We observed that several animation systems, though powerful and interesting, are generally heavy to implement, difficult to port onto different platforms, and usually not embeddable in Web browsers [1, 2, 6, 7, 10]. We pursue a light solution, which must be portable, easy to implement, fast enough in medium-sized computer environments, and embeddable in Web browsers. We introduce Fanky, a tool for animating 3D agents. For its realization a traditional FFD-based deformation algorithm has been adopted, but together with a new technology relying on SACs (Standard Anatomic Components) whose purpose is to improve system flexibility and modularity. From a technological point of view we decided to implement Fanky using the Java language and the Shout3D API [9]. This way we can rely on a true multi-platform system that might use the optional OpenGL acceleration features provided by Shout3D. This choice offers an advantage, in terms of portability, lightness, and adaptability. We decided to adopt the MPEG-4 standard as a description format of the animation streams [3, 4], which enables the integration of facial animation with multimedia communications and presentations and allows facial animation over low-bandwidth communication channels.

A. de Antonio, R. Aylett, and D. Ballin (Eds.): IVA 2001, LNAI 2190, pp. 242-243, 2001.

2. The Fanky System

Our goal has been to define an animation model that is effective, reliable, and gives good performances and results, and which is MPEG-4 compliant. The model we propose is partially based on Paradiso and al.' one, Tinky [5]. We extended it by introducing the concept of Standard Anatomical Component (SAC). A SAC is a facial region identified with its own properties and methods. Properties include skin elasticity, material, and mesh topology. Methods include the techniques applied in order to carry out the deformations or the animations. Each SAC is provided with its own animation method. In Fanky the technique of Free Form Deformations (FFD) has been adopted [8]. For each SAC a corresponding FFD box has been defined. The number and position of SACs has been defined in order to have a mapping between actions performed onto FFD control points and MPEG-4' Facial

Fig. 1. A screenshot of the expression editor panel.

Animation Parameters. A prototype of the system has been implemented, together with an expression editor, (Fig. 1) with which expressions and animations are produced.

References

1. Cassell, J.; Sullivan, J.; Prevost, S.; Churchill E.: Embodied Conversational Agents. The MIT Press, Cambridge, Massachusetts, 2000. ISBN 0-262-03278-3.
2. Capin, T.K., Pandzic, I.S., Noser, H., Magnenat-Thalmann, N., Thalmann, D.: Virtual Human Representation and Communication in VLNET Networked Virtual Environments. In: IEEE Computer Graphics and Applications, Special Issue on Multimedia Highways ,Vol. 17, No. 2, 1997, pp.42-53.
3. ISO/IEC IS 14496-1 Systems, 1999.
4. ISO/IEC IS 14496-2 Visual, 1999.
5. Paradiso, A.; Nack, F.; Fries G.; Schuhmacher, K. The Design of Expressive Cartoons for the Web – Tinky. In: Proceedings of ICMCS Conference, June 7-11 1999, Florence (Italy).
6. Parke, F.I., Waters, K. Computer Facial Animation, A K Peters. Ltd, 1996, pp. 96-99.
7. Pelachaud, C., et al. Final Report to nsf, in NSF Workshop on Facial Animation, 1994.
8. Sederberg, T.W., Parry, S.R.: Free-Form Deformations of Solid Geometric Models, SIGGRAPH '86.
9. Shout3D API, http://www.shout3d.com.
10. Smith, T.J., Shi, J., Granieri, J., and Badler, N.: JackMOO, An integration of Jack and lambdaMOO, Pacific Graphics, 1997.

Author Index

Lecture Notes in Artificial Intelligence (LNAI)

Lecture Notes in Computer Science